Oneness With God

An Analysis Of What It Means To Be Created In The Image And After The Likeness Of God

Ronald E. Richardson, Esq.

SECOND EDITION

Published by
Hybrid Global Publishing
333 E 14th Street
#3C
New York, NY 10003

Manufactured in the United States of America, or in the United Kingdom when distributed elsewhere.

Richardson, Ronald.
Oneness with God, 2nd. Edition
    ISBN: 978-1-957013-68-8
    eBook: 978-1-957013-69-5
    LCCN: 9781957013688

Cover design by: Julia Kuris
Interior design by: Suba Murugan
Author photo by: Brea Laroche

Table of Contents

Open thou mine eyes, that I may behold wondrous things out of thy law.

Psalm 119:18

Special thanks and my deepest love and appreciation go to my wife, Ella, whose steadfast support and love has made this book possible. I am also extremely thankful for Lyman Doster, Senior Pastor of The Greater Providence Missionary Baptist Church, Los Angeles, California., for his insightful comments.

INTRODUCTION

I found this book captivating and enriching with biblical information that will educationally heighten followers of Christian faith. Not only is its content filled with detailed information; but Mr. Ronald Richardson's testimony was enlightening. It is obvious he put concentrated study into critical issues affecting Christian culture. His presentation comes across as honest and straightforward.

Often when individuals commit to a Christian Church they are unaware of specific theological issues critical to spiritual understanding. These issues are important because they augment spiritual growth which should be the goal of all believers. The unawareness of new members is understandable because they are not students of the scriptures. Reading this book will not only fulfill theological needs of new members, but will enhance the knowledge of any believer who desires a better understanding of his relationship with God. It also answers questions related to how the Gospel Master Plan will affect Mankind.

I am confident anyone reading this book will be left full of appreciation for Whom he or she spiritually represents and why at times when they experience bouts of imperfection, God continues to bless them.

Reading this book will spiritually encourage and strengthen the believer's understanding of the faith. It will be clear God does not overlook Mankind because of imperfection; however, God expects a sincere effort from Mankind to demonstrate love to and trust in Him through our recognition of Yeshua HaMashiach.

I am absolutely convinced the reader will find a personal and spiritual satisfaction reading this book. By understanding chapters in this book, one will enhance spiritual commitment and realize the importance of living a devoted Christian life. Mr. Ronald Richardson deserves sincere gratitude for the dedicated work he put into writing this book.

Pastor Lyman Isaac Doster

PROLOGUE

The phrase "Believing attorney" has been viewed by some to be an oxymoron of sorts. On the one hand, whether deservedly or not, attorneys have the reputation that they will do whatever it takes to win for their clients even if it means violating the laws of God. On the other hand, an attorney who believes in Yeshua, be he/she Jew or Gentile, will seek to do only those things that are consistent with God's will even though a lawyer's interpretation of the law typically does not allow for concepts such as forgiveness or grace. Perhaps, this is why those law experts of Yeshua's day, the Pharisees, could not bring themselves to accept His gospel of grace, forgiveness and redemption. As with any believer, attorneys have surrendered their entire lives to Yeshua HaMashiach in the faith that His eternal, once and for all sin offering has freed them from the wages of their sins and, by grace, granted them eternal salvation. All believers, in and through Yeshua HaMashiach, have been reconciled with God and are, thereby, allowed to directly commune with Him daily and to fulfill their creative purpose, which is to become one with God in and through Yeshua.

It would appear, then, that it would be extremely difficult for an attorney to be a follower of Yeshua. However, just as Paul, a legal expert and a Pharisee, was won over to Yeshua, attorneys can likewise be called by God to accept Yeshua HaMashiach as their Lord and Savior. I know from experience. Yeshua HaMashiach is my Lord and Savior, and I am an attorney.

My law degree and over three decades of legal practice have trained me to appreciate the importance of detail and choosing the right words to convey the exact message intended. When briefing an issue before a court of law, the extent to which a lawyer possesses these talents will largely determine whether or not the court will agree with his interpretation of the law. This book does not address the ethical or moral issues surrounding a lawyer's interpretation of man's or God's law for the benefit of a client. Rather, it is an attempt to strictly construe the passages of the Bible, from the perspective of one who focuses on detail, to determine the intent of God with respect to why He created Mankind. Once Mankind's creative purpose is fully understood, the entirety of the Holy Bible can be put into proper perspective.

If ever there is a written work where the meaning of every word is critical to an understanding of the message contained therein, the Holy Scriptures, which are inspired by God, is such a work. Any analysis thereof will necessarily require an occasional review of the original text or a comparison of various translations. We must operate on the premise that every word contained therein was specifically chosen to convey this wonderful gospel…"the Good News."

By the guidance of the Holy Spirit, this book presents an analysis of the Holy Scriptures in an attempt to shed some light upon the mystery behind the creation of man in the image and after the likeness of God and the awesome role we were created to play in God's order of things. From the dawn of history to the present, man has striven to become God. Either he seeks to become the master of his own destiny or he seeks to exercise godlike powers over others, or both. This innate desire of man to become God can be traced back to the beginning; to the creation of man and to man's sin of selfish disobedience.

The Bible informs us that Mankind was made in the image and after the likeness of God. A review of the words chosen to describe the words "image" and "likeness" strongly suggests that Mankind was given the appearance, attributes, characteristics, and mannerisms of God. Further review of Biblical passages confirms the fact that these Godly traits were bestowed upon Mankind so that we can be perfect, holy physical temples, individually and collectively, for our perfect, Holy God. Essentially, we were created to become the physical manifestations of God to the same extent that Yeshua HaMashiach is the perfect, Holy embodiment of God. We attain this perfect oneness with God only because we are in Yeshua. We will have the same perfect oneness with God that Yeshua has because we are in Him and He is in us so much so that there is no distinction between Him and us. We will be what He is. We cannot be anything outside of Yeshua but we shall be mirror images of His earthly existence since He is in us and we are in Him. Everything Yeshua is we shall be because the extent of our existence is determined by the extent of Yeshua's existence.

Most denominations today do not teach of us becoming one with our Creator perhaps because of a concern of being viewed as advocating our elevation to the level of God. But this is exactly what the Holy Scriptures state is the creative purpose for Mankind. It is my humble prayer that Jew and Gentile believers come to a collective understanding of what the Bible actually says about God's creative purpose for Mankind.

By way of personal background, my salvation, in and through Yeshua, occurred midway through evening law school in 1983. I was dating an evening law student from another law school when we became aware that she was pregnant. I was a bachelor, and she was a single parent of one child. From my perspective, neither of us had an intimate, close and personal relationship with the Lord. We agonized over whether we should raise the child or have an abortion, but it seemed to me that the focus was on our professional careers instead of the life of the unborn child. Ultimately, we both agreed that an abortion would be in our best interests. If we considered the interests of the unborn child at all, it was of minor significance when compared to our interests. I knew what God's Word said about abortions but I decided that my self-interests were more important than God's interests concerning the life of the unborn child.

My relationship with the mother of the unborn child ended shortly thereafter. I am convinced that the abortion had something to do with our parting of the ways. I thought that this would have enabled me to have a fresh start, but it was only the beginning of my sorrows.

I was always somewhat fearless, to the extent that I tried to meet all challenges head-on, regardless of the consequences, especially if I thought I was right. The problem was I could not convince myself that the abortion was right. In fact, I became increasingly convinced that I had committed a great wrong. This was not something that I was going to be able to shrug off. It nagged at me at every turn. It was affecting my schoolwork, my employment and my every waking hour. I could find no rest or comfort. I knew that I could not bring back the life of this innocent child. I felt as if all was lost. I did not believe that any amount of success or fortune could erase the overwhelming sense of hopelessness and guilt that had taken over my life. I was not able to bury myself in my schoolwork or day job to rid myself of the shame and guilt.

I knew from my upbringing of an option that promised to remove all my burdens, including this most heavy one. That option is Yeshua. My situation was dire. I recalled Yeshua's promise that He would take on our burdens and forgive us our sins. I had to personally go before my Lord and Savior and put my faith in His promises on the line. I had to confess my sins and seek His forgiveness. If I was going to give all that I am to Yeshua, I had to have a face-to-face, heart-to-heart talk with Him. I could then tell Him how much of a mess I have made with my life and that I am totally relying on Him to keep His promises to forgive me unto salvation; to take on my burdens and to live in and through me from then on.

So, in deep contrition, I got on my knees and asked Yeshua into my life. Now that I was giving myself over to Him, it had to be 100 percent. My every breath, step and thought would be under His control for the rest of my life. Being aware of 1 Corinthians 3:2; 13:11 and 1 Peter 2:2, I understood that this would be a gradual spiritual growth process but my submission at that moment was total and complete. I gave my life to Yeshua and was spiritually reborn. As I stood up, I literally felt the guilt of a lifetime of sin fall off me. I had a similar feeling when Yeshua took away my addiction to smoking at my prayerful request years later.

I had a tremendous feeling of relief and freedom. It's the kind of feeling one gets when he knows that everything is going to be all right even though there is no earthly reason to feel that way. I continued to experience this same inner peace and joy every time I subsequently turned my burdens over to the Lord. I was convinced that my sins were forgiven and that Yeshua had accepted my invitation to come into my life. It was now His life to be lived through me and I welcomed Him. I cannot fully express the joy I have now that *Roe v. Wade*, and its progeny, have been reversed by the Unites States Supreme Court.

From the moment of my spiritual rebirth, I have asked God to explain, to the satisfaction of my soul, why He allowed a part of Himself to suffer and die for the sins of man? I knew the boilerplate responses to that question that have rolled off the tongues of believers for two millennia. However, I felt in my heart that there was more to this story. I am convinced that this was by inspiration of the Holy Spirit. So, I undertook to satisfy my inspired desire for clarity. I wanted to know the truth, the whole truth, and nothing but the truth concerning the reason for God's ultimate sacrifice for man.

As I delved into the Word of God in my quest to answer this fundamental question, the Holy Spirit allowed me to conceptualize God's creative purpose for man. The more I studied the Word of God, the more wondrous and awesome the answer became. I was so taken by the profoundness of God's creative purpose for every human being, as revealed to me through the Word of God, I felt compelled to write not only the first book but also this revised edition. I pray that I have been able to articulate the magnitude of the answer to this age-old question in such a way that any reader hereof will fully grasp its significance and revel in the indescribable joy, peace, and wonderment that comes with its understanding.

In order for God to become one with His highest creation, man had to be pure love; just as He is. This type of love is demonstrated by placing all other interests before one's own interests unconditionally and uncompromisingly. God knew that man, once given the gift of free will, would fail a test of unconditional and uncompromising love by choosing his interests over God's interests in direct disobedience to the command of God. Man needed a demonstration of exactly what type of love is required before he could become one with his Creator God.

So, God permitted Satan, one of His highest angelic creations, to intervene into God's obedience test of man through deception. You see, Satan fully understood God's creative purpose for man and had determined in his heart to wage a physical and spiritual rebellion against God to prevent man, a physical and spiritual creation of God, to become one with his Creator. Such a result would place man higher than Satan and the rest of God's spiritual and physical creations. Satan saw this test as an opportunity to initiate a rebellion against God in the physical, earthly realm making it impossible for God to become one with sinful man. This physical rebellion would be later accompanied by a spiritual rebellion. He, therefore, was more than willing to prove to God that man was unfit for such a high creative purpose.

As anticipated, through Satan's deception, Adam and Eve, our first parents, failed God's test of loving obedience. They were unable to demonstrate the unconditional selfless love that is of God; indeed, that is God. The consequences of their sin of disobedience required not only their physical deaths but also their spiritual deaths through eternal spiritual and physical separation from God. This same fate befell all Mankind because, as their progeny, we have inherited the same sin nature that caused them to sin.

However, God was prepared for this expected result. He knew before the creation of all things that man would require a personal demonstration of Godly love. This kind of selfless, unconditional love is usually given at great cost to the giver and at no expense to the given. It is graciously and freely given looking for nothing in return. It is love in its purest sense. That is who God is.

So, God initiated His plan to have a part of Himself, His spoken Word, take on flesh, through the person of Yeshua HaMashiach, and offer himself as the blameless and righteous sin offering for the remission of the sins of us all by suffering the most brutal and horrific persecution unto death that any man will ever have to endure for sins that He did not commit. Thereby, we were redeemed and restored to an existence that will allow us to perform that holy purpose for which we were created, as set forth in 2 Corinthians 6:16-18:

> And what agreement hath the temple of God with idols? for ye are the temple of the living God; as God hath said, I WILL DWELL IN THEM, AND WALK IN THEM; AND I WILL BE THEIR GOD, AND THEY SHALL BE MY PEOPLE.
>
> Wherefore, COME OUT FROM AMONG THEM, AND BE YE SEPARATE, saith the Lord, AND TOUCH NOT THE UNCLEAN THING; AND I WILL RECEIVE YOU,
>
> AND WILL BE A FATHER UNTO YOU, AND YE SHALL BE MY SONS AND DAUGHTERS, saith the Lord Almighty.

If we use nothing more than our God-given common sense, we must conclude that, as the spiritually reborn children of God, we are His offspring and thereby possess the same spiritual characteristics and attributes as God, our Father. This fact is affirmed in Acts 17:28 and Hebrews 12:9 which describe us as the offspring of God Who is the Father of Spirits. Yeshua is the perfect example of who we were created to be. However, the life of Yeshua demonstrates a caveat to us fulfilling our creative purpose. We must be submissive to the will of God to the same extent that Yeshua submitted to God's will. We must strive to be the least in the Kingdom of God in order to be the greatest. By this I mean that we must love all Mankind before ourselves and completely submit ourselves to the will of God, even unto death, because it is through this uncompromising obedience to God that we demonstrate our unconditional love for Him and can become one with Him. God, the Father, demonstrated the same unconditional love for us when He required His only begotten Son to make a sacrificial substitutional death for all of Mankind.

God, the Son, likewise demonstrated His unconditional love for man by being obedient to His Father unto death.

As children of God called to become one with Him, we eagerly await our glorification into our triune Godhead's mirror image after which we shall live and reign with, in and through Yeshua HaMashiach forever. Our spiritual rebirths and ultimate glorifications will perfect our personal and collective oneness with God.

This book discusses the nature and extent of our oneness with God which is exactly like the relationship Yeshua enjoys as God and yet as a human being. Indeed, Yeshua is the firstborn of all the children of God. God's greatest creation, HuMankind, was always intended to become one with God to the same extent that Yeshua is one with Him because we shall be Yeshua and Yeshua shall be us. Just the thought of being one with God to this extent is overwhelming. Yet this awesome reality is set forth in the Word of God, which is alive, true, and sure and, indeed, is a revelation and expression of God Himself.

God's Holy Word says that "EYE HATH NOT SEEN, NOR EAR HEARD, NEITHER HAVE ENTERED INTO THE HEART OF MAN, THE THINGS WHICH GOD HATH PREPARED FOR THEM THAT LOVE HIM" (1 Corinthians 2:9). As we currently exist, we cannot know the mind of God. As we will exist, we shall not only know the mind of God but shall also share the mind of God. Yeshua prayed that both Jew and Gentile be one with God just as He is one with God. Yeshua knew the mind of God. When we become one with God in Yeshua, then we shall come to know all things about God.

This book will provide, through the trained eye of a literalist, a glimpse into the will of God contained in the Word of God as it relates to why God created us in His image and after His likeness. Just as a lawyer would cite the legal basis contained in the law for any supposition or conclusion he might make, we shall review the biblical support for the gospel of Yeshua HaMashiach because it is inextricably connected with the creative purpose of Mankind. Through the ensuing chapters, we shall Scripturally examine what it means to be created in the image and likeness of God; why man had to be taught the very valuable lesson of being love just as God is love; and, what is in store for every person who is reconciled to his creative purpose in and through Yeshua HaMashiach, our Lord and Savior. The story of man in God's master plan has been told innumerable times. This book focuses on God's purpose behind the story. In the process of discussing Mankind's creative purpose, mysteries, which have been sealed for millennia, are revealed through the inspiration of the Holy Spirit.

I have always maintained that a client is best prepared for deposition or trial testimony by understanding the big picture. Similarly, understanding the big picture helps a child of God better deal with the day-to-day challenges of our spiritual walk with God. Praise be to God for choosing to restore us to our original estate and allowing us to house His spiritual essence and to thereby experience Him in a way that cannot now be fully imagined or appreciated.

It is my fervent prayer that this book will explain the gospel of Yeshua HaMashiach and the master plan of God for us in a way that the reborn children of God will be strengthened and encouraged to finish the race knowing that their future glorified states will mirror Yeshua in every respect. Yeshua is fully God and fully man. He is the first-born of all who are spiritually reborn in Him.

This book is also written for all those who have yet to accept the free gift of eternal salvation through Yeshua HaMashiach, in the hope that, with a better appreciation of who they were created to be and what is their predestination, they will fully understand why Yeshua is the only way to eternal life and oneness with God.

May God open our spiritual eyes and ears and grant us the wisdom to understand the fullness of His purpose for our creation in His image and after His likeness.

CHAPTER ONE

GOD'S MASTER PLAN— THE BEGINNING

A ny good legal analysis is most effectively performed when the issue to be analyzed is identified in the beginning. The issue presented here is why did God create Mankind in His image and likeness? A sub-issue is how does God intend to carry out His creative plan given Mankind's fallen state? To answer these questions, I will apply the Law of God, otherwise referred to as the Word of God, to the facts of my life, the facts of the lives of the men and women set forth in the Word of God, and, I submit, to the facts of the lives of every human being because, though separate and distinct, our individual and collective salvation is through the eternal life of Yeshua HaMashiach. Every human being who repentantly accepts the death, burial and resurrection of Yeshua for the remission of their sins are spiritually reborn in Yeshua and, through Yeshua, are restored to the image and likeness of God.

There is no eternal life outside of Yeshua but there is all the fullness of God in Him. Because Yeshua is fully God and fully man, so shall we be, upon our glorification, since we shall be literally in Him; being completely one with Him as He is one with God, the Father. God created Mankind to be everything that Yeshua is but only if we are in Him. We would have never known our creative predestination if Yeshua had not given up His heavenly throne, took on flesh, and shown us the why and the how of our creative existence. We have everything, in its absolute sense, in and through Yeshua, and nothing at all without Him. It is, literally and figuratively, all or nothing. Satan would have us believe that there are exceptions to this Truth but an analysis of the Word of God tells us there are no exceptions. It has always been God's creative intent, His master plan, to effectuate His perfect and holy will throughout all creation in and through His highest creation, Mankind, who would possess all His personality traits, characteristics, mannerisms and attributes as one with His only begotten Son, Yeshua HaMashiach.

Therefore, we shall begin our analysis of God's master plan to create a perfect universe, which would be ruled by Him through Yeshua and, therefore, through Mankind, His highest creation, by examining the creation process itself as set forth in the Holy Scriptures.

God's plan for all creation, including Mankind's role in it, was conceived and completed by God before the foundation of the world. The concept of time does not exist from God's eternal perspective. Time was introduced when God created the heavens and the earth. God, in His eternal omniscience, simultaneously experiences all things that occur from the beginning of time to the end of time. He is not constrained by time (Psalm 90:2). He is the ever-present consummation of everything from the beginning to the end. He is the All-in-All. God's constant state of everything-at-once existed before He spoke creation into existence. God's initiation of time allowed His present tense existence to be temporally played out. This fact alone boggles the mind. How can God, Who is a Spirit and Who experiences all things at the same time, create a means through which He is able to temporally manifest Himself through Mankind in a physical universe and, yet, remain the eternal, everything-at-the-same-time God? Until our glorification when we are one with God, we shall never be able to fully answer this question. However, we can certainly seek the Holy Spirit's guidance and inspiration as we delve into the Word of God in search of an answer to this question.

God intended no other created thing or being to have a significance greater than Mankind, who was created to be one with God, through the personage of Yeshua HaMashiach. I have chosen to refer to our Savior by His Jewish name because He is of the house of Judah and salvation is of the Jews (John 4:22), to the Jew first and then to the Gentile (Romans 1:16; 2:10). This is my personal preference and is not meant to suggest that all Christians should do the same.

It is generally agreed among Bible historians that the language Yeshua and His disciples spoke was a form of Jewish Palestinian Aramaic. Yeshua is the shortened version of the name Yeshoshua and its translation is "Jehovah is salvation." The Aramaic word for our Lord is Yeshua and the word for Messiah is Msheeka. Thus, in Aramaic, our Savior was referred to as Yeshua Msheeka. In Hebrew, He is Yeshua HaMashiach.

For centuries, the early church sought to distance itself from its Jewish roots through various means including violent persecution of the Jews. In the 4th century, the name Yeshua was removed from the New Testament of the Bible and replaced with Jesus, the English form of the Greek form of the Jewish/Aramaic name Yeshua. The actions of the early church created a chasm between Jews and Gentiles and a schism between Jewish and Gentile believers. However, Yeshua prayed for the unification of all believers and His prayer is being answered. This book assumes the Jewish roots of Yeshua as it addresses God's plan for oneness with Yeshua's Spiritual Body. Yeshua is the Head of His Spiritual Body, all authority in heaven and earth has been given to Yeshua and, consequently, to every member of His Spiritual Body whether they be Jew or Gentile.

From God's eternal, everything-in-the-present perspective, His elect among Mankind has already accomplished their creative purpose through Yeshua HaMashiach because the beginning and the end occur at the same time. From our temporal perspective, we cannot fully appreciate the fact that we were created to be so much more than our current temporal existence. The Scriptural Word of God does tell us that our creative purpose is so interconnected with all physical creation that, when Adam and Eve sinned, they and their progeny began to die and everything in the physical realm also began to die with them (Romans 8:18-22).

The redemption of Mankind was necessary for there to be an eternal, universal, glorified physical manifestation of God in and through man. God spoke creation into existence to be glorified by its magnificence. He also wanted His glorious heavenly Kingdom to be extended to the earthly realm (Matthew 6:10).

We shall see that, from a spiritual perspective, every person, born of Adam and Eve, has an eternal soul. Because Adam and Eve chose love of self over love of God, the fate of our souls is directly dependent upon whether we embrace God's perfect demonstration of unconditional love of others to the salvation of our souls. By this I mean that the Spiritual Body of Mashiach is not a created thing. It is eternal because Yeshua, the Word of God, is eternal. As members of His Spiritual Body, our spiritual souls are eternal just as He is eternal. We have eternal life because He is eternal life and we are in Him. Yeshua is the Alpha and the Omega in the present tense. Upon our spiritual rebirths, we were grafted into His Spiritual Body. This was achievable because the Spiritual Word of God took on flesh, lived among men (John 1:14), and lovingly sacrificed His sinless life for the remission of our sins.

God formed man of the dust of the ground and breathed into his nostrils the breath of life (Genesis 2:7). Yeshua is the Word of God and the breath of life (John 1:1; 14:6; Acts 17:25). In Yeshua is life which is the light of men and which lights every man that comes into the world (John 1:4, 9; 11:25; 14:6). Thus, Yeshua is the very spiritual breath of God that was breathed into the nostrils of Adam upon his creation. I have recently read that the pronunciation of YHWH is like the inhaling and exhaling of a single breath.

As the life of the flesh is in the blood (Leviticus 17:11), every person born of Adam has this same spiritual life. Yeshua does, in fact, light every person who enters the world through birth. As a result, every breath we take should be a testament to us that we have God's eternal breath of life in us. It is this breath of life that makes us living souls. Every human being has a spiritual, eternal soul which is physically alive through and by the breath of God and, thereby, capable of living in the physical realm and serving as physical temples for our Spiritual God.

The Holy Scriptures tell us that our God is comprised of three personages: God, the Word of God and the Holy Spirit. Our triune Godhead has always intended to enter the physical realm through Mankind for Their glory and honor. It was our creative purpose to have the Word of God breathed into us as the dust of the ground and to, thereby, become living souls, i.e., eternal souls that now abide in the flesh (John 6:63). Does this not explain why the only action required to make man in the image and after the likeness of God was the breathing of God, Himself, into the nostrils of man (Genesis 1:26-28; 2:7)? That life was the Word of God in Whom we exist and Who exists in us. Just as God is everlasting, Yeshua is also everlasting as the Word of God, the very breath of God. Our eternal, living souls were created by having this same everlasting breath instilled in us. Consequently, we shall eternally exist either completely separate and apart from God or completely one with Him. The fate of those who are apart from God is to share that place reserved for Satan and his followers, the eternal lake of fire.

We have the unperfected attributes, characteristics and mannerisms of God because our souls are from and of Him yet, our flesh has the sin nature of Satan, through Adam and Eve. This fundamental truth is essential in our understanding of why man was created in the image and likeness of God and, therefore, how man can be physically and spiritually one with his Creator.

The Bible often refers to the Book of Life which contains the names of every human being who was born with the Breath of Life in him. This would necessarily mean that, before the beginning, the names of Adam and Eve, and their progeny, were written in the Book of Life and were blotted out only if they died in their sins. Good works will not keep your name in that Book, only Yeshua can do that (Philippians 4:3; Revelation 3:5; 13:8; 17:8; 20:12,15; 21:27; 22:19).

In this chapter, we shall first consider the role each of the three personages of our triune Godhead played in the manifestation of God in the physical realm through the creation process. We shall then attempt to view creation from both God's eternal perspective and our earthly perspective. Finally, we shall discuss the role that faith has played in the creation of all things and the role it continues to play in the effectuation of God's will. The evidence set forth below points to but one inescapable conclusion and that is that all of creation, both physical and spiritual, are the means through which God manifests Himself in the physical and spiritual realms, all for His glory and honor.

Despite this fact, God allows the heavenly hosts and Mankind to choose to remain a part of him forever. Those who choose to have no sincere part in Him will be eternally separated from

God. That is true for the rebellious angels who will be cast into the eternal lake of fire and for those humans whose names have been blotted out of the Book of Life. They will share the fate of the fallen angels. Angels, who remained true to their God, will continue to perform their respective purposes for which they were created. Likewise, we, who have chosen to be justified through the blood of Yeshua HaMashiach, are given the privilege and honor to experience eternal oneness with God as members of the Spiritual Body of Mashiach and physical temples of our triune Godhead.

The Triune Godhead in Creation

The Bible states "In the beginning God created the heaven and the earth" (Genesis 1:1). The Hebrew word for God used in this text is *Elohim*, which is a plural form of the divine name signifying the existence of God, the Father, His Living Spoken Word Who took on flesh, and the Holy Spirit, the Ruach HaKodesh. This triune Godhead, composed of three separate, equal personages, is at the same time one deity, who is God (Matthew 28:19; John 10:30; 17:11, 21-24; 1 John 5:7).

Consider what Matthew was inspired to write. He said that Yeshua sent His disciples into the world to teach all nations and baptize them "in the name of the Father, and of the Son, and of the Holy Ghost" (Matthew 28:19). Notice that the use of the word "name" is singular. This demonstrates that this triune Godhead is one in every respect; so much so that a single name is used to refer to all three of them. In Isaiah 6:2-3, we discover that the seraphim cried to each other declaring "Holy, holy, holy, is the LORD of hosts." Again, the word "Lord" is singular. This threefold declaration of holy is for the threefold personages of God. In a later chapter, I discuss those passages of the Bible which establish that the children of God adopt the same name as that of our triune Godhead. This is God's affirmation that He intends for us to be one with Him in every respect.

In looking again at the Genesis creation account, we find that the Hebrew word for "created" is *bara*. Footnote 1:1 of the Book of Genesis in the Thomas Nelson Study Bible tells us that *bara* is a singular verb used with a plural noun *Elohim* (Genesis 1:1). What does this indicate? It is further confirmation of both the plurality and oneness of our triune Godhead in that They did the creating together as one. Indeed, when one looks at the creation passages contained in Genesis 1, every phase of creation begins with the phrase "And God said." The Orthodox Jewish Bible uses the Hebrew word *Elohim* in every instance to refer to God when creation was spoken into existence. Finally, and most importantly, *Elohim* is also used in Genesis 1:26 when God said "Let us make man in our image, after our likeness..." In this verse, God affirms the fact that all three personages of our triune Godhead spoke as one in the creation of all things because He uses the pronoun "us" to say who is making man.

Psalm 33:6 states: "By the word of the LORD were the heavens made; and all the host of them by the breath of his mouth." 2 Peter 3:5 echoes this fact by stating, "by the word of God the heavens were of old, and the earth standing out of the water and in the water." Psalm 148:1-6 command us to praise the Lord, for He created all things in heaven and on earth and established them forever by making a decree that shall not pass. That decree was an oral one, i.e., spoken one in the form of the second personage of our triune Godhead, the Word of God. According to Genesis 2:1-2, God rested on the seventh day of creation, having completed the creation of the heavens and the earth. Even though God made no creative oral commands on the seventh day, Yeshua, the Word of God, is still Lord of the Sabbath (Mark 2:7-8).

One may ask "Who is this Word of God?" The answer to this question is also revealed in the Holy Scriptures, which tell us that Yeshua HaMashiach is the Word of God (Luke 8:11; John 1:1, 14; Revelation 19:13). This begs the questions "How could the Son of God, Who was born thousands of years after Adam, participate in creation week as the Living Word of God?" and "How can we rationalize this if we interpret these passages literally?"

From a strict constructionist point of view, the references to Yeshua HaMashiach as the Word of God in the Holy Scriptures demand but one conclusion and that is that Yeshua is the *literal* Word of God Who took on flesh and dwelt among us as the only begotten Son of God (John 1:14; 1 John 1:1-2). Yeshua is the embodiment of every utterance from God. He is the breath of life (Genesis 2:7; Job 33:4) that is given to all men as an eternal gift (Romans 6:23). John 1:1 tells us that Yeshua, the Word of God, was with God in the beginning and, indeed, is God. Yeshua is the physical image of the invisible God and is the means through whom God's spiritual Kingdom shall be manifested on earth (Colossians 1:15-20).

Yeshua tells us that He is in the bosom of the Father (John 1:18) and that He came out from God (John 16:27). As the literal Word of God, Yeshua can only do what He hears the Father say (John 14:24). In fact, Yeshua's death and resurrection were the direct result of a commandment from God (John 10:7-18), specifically, verse 18. Taking this thought to its logical, literal conclusion, every act, great or small, performed by Yeshua during His earthly life was the fulfillment of the spoken commands of God. It necessarily follows, then, that, since we are members of the Spiritual Body of Mashiach, upon our glorification, we also will only do what God says in and through Yeshua. Indeed, we shall be completely conformed to the image of His Son, Yeshua

HaMashiach (Romans 8:28-30). The Apostle Paul instructs us to give thanks in everything as that is the will of God in Yeshua HaMashiach concerning us (1 Thessalonians 5:18).

However, it is God's will that our decisions to be one with Him, through Yeshua, be out of loving obedience because He first loved us by sacrificing His only begotten Son for the remission of our sins to the salvation of our souls. It must be a choice out of pure love and for no other reason. We must put our love for God above our love for ourselves. We must also put our love for others above our own self interests. The Apostle John tells us, in 1 John 4:7-12, that we must love one another because love comes from and is God. When we love, we demonstrate that we are spiritually born of God, that we know God and that God lives in us. We must mirror Him in every aspect, including His very essence which is His unconditional love.

Several translations of Genesis 3:8 state that Adam and Eve heard the voice of God walking in the garden. This would be none other than the Preincarnate Yeshua. Adam and Eve, apparently, were able to commune with the Preincarnate Word of God. They talked with Him daily. These were conversations between God and Mankind that appear to have been casual in nature. Now that we have been reconciled with God through the sacrificial death, burial and resurrection of Yeshua, we can have these same conversations with God all day, every day.

As the eternal Living Word of God, Yeshua is both one and equal to God, the Father, and God, the Holy Spirit. As mentioned earlier, John 1:1-3 confirm the oneness between God and Yeshua:

> In the beginning was the Word, and the Word was with God, and the Word was God. The same was in the beginning with God. All things were made by him; and without him was not anything made that was made.

However, when Yeshua became the Son of God, He subjected Himself to the authority of God, the Father (John 14:28; 1 Corinthians 15:27-28).

Yeshua is also the written Word of God since all Scriptures are inspired by God, the Holy Spirit. The Scriptures are alive with the presence of Yeshua HaMashiach, both in and of them. In Yeshua dwells all the fullness of the Godhead bodily (Colossians 2:9). As members of His Spiritual Body, we shall be glorified upon His return and shall fully appreciate this same fullness of God so much so that we shall be part of the All-in-All (Ephesians 1:22-23; 3:19).

The Holy Spirit, Who also proceeds from the Father (John 15:26), was intricately involved in the creation process, when He hovered over the face of the waters (Genesis 1:2) and adorned the heavens (Job 26:13). He continues to renew the earth and everything in it (Psalms 104:30). The Scriptures also tell us that the Holy Spirit can only say (and therefore do) what He hears the Father say (John 16:13). This is further confirmation that all three personages of the Godhead were involved in creation week as one (Genesis 1:1-2; John 1:3).

Creation and Evolution

A brief discussion about creation versus evolution is warranted. The question about whether Mankind, the earth and, indeed, the universe are the result of a supernatural creation process completed over a period of six days or an evolutionary process spanning millions, if not billions, of years is unequivocally answered in the first chapter of the Book of Genesis. In Genesis 1:5, God defines the first day as being night and day or an evening and a morning. In fact, God attributes so much importance to this definition of a day that He ends each day's creative work with the same definition of a day (Genesis 1:5, 8, 13, 19, 23, 31). Obviously, God sought to drive home the point that the creation of the physical and spiritual realms, and all that is in them, was accomplished in six literal days.

The Bible does not explain how our triune Godhead performed this supernatural feat. For that matter, it doesn't explain how any of the miracles of our triune Godhead were accomplished. We will most likely never fully understand the mechanics behind the wondrous works of God until we are glorified in Yeshua upon His return.

What the Bible does tell us about a day from God's eternal perspective is fascinating and may shed some light into the magnificent nature of God. For instance, we are told that one day to the Lord is as a thousand years, and a thousand years as one day (2 Peter 3:8). The first half of this verse could be literally interpreted to mean that each day is as an infinity to God because a thousand years are composed of approximately 365,000 days, each day of which is similarly like a thousand years and so forth and so forth such that, in the end, a day from God's eternal perspective consists of an infinite number of days. One day is like an endless eternity.

Based upon our interpretation of the first half of this verse, the second part of this verse would necessarily mean that, from God's perspective, infinity can occur in the span of one day. This would be consistent with those Biblical references which establish that God **is** "from everlasting to everlasting" (Psalms 90:2; 103:17; 106:48) and Yeshua **is** the Alpha and Omega (Revelation 1:11; 21:6; 22:13), emphasis on the present tense of the verbs. Our God is truly the beginning and the end at the same time.

It is of note that God did not create the universe and all that is in it on a second-by-second or moment-by-moment basis. Instead, creation was accomplished on a day-by-day basis over a period of six days. The Holy Scriptures do not elaborate on why God places significance on the completion of both night and day/evening and morning for a day to have transpired. Nor are we told why creation was measured in terms of days. Nonetheless, time appears to be defined by God in terms of a day. Indeed, we are told to take life day-by-day (Matthew 6:34). Consider Genesis 2:4 and 5:1-2, wherein God tells us that creation, including Mankind, was accomplished "in the day".

Since God is the Beginning and the End, at the same time, and does not reside in this temporal existence of ours, He is not limited to our temporal time frame and can supernaturally cram hundreds of billions of years into the span of one day. At the end of every day, God saw that His work was good. (Genesis 1:4, 10, 12, 18, 21, 25, 31). With God, all things are possible (Matthew 19:26).

Evolutionists cannot accept such an interpretation because it defies "science" and requires a leap of faith. This is a bit ironic since, as we shall see, faith is exactly what the Holy Scriptures say God used to form all of creation from things that are unseen.

The Role of Faith in the Creation Process

We know that God is faithful (1 Corinthians 1:9; 1 Thessalonians 5:24; 2 Thessalonians 3:3). The question is, "what is faith"? According to Hebrews 11:1, faith is defined as "the substance of things hoped for, the evidence of things not seen." The Greek word for "substance," in this context, is *hypostasis,* which means "assurance, confidence or realization." Therefore, faith is the assurance, confidence or realization of unseen things, which are hoped for. While this is a definition of faith, it begs the question how does faith accomplish this magnificent end result? The answer to that question starts and ends with Who our God is.

What does the Bible tell us about our God Whose limitless faith is able to bring into realization all unseen things hoped for? First and foremost, it tells us that God is love (1 John 4:8, 16). Furthermore, the Bible tells us that our God is the God of hope Who fills us with hope through the power of the Holy Spirit (Romans 15:13). These fundamental truths about the intrinsic nature of God is incredibly important because 1 Corinthians 13:7 tells us that it is love that believes and hopes for all things. Verse 8 of that same chapter tells us that love never fails. God's limitless love, therefore, is the underlying force that drives the execution of God's eternal faith resulting in the realization of all unseen hoped for things. Lamentations 3:22-23 inform us that God's compassions never fail, that they are new every morning and that His faithfulness is great. The Hebrew word for compassion is *rachem* which means tender love or great tender mercies.

The fact that God is pure, unadulterated, perfect love explains why He is holy (Psalm 99: 9), why there is no darkness in Him at all (1 John 1:5) and why He was able to declare that his creative efforts were good (Genesis 1: 4,10,12,18,21,25). Everything that God does is premised on love. Everything that God created was, therefore, good (Genesis 1:31). Since there is no limit to God, there must likewise be no limit to His love, His hope and, consequently, His faith. Anything and everything are possible for God Whose loving, hopeful faith has no boundaries. God's matchless loving faith hoped for and brought into realization every created thing, both physical and spiritual.

Since our God is pure, unadulterated love, His perfect will for all creation is premised on love. We can further answer the question of "why did God make man in His image and likeness." God wants to enjoy His perfect physical and spiritual creation through Mankind, His highest creation, in a love relationship that is equal to His relationship with His Son and His Holy

Spirit. In fact, as members of the Spiritual Body of the Son, we are now able to experience the same loving relationship the Son enjoys with His father for all eternity. All the love God has for His Son, He has for us because we are in His Son. Such a love is immeasurable. It is incomprehensible. It is beyond our understanding. Yet, it is our destiny as His children in Yeshua.

It may be difficult for some to comprehend how God's loving, hopeful faith can perform, from that which is unseen, such feats as the realization and sustainment of His spiritual Kingdom, an entire universe, and all that is in it. However, the Holy Scriptures are replete with instances in which God's loving, hopeful faith is the underlying source behind the performance of wondrous miracles of healing and deliverance.

As we look further at Genesis 1:1, we find that the Hebrew word for "heaven" is *shamayim,* the root of which is *shameh,* which means "heaven seen and unseen." This suggests that all things, visible and invisible, were created "in the beginning." This includes all matter, from huge planets to microscopic atoms, molecules, or particles. It also includes all things spiritual, such as the angels. This is confirmed in Colossians 1:16-17 which state

> For by him were all things created, that are in heaven, and that are in earth, visible and invisible, whether they be thrones, or dominions, or principalities, or powers: all things were created by him, and for him: And he is before all things, and by him all things consist.

God's faith is absolute and limitless. It is so sure that it is, for all practical purposes, actual knowledge. With this kind of loving faith, God can realize and sustain anything.

God's words are true and faithful (Revelation 21:5). God demonstrated the faithfulness of His words in a mighty way during creation week. When God said "Let there be light" (Genesis 1:3), His living words were able to effectuate His command because of the power attendant with His limitless faith.

Hebrews 11:3 tells us that:

Through faith we understand that the worlds were framed by the word of God, so that things which are seen were not made of things which do appear.

Thus, God's faith is the only means by which the unseen can be realized (Hebrews 11:1). Indeed, this degree of faith cannot be fully appreciated by man. To create the universe and all that is in it, with the intricate order and arrangement of it all, takes a great and intelligent mind beyond our imagination, with faith too powerful and awesome to describe. Without our triune God's faith, the universe would not exist, and through this limitless faith the universe consists, that is, holds together. The Bible tells us that God upholds all things by the word of His power (Hebrews 1:3). The power of our faithful God manifests itself through Yeshua HaMashiach, His spoken word.

Also, because God is always the same yesterday, today, and forever, His level of faithfulness never decreases, nor can it increase. All that He has made to be realized will always exist in the form He wills it to be (Hebrews 13:8; Malachi 3:6).

The Role of Faith in God's Master Plan for Man

In order to be one with God, man must have the full measure of God's love and faith. Acceptance of what the Bible says about the role that God's loving faith played in the creation process requires the same loving faith on the part of the child of God. Indeed, in His eternal master plan for Mankind, God intends that

His loving faith play an equally vital role in the life and salvation of each of His children. 1 John 4:12,16 inform us that when we love our fellow man, we demonstrate our belief in the love God has for us. God, thereby, dwells in us and His love is perfected in us. During His earthly ministry, Yeshua placed heavy emphasis on the power of faith (Matthew 9:2, 13:58). He placed an equal emphasis on love (John 15:9-13). Through Yeshua, every reborn child of God exhibits these Godly traits (1 Thessalonians 5:8, 1 Timothy 1:14, 2 Timothy 1:13).

The apostle Paul informs us, in Romans 1:20:

For the invisible things of him from the creation of the world are clearly seen, being understood by the things that are made, even his eternal power and Godhead, so that they are without excuse.

The context of this verse is that our invisible God is revealed to every one of us through all of creation, which can be clearly seen. However, it requires loving faith for us to see that the world and everything in it is a revelation of God's eternal power and divine loving nature.

No man has ever mastered loving faith to the extent that God has. However, in our soon-to-be-glorified states, when we are one with Him, our mastery of His faith, driven by perfect love, will allow us to create and sustain to the same extent that God can according to His perfect will. This is only possible because God will be so much a part of us, and we apart of Him, that His love and His faith will become our love and our faith, His will, our will. Just as Yeshua could only do as He heard God say, we, who will be in Yeshua and perfect mirror images of Yeshua, also will only be able to do as we hear God say.

The writer of the Book of Hebrews introduces the definition of faith with the word "Now." There has been much discussion as to what meaning the writer of Hebrews intended for the word "Now" in this verse. I am reminded of a sermon, given by Bishop Clifford M. Johnson, Jr. several years ago, in which he stated the word "now", in the context of Hebrews 11:1, could serve equally as an adverb, conjunction, noun, adjective, or interjection. Bishop Johnson went on to explain that, as an adverb, the word "Now" would mean "at the present time," "at this moment," or "at once." This passage, then, would mean that the faith one currently possesses is the substance or realization of things hoped for.

He further noted the word "Now" could serve as a conjunction, thus connecting the message of Chapter 10 of Hebrews to that of Chapter 11. The message of Chapter 10 is that Yeshua's once-for-all sacrifice has replaced the old covenant's yearly animal sacrifice, thereby allowing all who believe in faith to have direct access to the throne of God. The message of Chapter 11 is that true faith is the means of realizing the promises of the new covenant.

Completing the discussion, Bishop Johnson said as a noun, the word "Now" would simply mean "the present time." As an adjective, it would mean "of the present time." Finally, as an interjection, it would signify a preface or resumption of the writer's previous remarks.

Could it not be that the Holy Spirit, Who inspired the writer of Hebrews, intended for the word "Now" to function in *each* of these ways simultaneously? You see, the word "Now" introduces and connects the most important word, "faith." In other words, the faith that each child of God possesses concerning his or her salvation through Yeshua HaMashiach is the means through which his or her salvation will be realized. Through faith, we abide in God, and He in us. His faith becomes our faith. Yes, "now" is a catch word to get our attention and means all modes.

Romans 12:3-6 tell us that each member of the Body of Mashiach has been apportioned a measure of faith sufficient to perform the spiritual gift(s) given to each of us. God, the Father, has given every child of His differing gifts, such as prophecy, teaching, exhortation and ministry. He, therefore, has equipped us with enough faith to exercise these gifts. Only upon our perfection, in and through Yeshua, will we be able to fully appreciate, through demonstration, God's matchless faith.

The apostle Paul wrote: "Faithful is he that calleth you, who also will do it" (1 Thessalonians 5:24). We were predestined before the foundation of the world to be heirs of salvation and fellow brethren of Yeshua HaMashiach. Our God, Who is faithful, will make this a realization. Whoever is spiritually born of God overcomes the world, and the victory that overcomes the world is our faith (1 John 5:4). Scripture reminds us that we are saved by the hope of what is not seen, and we patiently wait for it (Romans 8:24-25).

Now then, since faith is the realization of things hoped for, anything we are inspired by the Holy Spirit to ask of God, according to His perfect will, whether it be as intercessors for others or on our own behalves, must first be lovingly hoped for, and we must wait patiently for it to be realized. The faith of God, who lives in and through us, will bring it to realization. We walk by faith and not by sight (2 Corinthians 5:7). This faith comes by hearing, and hearing by the Word of God (Romans 10:17). It is the faith of God by and through which our salvation has been assured. Since God is the author of our salvation, according to Hebrews 5:9, His limitless faith will ensure that we are indeed saved.

As the children of God, we are of one faith. For it is written in Ephesians 4:4-6:

There is one body, and one Spirit, even as ye are called in one hope of your calling; One Lord, one faith, one baptism, One God and Father of all, who is above all, and through all, and in you all.

We, therefore, must be very careful of what we say when we are in the Spirit, because when we speak, our faithful God, Who in-dwells us, lives in our words and, therefore, they have power. 2 Corinthians 4:13 states:

We having the same spirit of faith, according as it is written, I BELIEVED, AND THEREFORE HAVE I SPOKEN, we also believe,
And therefore speak.

When our triune Godhead is fully in us and we in Them, we can faithfully tell a mountain to remove to another place, and it will do it. Nothing shall be impossible for us (Matthew 17:20). It all depends on the extent to which we are willing to let God's loving faith manifest itself through us.

The Scriptures warn us not to let any corrupt communications proceed out of our mouths but only that which is good for teaching, so that it may minister grace unto the hearers (Ephesians 4:29). What we say and how we say it is extremely important for a child of God who is one with Elohim because Peter tells us that, when we speak, we are to do so as one who speaks the very words of God (1 Peter 4:11).

Indeed, Matthew 12:36-37 tell us that we will ultimately be judged by the words that proceed out of our mouths. We are told in Proverbs 14:5 that a faithful witness will not lie. In James 3:8-10, we are cautioned to be careful with our tongue, lest we curse men who are made after the likeness of God. In other words, should we curse others, we are cursing creations of God, including reborn children of God, all of whom have been made in the image and the likeness of God.

Ephesians 2:8 tells us that, by grace, we are saved through faith. Once saved, we cannot lose our salvation (John 6:27, 37-40). We are spiritually reborn of God and therefore have His spiritual genes in us. We can no more rid ourselves of God's spiritual genes than we can the genes we are physically born with. Just as our physical genes determine our physical mannerisms, attributes and characteristics for the duration of our physical lives, our spiritual genes also are with us for the duration of our eternal spiritual lives and determine our spiritual mannerisms, attributes and characteristics which, when we are spiritually re-born of God, fully mirror His mannerisms, attributes and characteristics.

The assurance of our salvation is the result of our spiritual genetic relationship with God upon our spiritual rebirths. Yeshua confirms this fact by assuring us that, once joined with us as one, He will never leave us (Matthew 28:20, Hebrews 13:5). Thus, no one is able to pluck us out of the hand of Yeshua or God, the Father, since They are one (John 10:25-30). Remember, God, the Father, is currently enjoying our physical and spiritual perfection in and through Yeshua because all of time happens at once from His eternal perspective. However, we, in the earthly realm, must live out, through faith, what God is now experiencing. We cannot lose what eternally is.

Some have cited John 15:2 to support the contention that the saved can lose their salvation. Let's carefully examine this verse:

Every branch in me that beareth not fruit he taketh away: and every branch that beareth fruit, he purgeth it, that it may bring forth more fruit.

These words of Yeshua have been incorrectly interpreted to mean that the children of God, who abide in Mashiach and are therefore saved, will be removed from Him and, inferentially, lose their salvation if they do not bear fruit. Nothing could be further from the truth. It is the branches who are not connected to the true vine, and, therefore, are not in Yeshua, that bear corrupt fruit, are cast into the fire and are burned (John 15:6). Every tree is known by its fruit (Luke 6:43-44).

To clearly understand what Yeshua is telling us in John 15:1-7, we need to have an appreciation of what is involved in the growing of grapes. Bruce Wilkinson, in his book, *Secrets of the Vine*, gives us an excellent explanation of the process of growing grapes. He states that the vinedresser never cuts off and discards branches that bear no fruit. Instead, he lifts the nonproductive branches off the ground, cleans them up and secures them on the trellis, thereby enabling them to bear fruit. Wilkinson suggests that the King James translation of Scriptures, such as Matthew 14:20; 27:32; and John 1:29, lends to multiple interpretations of the Greek word *airo* including "take away," "take up," "lift up," or "to bear." I agree with Wilkerson's conclusion that, in the context of John 15:1-7, the correct interpretation is "take up" or "lift up." If a believer is not bearing fruit, God lifts up that child of His and cleanses that person's heart and soul so that spiritual fruit-bearing can begin.

I can tell you from my personal experience that this cleansing process can sometimes be a very painful or difficult process. My salvation came about after I participated in an abortion, the taking of the life of my unborn child. This horrific tragedy made my life unbearable until it brought me to my knees in submission to Yeshua Who washed away my sins through the shedding of His eternal, blameless blood. It took the sacrifice of this yet-to-be-born life for me to be saved and to begin to bear spiritual fruit. That child is automatically saved because it died in its innocence. I am reminded of the Biblical reference about the death of King David's first child with Bathsheba wherein, after the death of the child, David said he will go to the child (2 Samuel 12:15-23). I look forward to the day when I will go to my child and thank this person for my eternal salvation at his/her expense.

With respect to branches that are already bearing fruit, Wilkinson informs us that the vinedresser prunes these branches so that they may bear even more fruit. Both forms of purging are oftentimes painful. However, any branch (that is, believer) who is united to the true vine, Yeshua, cannot be cast away. Virtually every servant of God, including the Old Testament prophets and Yeshua's disciples, were made to endure trying times so that they would be able to bear increasingly more spiritual fruit. Fruit-bearing, you see, is part of the Creator's master plan for every child of His. The New International Version of James 2:22 tells us that our faith and actions work together to the perfection or completeness of our faith.

The importance of faith in the life of a child of God, according to God's master plan, cannot be overstated. The Holy Scriptures are replete with examples of the power of God's faith when exercised by man, causing his unseen hopes to be realized immediately or over time. Indeed, our hope in the Lord strengthens us (Isaiah 40:31).

Examples of the immediate realization of unseen hopes through faith are when Yeshua spoke healing into the nobleman's sick son which occurred at the moment the nobleman believed Him (John 4:43-53), when Yeshua healed the servant of the centurion the selfsame hour of his expression of faith in Yeshua's authority over all things physical and spiritual (Matthew 8:5-13), when the woman, who suffered from an issue of blood for twelve years, was immediately healed upon touching the garment of Yeshua (Luke 8:43-48) and when the unwavering faith of Joshua allowed him to command the sun and moon to stay still for the span of one day while the Israelites defeated the Amorites (Joshua 10:12-14).

In addition, in the Acts of the Apostles, Luke describes the healing of a lame man through the apostles Peter and John:

And his name through faith in his name hath made this man strong, whom ye see and know: yea, the faith which is by him hath given him this perfect soundness in the presence of you all. (Acts 3:16)

In this passage, Peter is telling those gathered around the man, who was healed, that it was the man's faith in the name of Yeshua that allowed the faith of Yeshua to immediately make him strong. Luke 14:2-4 and 18:41-43 are two further examples of how man's faith, in and through Yeshua, can immediately heal infirmities.

Through faith, unseen hopes can also be realized over time, as was the case with Moses and Abraham. We are told that by faith Moses "forsook Egypt, not fearing the wrath of the king: for he endured, as seeing him who is invisible" (Hebrews 11:27). Yeshua told us that Abraham rejoiced to see His day, and Abraham saw it and was glad (John 8:56). The only way for our father Abraham (Romans 4:1-16) to see Yeshua's day was by faith through his spiritual eyes. Thus, by faith, we can see God, who is invisible.

That is why the writer of Hebrews goes to such great lengths to testify about the power of faith in anointed people of God throughout the ages. These men and women knew that their unseen hopes would eventually be realized because of their faith in the Word of God (Hebrews 11:4-40).

The faith of our triune God, when called upon through our God-given faith, will never fail us and will give us perfect soundness (Acts 3:16). It necessarily follows that the realization of our unseen hopes is limited only by the extent of our faith in God's faithfulness, which is determined by the extent of our intimacy and oneness with God. That, in turn, is determined by the extent of our reading, hearing and obedience to the Word of God (Romans 10:17). The more we abide in God and He in us, through constant, intimate and prayerful communion with God, the more access we have to His limitless faith (1 Thessalonians 5:17).

When we ultimately attain our incorruptible states, our faith will be one and the same as God's limitless faith because of our complete oneness with Him. In such a state, all unseen things lovingly hoped for will, pursuant to the perfect will of God, be realized unto the glory of God, including the literal movement of mountains, because we shall possess absolute faith, having no doubt (Matthew 21:21).

However, we do not have to wait until we are glorified with Yeshua to experience God's limitless faith. As spiritually reborn children of God, we have direct access to God's limitless faith now. All we have to do is demonstrate our uncompromising and unconditional love for God by letting God live in and through us. The more we die to self, the more God lives in and through us. As a result, whatever we ask for in faithful prayer, we shall receive insofar as it is the will of God (Matthew 21:22).

God does this for us because Yeshua is the author and finisher of our faith (Hebrews 12:2). Our unseen salvation is realized, through the grace of God, by our hope and faith in the name of Yeshua, Who is God. Yes, we can do all things through Yeshua who strengthens us (Philippians 4:13). The Holy Spirit also strengthens us as we eagerly wait for our hope of righteousness to be realized through faith (Galatians 5:5). Once realized, we will be like Yeshua in every respect (2 Corinthians 3:18).

Because of our faith in Yeshua HaMashiach, God imputes— that is, puts into our account—the righteousness of Yeshua (Romans 10:3-4, Philippians 3:9). The definition of the word "impute," as contained in *Black's Law Dictionary*, can be paraphrased using a Christian analogy as follows: "Righteousness is imputed to a child of God when it is ascribed or charged to him, not because he is personally cognizant of it or deserving of it, but because another is, namely, Yeshua, HaMashiach." Another analogy would be the imputation of sin to the sinner as a violator of God's law whether done intentionally or otherwise because the purpose of the law is to reveal sin (Romans 3:20). It's the law that generates the imputation of sin (Romans 5:13) just as it is the righteousness of Yeshua that creates the imputation of righteousness in the children of God.

It is this same righteousness that enables us to be transformed into the express image of Yeshua, who is the express image of God. This transformation will not be totally complete until we are given our incorruptible bodies and become completely one with God, just as Yeshua is one with God in glory. In the meantime, our ever-maturing faith through Yeshua HaMashiach will allow us to realize our unseen hopes, some sooner than others. For example, Mark 8:22-26 provide an account where it took Yeshua two tries to restore sight to the blind man. Obviously, Yeshua didn't need two attempts to give sight to this man. This passage infers that the faith of the blind man was insufficient for him to receive full sight on the first attempt but was enough to give him clear vision on the second attempt.

Only true, loving faith, which stems from Yeshua, can bring about the realization of the unseen hopes of every child of God who is to be glorified unto God in the image of Yeshua. Even a little bit of faith in Yeshua can do miraculous things (Luke 17:6). All other faith is vain. And what is vain faith? In 1 Corinthians 15:1-19, the apostle Paul tells us that, should the Gospel be not true, then our faith is vain and we perish. *The Thomas Nelson Study Bible*, in footnote 15.2 of 1 Corinthians, describes in more detail the distinction between vain, Godless faith and true faith in the Gospel of Yeshua. The footnote explains that, in Chapter 15 of 1 Corinthians, Paul uses three Greek words to describe vain faith. The first word is *Eikei* which means "without effect." In other words, faith without Yeshua HaMashiach cannot effectuate the realization of unseen hopes. The second word is *Kenos,* which means "without success," "without truth," and "without basis." Clearly, this kind of faith, lacking as it does any divine basis, cannot successfully realize unseen hopes. The third word the apostle uses in this chapter to describe vain faith is *Mataios,* which means "useless." This type of faith is a waste of time because it can do nothing for the believer. Of note is the fact that, because of the vain faith of the Nazarenes, Yeshua could do no mighty works there (Mark 6:1-6).

Anything that is not of the limitless faith of God is sin (Romans 14:23). The devils believe that there is one God (James 2:19), but they will never realize their unseen hopes of usurping God's authority and ruling the heavens and the earth in God's stead because their faith is not grounded in Yeshua, the Word of God. Baseless, vain faith cannot bring about the realization of unseen hopes. In fact, to feign true faith is justification for immediate condemnation. Yeshua symbolically demonstrated this point through the story of the fig tree (Mark 11:13-14). A factual example of immediate condemnation, resulting from the exercising of vain faith, is that of Saul, who offered burnt offerings to God in Samuel's stead (1 Samuel 13:9-14) and disobeyed God's command concerning the destruction of the Amalekites (1 Samuel 15:1-11). These acts of vain faith by Saul brought down God's immediate judgment upon him. Clearly, it is impossible for the unseen hopes of a person, whose faith is vain, to be realized.

There is only one true faith, and the only source of that faith is our triune Godhead (Ephesians 4:4-6). We can be faithful only because God is faithful. We comprise the Spiritual Body of Yeshua, who is the faithful witness (Revelation 1:5, 3:14). If we ask anything of God, in His faith, wavering not, it shall be given unto us (James 1:5-6). However, we should only ask for unseen hopes that are in furtherance of God, the Father's, holy will. The realization of these hopes would then be the effectuation of His perfect will to His honor and glory.

True faith is demonstrated through the fruits of our faith by our works. True faith works not for salvation, but because of salvation. The works, which are the consequence of true faith, do not bring about salvation. Instead, they are the natural and practical result of salvation.

James, the brother of Yeshua, tells us that just as the body without the spirit is dead, so faith without works is dead (James 2:26). He writes:

What doth it profit, my brethren, though a man say he hath faith, and have not works? Can faith save him? ... Even so faith, if it hath not works, is dead, being alone. (James 2:14, 17)

According to James, for faith to have any effect, the believer must be willing to engage in acts in furtherance of his acknowledged faith. This is the fruit-bearing I referred to earlier. Yeshua said "According to your faith be it unto you" (Matthew 9:29). It was faith in the underlying faithfulness of God that formed the basis for His miraculous ministry. Yeshua taught with authority (Matthew 7:29). He gives this same authority to those who believe in Him in faith. For instance, He gave it to His disciples (Luke 9:1), and they were able to exercise this God-given authority according to the measure of their faith (Mark 9: 14-29).

Paul asserts that the members of the Body of Yeshua have been given measures of faith proportionally through Yeshua HaMashiach according to the determined grace of God (Romans12:3-8). HaMashiach is the source of all grace and faith, which He distributes proportionately to His brethren according to His Father's good pleasure. In a later chapter, we will discuss how the children of God, being members of the Spiritual Body of Mashiach, have different functions requiring varying levels of faith and suffering, just as the physical members of Yeshua's physical body had different functions and levels of suffering. The measure of faith given and the degree of suffering attributed to every member of the Spiritual Body of Mashiach is determined by the specific function each member is asked to perform.

Every child of God, being a member of the Body of Messiah, has the faithfulness of God living in him and through him. We are one in body, spirit, hope, and faith, yet every one of us has differing gifts to be used according to the proportion of faith given to us by Yeshua HaMashiach (Ephesians 4:4-7). It is the oneness of our collective faith, which is the faith of God, that ensures our salvation and the realization of all that is promised to us as heirs of salvation.

Faith, you see, is extremely important in the life of a believer. It allows us to use our spiritual senses and gifts. According to Yeshua, that's why He used parables (Matthew 13:9-16, Mark 4:33-34). Those who have no faith will hear these parables and yet not hear, they will see and yet not see. They will not understand with their heart. However, blessed are our eyes for they see, and our ears, for they hear (Matthew 13:10-17). Faith opens our spiritual eyes and ears. It causes us to understand the Word of God.

Envision, if you will, that every human being has a life car that proceeds down the road of life until the fuel runs out and death ensues. From birth, we are taught how to drive that car and eventually to take control of our life car's steering wheel so that we can maneuver our way through our respective courses of life. Since everyone wants to be in control of his own life, we can't wait to take control of our respective life cars and instinctively balk at the thought of letting someone else drive our life cars.

When we accept the death, burial and resurrection of our Lord and Savior Yeshua HaMashiach for the forgiveness of our sins and the salvation of our souls, in faith, and are thereby spiritually reborn, we relinquish control of the steering wheels to our life cars and give them over to our invisible God. We do so because we trust in His Word that, with Him behind our steering wheels, we shall never run out of fuel (John 7:38, 11:26) and He will direct our paths (Proverbs 3:6).

Now our jobs and worldly possessions are in that car. For those of us who have families, our families are in the back seat. We, therefore, surrender to Yeshua all that we are responsible for in life. It is helpful for us to remember that everything and everyone we receive on earth is from God (John 3:27). Nonetheless, it takes a leap of faith to move over to the passenger seat and let our invisible God drive our life cars, especially when we see life's stop signs, turns, traffic, potholes and the like, directly in our paths.

As our invisible God begins to drive our life cars, we nervously gaze with our earthly eyes at what appears to be an empty driver's seat. Every bone in our bodies anticipates a wreck with potential fatalities. We instinctively want to snatch control of that steering wheel and rely on what we can physically see instead of on what we cannot physically see (faith).

However, Yeshua, Who is the author and finisher of our faith (Hebrews 12:2), abides in us and keeps us still. The more we observe God weaving in and out of traffic, avoiding the potholes, and otherwise being true to His Word, our faith matures and we are at peace. Of significance is the fact that God's Word tells us not only will we be saved, but also our households (Acts 16:31). This happens because our family members are also in the car with us. They see the life car being maneuvered through the perils of life without a physical driver. They see the continued realization of the things hoped for, in faith, by the head of their household and embrace that faith for themselves.

When nonbelievers observe us safely proceeding through life, content and at peace in the passenger seats of our life cars without any apparent driver behind the steering wheels, they marvel at our ability to faithfully remain at peace, despite life's travails. They question the source of our remarkable faith and say to themselves that there must be something to this invisible God of ours. Hopefully, they will be encouraged to similarly relieve themselves of the stress and burden of driving their life cars until the fuel is depleted or they wreck and turn that responsibility over to God, Who promises that the fuel will never run dry and that our life cars will always remain on course—His course.

In 1993, I was part of a team that tried an eight-month common issues trial on the issue of liability against multiple defendants on behalf of approximately 8,500 plaintiffs who alleged various diseases caused by their exposure to asbestos. Because of the size of the litigation, there were a number of attorneys who were members of the plaintiffs' trial team and I was one of three lawyers who were responsible for openings and closings. My father passed away in the early months of the trial from a massive heart attack. In deep despair, I asked God to see me through this trial. I watched Almighty God move throughout the trial. In the end, we settled with most of the defendants and obtained a judgment against the remaining six who ultimately settled. The collective recovery for our clients was one of the largest in the State of Maryland.

Another occasion when I watched God order my steps through a six-month trial occurred in 2011. My firm represented over hundreds of homeowners in Baltimore County who sued Exxon Mobil for the contamination of their wells caused by the release of 26,000 gallons of gasoline from a local Exxon gas station in 2006. Plaintiffs sued for property damage only. Because of the magnitude of this litigation, a sizeable trial team was again assembled.

Because of the well-contamination, the plaintiffs were unable to drink, shower or use their well water for anything. Exxon, along with the Maryland Department of the Environment, determined that only those homes located within a certain radius of the station should receive bottled water. Exxon chose to stick with this determination even though the wells of homes located twice the distance of the radius were contaminated. Even homes located within feet of the line of demarcation were denied bottled water.

Initially, I volunteered to assist wherever needed. As God would have it, I took on more and more responsibilities until, by the time of trial, I was asked to share opening and closing statements. In fact, I closed out the openings and the closings. During the trial, it became apparent that the jury was not buying Exxon's defense. During my closing, I spent three hours covering the damages for each of the homeowner plaintiffs. The jury took copious notes, especially the foreperson. The jury returned a verdict of $500 million in compensatory damages and $1 billion in punitive damages. Unfortunately, that verdict was overturned on appeal and Exxon eventually settled.

The jury created a framed memorial poster of the trial that included photos of every juror, including alternates, and the details of the verdict. A copy of the framed poster was given to the judge, his court clerk and every member of the jury. I was the only lawyer on either side of the isle who was honored with a framed poster. This is what can happen when we let God be in control.

As the faithfulness of our triune Godhead becomes our faithfulness, we develop into illuminating lights of varying degrees in this otherwise dark world. We allow the lost to see that, through the death, burial and resurrection of the Word of God, our Lord Yeshua HaMashiach, salvation is at hand for all who are willing to accept it on their behalf through faith.

Once our faith endures to the end, we shall eat of the Tree of Life, as we were originally intended to do (Revelation 2:7). It is crucial that we understand the importance of faith, not just in the redemption of Mankind, but in God's original master plan for Mankind, conceived and, indeed, promised, before the beginning and put into temporal effect at creation (Titus 1:2).

According to the order of things as determined by God in the beginning, the chosen people of God, who are spiritually begotten of Him, will become mirror images of Yeshua. We will abide in Him and He will abide in us. When He is seen, we are seen, and when we are seen, He is seen. That is why God sees Yeshua when He looks at His spiritually reborn children who comprise the Spiritual Body of Mashiach. Since God's definition of "righteous" is Yeshua HaMashiach (1 John 2:1), we are righteous before His eyes because Yeshua is righteous.

In *Webster's New World Dictionary,* "righteous" is defined as "acting in a just, upright manner; doing what is right, virtuous; morally right, fair and just." In a legal context, "righteous" means obeying the law, free from blame. Any transgression of man's law requires a penalty to be paid that is commensurate to the severity of the transgression. In contrast, however, any act in violation of God's law, regardless of severity, requires the same penalty: death through eternal damnation and separation from God. This damnation is horrific in that it involves the most excruciating pain and suffering that is constant and never ends. There is no hope of a break, reprieve or rescue. For the damned, there is no light, love, rest or peace, only darkness and unimaginable torment. Separation from God ensures that this terrible situation never changes or ends.

Because of our sin nature, passed down to every person born of Adam and Eve, no person can be righteous under God's law (Romans 3:10) and, therefore, are destined for this disastrous fate. However, Yeshua, having Adam's and Eve's sin nature, was also born of God, remained obedient to God and, therefore, was righteous throughout His earthly life. He lovingly gave up His sinless life so that we would not have to suffer eternal damnation or eternal separation from God, though our transgressions demanded it. Yeshua voluntarily paid God's penalty for the sins of the world. The only requirement is that we accept His sacrifice on our behalf in the faith that God will deliver on His promise of eternal salvation. Incredibly, many refuse to do so.

Instead, they choose to find their own way to eternal life just as Adam and Eve chose to do in their moment of sin. All who accept Yeshua's sacrifice on their behalf take on the image and likeness of Yeshua, become righteous before God and have eternal life. All who do not accept Yeshua's sacrifice are eternally damned. Yeshua is the firstborn and the head of His Spiritual

Body composed of those who were made righteous because of their acceptance of His blameless death on their behalves. Once we take on His image and likeness, we become one with Him. Since there is no limit to what Yeshua can do, there is no limit to what we, who are one with Him, can do. Our imaginations cannot begin to see what glorious things we can accomplish now and when we are completely one with God, as we were originally intended to be before the beginning.

It is often asked, when shall our glorification with God occur? This same question was asked of Yeshua by His disciples. The apostle Matthew, in Chapter 24 of his Gospel, transcribes Yeshua's response to this question. He identifies the signs of the times that are associated with His return and our glorification in and through Him. Many biblical scholars believe that we are living in the days during which these signs are occurring. With every passing day, there is an increasing polarization between those who accept the ways of the world and those who accept God's ways. Eventually, the spiritually reborn children of God will stick out like sore thumbs from the world's perspective and like bright beacons of light in an otherwise dark world from God's perspective. Inevitably, the world will seek to put these lights out but they shall not succeed.

Although some have, many of God's chosen people, the Jews, have yet to accept Yeshua as HaMashiach but have always anticipated the day when Messiah would subdue their enemies, rid the world of evil, and rule justly and with authority from the throne of David forever and this shall indeed happen. However, God's creative purpose for man would not be served if, upon Yeshua's triumphant return, Mankind would be damned to eternal separation from God because of our sins. The wages of the sins of the world had to be paid first. Mankind would then be able to not only reign with Yeshua but also become one with Him upon His triumphant return. The salvation of Mankind had to be achieved before our unification with God. The gospel of Yeshua is the power of God unto salvation to everyone that believes; to the Jew first and also to the Greek (Romans 1:16).

We have discussed in this chapter how our triune Godhead, through faith, created all things, and how each of His children has access to this limitless faith. In the next chapter, we shall discuss why man is the only created being to have access to this faith and we shall delve deeper into why God created man in His image and after His likeness. Through the death, burial and resurrection of His Son, Yeshua HaMashiach, God has successfully restored unto Himself the called among Mankind, and all physical things created during Creation week. His master plan is close to completion.

Very soon God's elect among Mankind will become completely one with God through Yeshua HaMashiach, and all will be perfect as was originally intended. All that is left to be accomplished is for every person, who is called by God, to have an opportunity to accept God's free offer of redemption through the blood of Yeshua's substitutionary sacrifice. However, God allotted a certain amount of time to execute His master plan. Once that time has elapsed, God's offer of salvation will be taken off the proverbial table.

Now the questions are: Are you saved in and through Yeshua HaMashiach? Have you, by faith, accepted His free offer of pardon and of salvation? Is your faith a living and vital faith, or is it a vain and baseless faith? After all, it does make a difference. Your answers to these questions have eternal consequences, and time is running out. Each new second and each new breath present new opportunities to establish an eternal relationship with our triune Godhead. Let's not waste them.

CHAPTER TWO

THE CREATION OF MAN IN GOD'S IMAGE, AFTER THEIR LIKENESS

In this chapter, we shall take a closer look at what it means to be made in the image and after the likeness of our triune Godhead and its implications for us as believers in Yeshua. Every human being was created to look like and have the characteristics of God so that we may be compatible enough with Him that He can abide in us and we in Him as one. We must be holy because He is Holy. Our sins have made us incompatible for this purpose, but our redemption in Yeshua has allowed us to be transformed into the image and likeness of Yeshua, Who is the express image of God. Thus, we are restored to our originally created state.

The Creation of Man

Genesis 1:26-27 tell us that, on the sixth day of creation week, God said:

> Let us make man in our image, after our likeness.... So God created man in his own image, in the image of God created he him; male and female created he them.

The Hebrew word for "image" is *tselem*, which means "resemblance." The Hebrew word for "likeness" is *demuwth*, which means "manner or similitude." Therefore, man was made to resemble the appearance and to have attributes similar to those of God. Adam and Eve and their progeny were truly created to mirror God in every way. It is, therefore, appropriate to conclude that, before their fall, Adam and Eve were the unperfected physical manifestations of God on earth. Being one with God, albeit through innocence rather than glory, their pre-Fall relationship with God was so close that it must have been extremely debilitating for Adam and Eve to grasp what they had lost as a result of their sin of disobedience.

Adam was given a mind of his own so that he, by his own volition, could be fully persuaded to obey or disobey God for no other reason than because he loved his Creator more than he loved himself (Matthew 22:37, Romans 14:5). Every soul was created to have a body and a mind. This is exactly the makeup of our triune Godhead.

Yeshua HaMashiach is head of the Body of God, and we, the children of God, comprise the Body of Yeshua (Romans 12:5, 1 Corinthians 12:12-14). There are passages too numerous to cite that establish the fact that the Holy Spirit is the Spirit of God (e.g., Matthew 28:19, John 14:26) in Whom the children of God live (Galatians 5:25). Leviticus 24:12; 1 Samuel 2:35; Romans 8:27; 11:34, and 1 Corinthians 2:16 all talk about the mind of God the Father, God the Son, and God the Holy Spirit. Mankind was created to be "filled with all the fullness of God" (Ephesians 3:19)—soul, body and mind. Colossians 2:9 tells us that in Yeshua HaMashiach dwells "all the fullness of the Godhead bodily." As members of the Body of Yeshua, we are indwelt by the same fullness of the Godhead that dwells in Yeshua. We can only be what Yeshua is and He is the fullness of God in the flesh (John 1:14).

Man's Endowment with the Appearance and Characteristics of God

With respect to our being created in the image of God (Genesis 5:1-2; 9:6), what do the Holy Scriptures tell us about what God looks like? John 4:24 tells us that God, the Father, is a Spirit. Ezekiel 1:26-28 provides a limited description of the appearance of God:

> And above the firmament that was over their heads was the likeness of a throne, as the appearance of a sapphire stone: and upon the likeness of the throne was the likeness as the appearance of a man above upon it.
>
> And I saw as the colour of amber, as the appearance of fire round about within it, from the appearance of his loins even upward, and from the appearance of his loins even downward, I saw as it were the appearance of fire, and it had brightness round about.
>
> As the appearance of the bow that is in the cloud in the day of rain, so was the appearance of the brightness round about. This was the appearance of the likeness of the glory of the LORD. And when I saw it, I fell upon my face, and I heard a voice of one that spoke.

According to these verses, God, the Father, has the appearance of a man with the loins of a man. Nothing else is said about the appearance of God. Instead, these passages provide us with a vivid description of the glory of God, the likes of which we have yet to fully attain. From the waist up, God's glory looks like the color of amber that appears to have fire around and within it. The glory surrounding His lower body has the appearance of fire, but with a brightness around it (Ezekiel 8:2). The throne of God has a rainbow around it (Revelation 4:2-3). 2 Corinthians 3:18 states that every one of God's children, once glorified, will have the same glory as the Lord.

> But we all, with open face beholding as in a glass the glory of the Lord, are changed into the same image from glory to glory, even as by the Spirit of the Lord.

According to Romans 8:29-30, this is our predestination.

> For whom he did foreknow, he also did predestinate to be conformed to the image of his Son, that he might be the first-born among many brethren.
> Moreover whom he did predestinate, them he also called: and whom he called, them he also justified: and whom he justified, them he also glorified.

The glory of our Lord and Savior, Yeshua HaMashiach, is the same glory of God, the Father (Matthew 16:27). Though created, both physically and spiritually, in our triune Godhead's image, that is, appearance, God's glory was withheld from Adam and Eve pending their passing God's test of loving, selfless obedience.

Equally important as being made to look like the image of God is the fact that we were also created to have the characteristics and mannerisms of God. Since our triune Godhead is one, the attributes of any one of Them are the attributes of all of Them. The more our oneness with God is perfected, the more Their attributes become our attributes. This is what it means to be created after Their likeness.

With respect to the attributes of God, the Father, the Holy Scriptures tell us that God is perfect (Matthew 5:48). God, the Father, cannot lie (Numbers 23:19, Titus 1:1-2, Hebrews 6:18). He is truth; is without iniquity, just and right (Deuteronomy 32:4, Psalm 31:5). He is holy (Leviticus 11:44-45, 1 Peter 1:15-16), light (1 John 1:5), almighty (Genesis 17:1) and the great I

AM (Exodus 3:14). He is love (1 John 4:8,16), and He is faithful (Deuteronomy 7:9; 1 Corinthians 1:9; 1 Thessalonians 5:24). Job 37:23 tells us that we cannot figure Him out. Man was created to possess the same Godly characteristics. Because God will fully indwell and be completely one with us, we shall also be almighty, perfect, truthful, holy, love, faithful and incapable of being fully understood by an imperfect man. We shall be light in which nothing dark or evil can dwell. We were created, not only to experience love, but to be love having uncompromising, unconditional, pure love as our very nature.

1 Corinthians 13:1-13 explains, quite well, the characteristics of Godly love. Specifically, verse 13 describes Godly love as being greater than the limitless faith of God which created and sustains all of creation. This makes perfect sense when verse 7 is considered. That verse says that love "Beareth all things, believeth all things, hopeth all things, endureth all things." We learned from the previous chapter that faith is the realization of all things hoped for (Hebrews 11:1). Faith is the means through which all things hoped for by God's love is realized. God's love is needed first and then His faith brings all things hoped for, through love, into realization and sustains it.

According to 1 Corinthians 13:4-8, all who possess this kind of love endures long suffering, does not envy, is humble, behaves properly, seeks no personal gain, is not easily provoked, has no evil thoughts, rejoices in truth and not iniquity, bears, believes, hopes for and endures all things and never fails. We were created to have this kind of love…God's love. We were meant to have this wonderful attribute of God, the Father, and to have each of His attributes described in Scripture. Thus, it is our creative function to share in the experience of God, the Father. We shall participate with Him in the performance of whatever is in His mind to do.

As the second personage of our triune Godhead, Yeshua, HaMashiach, being the literal Word of God, can be nothing but consistent with Almighty God, the Father. When God speaks, Yeshua is the words that are spoken. God, therefore, speaks living words consisting of Himself.

Yeshua said, "I am the resurrection, and the life: he that believeth in me, though he were dead, yet shall he live" (John 11:25). John 1:4 says about Yeshua: "In him was life; and the life was the light of men." These passages imply that Yeshua, being the every utterance of God, can only speak that which is of God, namely spirit and life.

In Psalm 12:6, it is written:

The words of the LORD are pure words: as silver tried in a furnace of earth, purified seven times.

Hebrews 4:12-13 describe the Word of God as being alive, powerful, sharp enough to divide asunder soul and spirit and joint and marrow, able to discern the thoughts and intents of the heart, and able to see all things hidden and open. John 14:6 says that Yeshua, the Son of God, is the Way, the Truth, and the Life. Hebrews 7:26 tells us more about the attributes of Yeshua, the Son of God. It describes Yeshua as "holy, harmless, undefiled, separate from sinners, and made higher than the heavens."

A wonderful description of the characteristics of Yeshua and, consequently, every child of God, is given by Yeshua Himself in what is commonly referred to as the Beatitudes (Matthew 5:1-12). Such children are poor in spirit, mourners, meek, hungry and thirsty for righteousness, merciful, pure in heart, peacemakers and persecuted for righteousness' sake. These verses describe the Godly characteristics of the children of God, who are conformed to His image (Romans 8:29).

John 1:4 describes Yeshua as being the life which is the light of men. It is this very life force that will sustain us throughout eternity as members of the Body of our Messiah. All that the incarnate Yeshua is, we were created to be, and shall be, upon our glorification. In and through Yeshua, we shall judge all matters and nothing shall be hidden from us. Through Yeshua, we shall also be the Way, the Truth and the Life. Through Yeshua HaMashiach, we shall be the life force of all creation, in heaven and on earth.

We, who are in Yeshua, will come to know His love which is now beyond knowing (Ephesians 3:19). It is our creative purpose to be the physical manifestations of God in Yeshua. How exciting it will be to experience God to this unimaginable extent. How exciting it is to know that we were created to be God in the flesh only because we are in Yeshua Who is God in the flesh. Yeshua proclaimed that, as the Son of God, He and His Father are one (John 5:18; 10:30; 17:11, 21-24). As members of His Spiritual Body, His proclamation becomes our proclamation. Through Yeshua HaMashiach, we are also the children of God and are one with Him. Such a reality is almost too incredible to believe. Yet, the Holy Scriptures tell us that this is our predestination according to the will of God.

With respect to the third personage of our triune Godhead, there are also numerous Scriptural references that describe the attributes of the Spirit of God, who is also referred to as the Holy Ghost, the Ruach HaKodesh. The Holy Ghost is described as the seven Spirits of God that have been sent forth into all the earth (Revelation 4:5, 5:6). In Isaiah 11:1-2, God defines the sevenfold Spirit of God as being the Spirit of the Lord, the Spirit of Wisdom, the Spirit of Understanding, the Spirit of Counsel, the Spirit of Might, the Spirit of Knowledge and the Spirit of the

Fear of the Lord. Since we were created to be one with the Holy Spirit in that the Spirit of God indwells us and we indwell Him, we were created also to possess the fullness of the Spirit of the Lord, Wisdom, Understanding, Counsel, Might, Knowledge and Fear of the Lord. We shall be all wise, all understanding, able to counsel in all matters, almighty, all knowing and in total fearful reverence of our Lord God.

1 John 5:6 tells us that it is the Spirit that bears witness to all things because He is the Spirit of Truth. Other scriptural passages describe the Holy Ghost as the Spirit of Faith (2 Corinthians 4:13), the Spirit of Adoption (Romans 8:15), the Spirit of Grace (Hebrews 10:29) and the Spirit of Glory (1 Peter 4:14). All of these are additional characteristics of the Ruach HaKodesh in whose likeness all of Mankind were created. We shall be the physical manifestations of all that the Holy Ghost is.

Galatians 5:22 tells us that the fruit of the Spirit is love, joy, peace, long-suffering, gentleness, goodness, faith, meekness and temperance. All of the attributes of the Spirit of God can be ascribed to Yeshua and to God, the Father. Yeshua's entire earthly experience was a constant exhibition of these fruits of the Spirit. Similarly, every child of God was created to produce the same fruit, having as we do the same characteristics as that of the Holy Spirit. Envision, if you will, millions, and perhaps billions, of people, all saved by the grace of God through Yeshua HaMashiach, being all about love, joy, peace, long-suffering, gentleness, goodness, faith, meekness and temperance, yet, also being all that our triune Godhead is in terms of power, wisdom, knowledge and love.

Everything, and more, that Mankind has striven to achieve, independent of God, was always intended to be our creative inheritance. There is absolutely nothing that we could attain in this world that could come remotely close to what is in store for the children of God. Knowing this helps us to better appreciate what Yeshua was telling us when He said that there is no profit or gain in possessing the whole world if, by doing so, one loses his eternal soul (Matthew 16:26, Mark 8:36, Luke 9:25). We lose everything without God but we gain everything through eternal oneness with God. Revelation 21:7 confirms this fact:

He that overcometh shall inherit all things; and I will be his God,
And he shall be my son.

While it is important for every child of God to know that he or she was created to possess all of the characteristics, mannerisms and attributes of each of the three personages of our triune Godhead, it is equally important for the children of God to know that these traits are mutually inclusive. By that I mean, just as They three, being separate personages, are one with each other and share each other's traits, so we also share the traits of all three personages. The way for us to enter into this perfect Godly oneness is through the personage of Yeshua. Once this is accomplished through the perfection of our spiritual re-births, every characteristic, mannerism or attribute of God will be shared by all of His children through Yeshua HaMashiach.

For instance, let's consider two of the Holy Spirit's characteristics, namely wisdom and understanding. James 3:17 describes Godly wisdom as being pure, peaceable, gentle, easy to be entreated, full of mercy and good fruits, without partiality and without hypocrisy. According to the Holy Scriptures, wisdom and understanding are likened to valued hidden treasures. Proverbs 2:1-6 instruct us to search for wisdom and understanding as if they were hidden treasures. Indeed, happy is the man who finds wisdom and gets understanding because he shall enjoy a long, pleasant and peaceful life and have riches and honor (Proverbs 3:13-24).

These same verses also tell us that it was with wisdom that our Lord founded the earth and with understanding that He established the heavens. Yeshua tells us that the Kingdom of heaven is like unto treasure hid in a field (Matthew 13:44). Colossians 2:1-3 inform us that the treasures of wisdom and knowledge are hidden in God, the Father, and Yeshua HaMashiach. We find and, therefore, make a part of our natures, the Holy Spirit's characteristics of wisdom and understanding through God and Yeshua when we obey the Word of God (Proverbs 8). Our perfect oneness, through Yeshua, with each of the three personages of our triune Godhead, allows for the type of Godly unity as set forth in Ephesians 4:4-6.

As the possessors of the characteristics, mannerisms and attributes of God the Father, God, the Son, and God, the Holy Ghost, through and in Yeshua, we have found and, in fact, share the formerly hidden treasures of wisdom and understanding.

Adam and Eve were the greatest among all creation. However, they, and their progeny, lost the opportunity to experience these Godly characteristics upon their fall, but will possess them upon their redemption, resurrection and ultimate glorification. These attributes currently exist in every spiritually reborn child of God and they will become the whole of our nature upon the perfection of our faith when we are similarly glorified in Yeshua HaMashiach.

Set forth below are but a sample of the passages in the Holy Scriptures which establish that, even in our yet to be glorified states, the spiritually reborn children of God can presently exhibit the characteristics of our triune God:

With all lowliness and meekness, with long-suffering, forbearing one another in love (Ephesians 4:2).

Strengthened with all might, according to his glorious power, unto all patience and long-suffering with joyfulness (Colossians 1:11).

Put on therefore, as the elect of God, holy and beloved, bowels of mercies, kindness, humbleness of mind, meekness, long-suffering (Colossians 3:12).

But thou, O man of God, flee these things; and follow after righteousness, godliness, faith, love, patience, meekness (1 Timothy 6:11).

One of the Godly attributes that Adam and Eve were not endowed with was the ability to discern the thoughts and intents of the heart, that is, they were not omniscient. Instead, they were given innocence. Had Adam and Eve been omniscient, they surely would have seen through Satan's deception. It was their desire to become wise, with its attendant ability to discern between good and evil, that caused them to disobey God.

If Adam and Eve, through obedience, had eaten from the Tree of Life instead of from the Tree of the Knowledge of Good and Evil, they would have immediately received immortal, glorified bodies and would have secured their eternal status as the greatest of God's creations (Genesis 3:22-24). The millions and, indeed, billions of offspring of a glorified Adam and Eve (Genesis 1:28) would be the glorified children of God (1 John 3:1). Because of their sin of disobedience, we, who have accepted God's redemption unto salvation, are the physical temples of God yet to be glorified. We possess all the spiritual and physical characteristics of our triune God but our ability to exhibit these qualities is yet to be perfected.

The Purpose for Man's Creation

God gave to Mankind authority and dominion over the earth and all created things in it (Genesis 1:26-28). Every created thing, with the exception of Mankind, was created to exist as an entity separate from God, yet sustained by Him. They reap the benefits of being creatures of God and honor God through their very existence. Mankind, however, was created to be one with God, to be the physical temples in whom God would indwell and through whom God would physically exercise dominion and authority over all creation. This is the physical and spiritual oneness that Mankind was created to have with our God. Not only was God originally intended to dwell in our physical bodies, we were also created to maintain a spiritual oneness with God.

It is difficult for us to comprehend this type of oneness with God that is described and prayed for by Yeshua in John 17. This is because it is our nature to want to be in control of our lives and we consider it an intrusion for someone else to dictate how we live. We do not realize that we have never maintained control of our lives. We are either servants of Satan or servants of God. Unless we accept Yeshua as our Savior, our lives are already lost, destined for destruction. Only by allowing God's life to merge with ours through our spiritual rebirths in and through Yeshua, can we eternally save our lives.

There are some who contend that all spiritual roads ultimately lead to the same God. This universalistic approach assumes the validity of every faith and, at its core, bases salvation on the performance of good works. In other words, if you live a good enough life, you may be granted eternal life no matter what faith you may adhere to.

However, any true child of the only living God knows this to be not true and to be inconsistent with the Holy inspired Word of

God. John 11:25 tells us that Yeshua is the resurrection and the life and that anyone who believes in Him, though he were dead, shall live. Yeshua also said, in John 14:6, that He is the way, the truth and the life, that no man comes to the Father but by Him. The Thomas Nelson Study Bible, in footnote 14:6, points out that Yeshua is making it very clear that He *is* the way. There is no other way!

This is extremely important. So much so that I will repeat it throughout this book. Yeshua expounded on this point in John 15:4-6:

> Abide in me, and I in you. As the branch cannot bear fruit of itself, except it abide in the vine; no more can ye, except ye abide in me.
>
> I am the vine, ye are the branches: He that abideth in me, and I in him, the same bringeth forth much fruit: for without me ye can do nothing.
>
> If a man abide not in me, he is cast forth as a branch and is withered; and men gather them, and cast them into the fire, and they are burned.

There is no eternal life without Yeshua. He is the breath of our everlasting God Who took on flesh to be the ultimate and final sin offering for man. When He rose from the dead unto eternal life, the souls of every saved person rose with Him and in Him. We have eternal life, not only because of what He did but also because we are in Him. There is no eternal life outside of the Spiritual Body of Yeshua. That is why Yeshua tells us we can do nothing outside of Him. He further tells us that those who do not abide in Him and He in them are destined for eternal damnation in the lake of fire (Revelation 20:15).

This form of mutual inhabitation explains why Yeshua would say He would spew out of His mouth those who are lukewarm to Him (Revelation 3:15-16). As I stated, Yeshua is the breath of our eternal God Who was breathed into all Mankind and, indeed, into all flesh (Genesis 2:7; 6:17, 7:15, 22, Job 33:4). However, only in man did God's breath create eternal spirits (Genesis 2:7). When we physically die, our spirits leave our fleshly bodies but they continue to exist. The extent of our eternal existence depends on whether we remain in Yeshua and He in us. We will experience eternal life in the only source of eternal life or we will experience eternal death, completely separated from God, in utter darkness and suffering.

It would also explain why God would tell us, in His Holy Word, that He will never leave us nor forsake us and is always with us (Deuteronomy 31-6,8, Joshua 1:5, Matthew 28:20, Hebrews 13:5). Yeshua created and maintains everything because all things are in Him (Colossians 1:16-17; Hebrews 1:3). According to the Thomas Nelson Study Bible, the literal translation of the word "by," in this text, is "in." Thus, the existence of all things is maintained by the power of Yeshua because they are *in* Him. Yeshua will never leave nor forsake anything or anyone who is in Him.

We need not be afraid of God living in us and we in God. The same cannot be said of those who live in Satan and he in them. Because of the nature of our God, we should be excited to live in God and to have God live in and through us. When we are made perfect in Yeshua upon His return, God will be our every breath, our every thought and the purpose of our every act. When we are one with God to this extent, God truly abides in us and we in God.

God gave me an excellent real-life illustration of what it means to be one with God to this extent. I was playing a round of golf with three friends: two were saved, and one was not. We were playing a competitive round of golf for bragging rights only. The object of golf is to put the ball in a hole several hundred yards away with the least amount of strokes. One of my tee shots landed directly behind a tree. I would have to take a penalty stroke to put the ball in play.

As I approached my ball and realized my dilemma, I was immediately tempted to move my ball away from the tree and play it without taking the penalty stroke. I looked around and confirmed that none of my friends would know of my deception. Because God lives in me and I in Him, He plays with me and does everything with me. Therefore, I knew that God would know and that I risked immediate chastisement if I did this deceitful act. Revelation 3:19 states "As many as I love, I rebuke and chasten: be zealous therefore, and repent." I fully expected to end up taking a penalty stroke one way or the other before this round of golf was over.

Then God spoke to me and said, "If you deceitfully move that ball, you would be effectively keeping Me from playing through you. I caused you to hit the ball behind the tree for any of a number of reasons. For instance, I may want you to lose today so that I may be glorified through the way you magnify Me in your loss in the presence of your friends, saved and unsaved. Or, I may want you to win today, but only after you have grown closer to Me through the trials and tribulations of the game. Your victory would be only as I have laid it out for you. Yet, further still, I am actively playing the round of golf with your two saved friends as I am with you, effectuating My will in the lives of My children. Finally, I may be using My involvement in this entire golf outing to reach out to your unsaved friend. He may come to accept My Son as his Savior upon observing Me through you and your saved friends. Indeed, I am doing all of these things and more. In order for Me to do so, you must relinquish control and let Me live through you. Now that My Spirit is merged with your spirit, everything that happens in your life is orchestrated by Me, and it is not for you to disrupt my work with your selfish agendas."

I am happy to say I did not move my ball from behind the tree. I took a penalty stroke and proceeded with the round of golf, but the game took on added significance. Whether I win or lose in golf, or any other endeavor in life, the outcome is only important to me as it relates to the will of God. I now realize that I can be at peace regardless of the trials and tribulations of life. I further realize that God is an active participant during every second of my life, to the furtherance of His good work. His is exactly what I prayed for during my spiritual rebirth many years ago. The extent of my spiritual maturation determines the degree to which I am able to be used by God. God truly abides in me, and I in God.

Just as every living creature gives glory and honor to God by being what they were created to be, Mankind also gives God glory and honor by being what we were created to be. However, He will not force Himself upon us. We have to willingly honor Him by lovingly giving ourselves over to Him. In return, we become one with Him and will forever abide in God and He in us, in answer to the high priestly prayer of our Lord and Savior Yeshua HaMashiach (John 17). Our physical bodies become temples in which our spirit, which is forever merged with the living Spirit of God, abides as one (1 Corinthians 3:16-17, 6:15-20).

In preparation for this holy union with God, Mankind was created to be compatible with God by possessing the attributes and characteristics of God. Up until Mankind's fall, there was no way to distinguish between the attributes and characteristics of God and those of Adam and Eve. Adam and Eve communed with God in a way that allowed them to exercise all the power, dominion and authority of God. They were the most powerful beings created by God, and they ruled the world with their God-given authority. It is called the "fall of man" because Adam and Eve enjoyed a far higher state of existence before they sinned.

Mankind is the apex of all of God's creations. No other creature has a more important role in God's master plan to manifest Himself in the physical realm. Thus, Mankind was the last to be created. We were created to be the holy, physical temples of God. Our unified relationship with God will allow us to participate with God as He exercises His dominion over all creation. Because of this glorious function, unlike any other created thing, we were created in the image and after the likeness of our Creator. It is our intended function that defines our significance and thus our place in the creative order of things. Absent this utility, we would be just like every other created thing, in our own image and after our own likeness.

This holy privilege is now destined for those of us chosen and called according to God's purpose. God becomes spiritually one with every child of His at the moment of their voluntary spiritual rebirths. That oneness becomes complete upon our glorification when Yeshua returns. We will be inseparable from God to the same extent that Yeshua is inseparable from God. Yeshua and God, the Father, are one (John 10:30).

What it actually means to be a child of God is almost too incredible to comprehend. God is all-knowing, all-powerful and all-present. Because we were made in God's image and after His likeness, we were created to also be all-knowing, all-powerful and all-present, and yet not us, but God who lives in and through us. We possess these awesome qualities only because God does. We must encourage each other unabashedly with this message and spread the good news to those who are lost.

The fact that we were created to possess the mannerisms, characteristics and attributes of God is a clear indication that our creative purpose requires us to be mirror images of God. The revelation of that requirement is unequivocally set forth with precise bluntness by Yeshua Himself as recorded in the Gospel of John.

In John 17, Yeshua interceded on behalf of Jewish and Gentile believers and prayed that they would become one with each other and with God just like Yeshua is one with Him. In fact, Yeshua told His disciples in John 10:16 that other sheep will be added to His Jewish sheep to make one flock under one shepherd. I did not fully appreciate the significance of this prayerful request of Yeshua until the Holy Spirit led my wife and I to the 100th anniversary conference of the Messianic Jewish Alliance of America that was held at Messiah College. Messianic Jews from all over the world gathered in one place and were of one mind in the unification of both Jew and Gentile in Yeshua HaMashiach. It was an experience beyond measure to worship God as one with them in and through Yeshua HaMashiach. Yet, the vast majority of Gentile Christians are unaware of or have ignored the existence of Messianic Jews. From a purely Gentile perspective, it appears that, for centuries, these two components of the Spiritual Body of Yeshua have maintained a relationship more akin to a collaborative competition than a relationship of unified oneness.

It was at this historic conference that my wife and I learned, through the teaching of Pastor Raleigh Washington, and others, that Yeshua's prayer, contained in John 17, will not be fully answered until Jew and Gentile believers are united as one (Ephesians 2:14-16, John 13:34-35, 17:21), a reality that has yet to occur. Over 2,000 years ago, it was the Jews who first believed that Yeshua is the Messiah to the salvation of their souls. Through these Messianic Jews, salvation came to the Gentiles.

However, since the early days of the church, the role of Jewish believers in the Body of Yeshua have, for all practical purposes, been ignored by the much larger Gentile component. Messianic Jews have been forced to worship Yeshua independent of their Gentile counterparts. Without any meaningful Jewish participation, many Gentiles lost their way by embracing a belief system that embraces tolerance, tradition and freedom of expression.

But God, over the past few centuries, has brought about the re-emergence of Jewish believers whose numbers are growing exponentially. These Jewish believers understand the importance of John 17:21 and are no longer willing to remain silent. Instead, they are actively engaged in collaborative efforts with Gentile believing groups, such as Promise Keepers, to unite both Jew and Gentile believers in Yeshua HaMashiach. Once accomplished, there is nothing left but the glorification of all believers into perfect oneness with our triune Godhead, in and through our Messiah, for Yeshua's prayer to be fully answered.

God has always understood that a united Mankind could accomplish all that it desired to do (Genesis 11:1-9). So, it is not surprising that Yeshua prayed for a united body of believers in John 17. He fully understood how powerfully productive a truly united Body of Yeshua would be. According to the Ambassadors of Christ Network, the unification of Jewish and Gentile believers will be the fulfillment of Revelation 11:8-12. They believe these two groups of believers may be the two witnesses, which are the two olive trees and two lampstands, who will be empowered by the Holy Spirit to spread the Gospel at the beginning of the seven-year tribulation period. While this may or may not be true, Jewish and Gentile believers shall be unified in answer to Yeshua's prayer.

For us to become united as one with God, individually and collectively, whether Jew or Gentile, to the same extent that Yeshua is one with Him, we have to choose God's way over our own sinful way. God cannot co-exist with sin. Since we have all sinned, our salvation can only be through the remissive blood of Yeshua HaMashiach, Who is our mediator (Hebrews 9:15). We must give up our individual existence independent from God because the only existence separate from God is physical and spiritual death. We are required to lose our lives and all the benefits thereof so that we can regain them, and yet not our lives, but God's life in us.

Specifically, John 17:11, 21-23 tell us that Yeshua prayed that both Jew and Gentile become one with each other and with God, the Father, as He is one with Him. The significance of John 17, in its entirety, and specifically these four verses, in terms of understanding what our triune Godhead intended all believers to be when They made us in Their image and after Their likeness, cannot be overstated. It is important enough that we should look at the issue of oneness set forth in these four verses as translated in the New Living Translation (NLT), the New King James Version (NKJV), the New American Standard Bible (NASB) and the English Standard Version (ESV).

John 17:11 NLT Holy Father, keep them and care for them—all those you have given me—so that they will be united just as we are.

   NKJV Holy Father, keep through Your name those whom You have given Me, that they may be one as We are.

NASB	Holy Father, keep them in Your name, the name which You have given Me, that they may be one even as We are.
ESV	Holy Father, keep them in your name, which you have given me, that they may be one, even as we are one.
John 17:21 NLT	My prayer for all of them is that they will be one, just as you and I are one, Father— that just as you are in me and I am in you, so they will be in us.
NKJV	[T]hat they all may be one, as You, Father, are in Me, and I in You; that they also may be in Us.
NASB	[T]hat they may all be one; even as You, Father, are in Me and I in You, that they also may be in Us.
ESV	[T]hat they may all be one, just as you, Father, are in me, and I in you, that they also may be in us, so that the world may believe that you have sent me.
John 17:22 NLT	I have given them the glory you gave me, so that they may be one, as we are.
NKJV	And the glory which You gave Me I have given them, that they may be one just as We are one.
NASB	The glory which You have given Me I have given to them, that they may be one, just as We are one.
ESV	The glory that you have given me I have given to them, that they may be one even as we are one.

John 17:23 NLT	I in them and you in me, all being perfected into one.
NKJV	I in them, and You in Me; that they may be made perfect in one.
NASB	I in them and You in Me, that they may be perfected in unity.
ESV	I in them and you in me, that they may become perfectly one, so that the world may know that you sent me and loved them even as you loved me.

In John 17:11, our Lord and Savior prays that God, the Father, will keep out of the world all believers, Jew and Gentile, who are called "in His name." We know that God the Father, God, the Son, and God, the Holy Ghost all carry the same name (Matthew 28:19). We also know that the whole family in heaven and earth carry the same name (Ephesians 3:15). So one interpretation of this phrase would be that, when we abide *in* Yeshua and Yeshua abides *in* us, we are, literally, *"in* His name" (John 15:7). By that I mean that we possess all of our triune's Godhead's character traits, albeit not in their perfected state.

For instance, when the name of the Lord was proclaimed to Moses, the name consisted of character attributes such as merciful, gracious, longsuffering, abundant in goodness and truth and forgiver of sins for those who seek it (Exodus 34:5-7). Thus, the name of God is like a state of being, a reputation. To take on His name means to represent Who He is.

To take this thought a step further, God told Moses to tell the children of Israel that His name is I AM (Exodus 3:14). In other words, "I exist." Because God is and forever shall be, we, who are in His name, also are and forever shall be. Because God is, we are. When we exhibit, through the Holy Spirit, the characteristics, mannerisms, attributes and existence of our God, we are, in effect, physical manifestations of God on earth and, thus, "in His name". As members of the Spiritual Body of Yeshua, we are truly in Him. Hence, when we ask anything while living "in His name" or in this representative state, it will be granted unto us (Psalm 63:3-4; John 14:13-26).

When we faithfully live out our lives in the name of our triune Godhead, we become partakers of God's divine nature adding virtue to our faith, knowledge to our virtue, temperance to our knowledge, patience to our temperance, godliness to our patience, brotherly kindness to our godliness and charity to our brotherly kindness (2 Peter 1:3-5). Just as Yeshua used virtue to heal many, we, who are "in His name", can also heal using this same virtue (Mark 5:30, Luke 6:19, Luke 8:46). Of course, we will never be able to attain this state of being if we are not obedient to the commands of our Lord and Savior, Yeshua HaMashiach (John 14:15, 1 John 3:22-24).

Another interpretation of John 17:11 is as follows: if I were to keep a child and raise him in my name, I, in essence, would be adopting him, and he would have my name. He would be an heir to all of my possessions and would share in the daily responsibilities of managing the family's affairs. When this verse is viewed in the context of the other three verses, we have some measure of appreciation as to what Yeshua may have meant by asking God to keep us in the name of our triune Godhead. When our God abides in us and we in Him, we are adopted by Him. As a consequence, we take on His name and all of the benefits and responsibilities associated therewith. Galatians 4:4-7 state:

> But when the fullness of the time was come, God sent forth his Son, made of a woman, made under the law, To redeem them that were under the law, that we might receive the

adoption of sons. And because ye are sons, God hath sent forth the Spirit of his Son into your hearts, crying, Abba, Father. Wherefore thou art no more a servant, but a son; and if a son, then an heir of God through Yeshua HaMashiach.

The Thomas Nelson Study Bible, in footnote 4:5 of Galatians, informs us that the Greek word *huiothesia* is used for the phrase "adoption of sons" and means sonship conferred as opposed to sonship by birth. Yeshua is the only Son of God by birth. Through our faith in Yeshua, we are adopted as sons of God, the Spirit of Yeshua lives in our hearts and we are heirs of God through Yeshua (Ephesians 1:3-12).

We are not only adopted by God and given all of the privileges, rights and responsibilities attendant to one who carries His name, but we also literally live in His name and He lives in us. Thus, when we ask anything, while in this state of mutual inhabitation "in His name," God, the Father, will do it (John 14:14, 16:23). We have to abide in our God and He in us in order for us to be in a position to have our prayers answered. So many of us end our prayers to God with the perfunctory "In the name of Yeshua HaMashiach, our Lord and Savior" without appreciating that it is our spiritual relationship with God that determines whether we are "in His name" and it is God, the Father, Who answers our prayers (John 16:23). Our prayers are answered because God abides in us and we in Him, not because we rotely call upon His name at the end of every prayer. It is only then that we are truly "in His name." This mutual indwelling between the children of God and their Father will result in a unification that mirrors the oneness Yeshua has with His Father. Consequently, just as Yeshua forgave sins, so are we, in whom our Father dwells, able to do likewise (Matthew 9:1-8, John 20:23).

Verse 21 defines the unification the children of God will experience when they become one with each other and with

God, their Father (John 10:30). In other words, we will all be in each other (John 14:20). This oneness does not come about solely as a result of souls joining with God individually. It also comes about when all reborn souls, Jew and Gentile alike, join with one another and with God collectively, much like a marriage (Ephesians 4:4-6, 5:30-32). Just as a woman gives up her identity and takes on the identity of her husband, so does each child of God the moment of his or her spiritual rebirth into the family of God.

This type of oneness is inseparable, and the component parts are indistinguishable. A great example of this type of oneness is Psalm 95. In that Psalm which, as all Scripture, is inspired by the Holy Ghost, the author is depicted in the first person as both David and God. Verses 1-7 has David as the author, verses 8-11 has God has the author. David, who wrote the entire Psalm, does not refer to God in the third person as would be expected when he is writing about what God said. It is as if they are both the simultaneous authors of the Psalm. What a wonderful display of oneness between God and man, His highest creation!

Oneness to this extent gives God, the Father, full and complete control to be all that He is through us, individually and collectively. Yeshua tells us in John 14:10 that the two-way habitation between Him and the Father does not allow Him to speak on His own authority. It allows God, the Father, to speak on His own authority through Yeshua. When we become one with God to this extent, we will not do anything on our own authority. God, the Father, will be doing everything through us on His own authority.

Verse 22 of John 17 describes how this oneness will be effectuated. Yeshua gives us the same glory that God gave Him. Yeshua demonstrated the glory God gave Him at the transfiguration (Luke 9:28-30). We are being transformed daily into this same glory by the Holy Spirit (2 Corinthians 3:18). It is this transformation that enables us to become completely one with our triune Godhead.

Verse 23 further explains that, as we become more and more in God and God in us, God's glory becomes more and more our glory as we are perfected into one. As members of the Body of Yeshua, we are in Yeshua and He is in us. Since Yeshua and God are one, we are also in God and God is in us. It is only through this type of indivisible unity that we can look and act like God. It is only through this form of oneness that we can truly say that we are in the image and after the likeness of our triune Godhead. I constantly repeat this theme because I believe that it cannot be said enough. The reality of Mankind's creative purpose is so amazing that I cannot think of anything more important to impress upon the world.

Since Yeshua is described as the faithful witness in Revelation 1:5, the unlimited faithfulness of His prayer, contained in John 17, will cause it to be answered. Yeshua never made a petition to God, His Father, that was not realized. After all, He is Himself God. The first scriptural indication that Yeshua's faithful prayer in John 17 was being realized was His resurrection (Matthew 28:1-8). Another occurred on the day of Pentecost when those gathered "were all with one accord in one place" (Acts 2:1).

Upon each of them receiving the Holy Spirit, they knew that Yeshua is in the Father, that the Father is in Yeshua, that they are in Yeshua, that Yeshua is in them, that they are in God, and that God is in them (John 14:20). They knew that they were all one with their triune Godhead. They immediately demonstrated the awesome power attendant to their oneness with God by inspirationally and miraculously spreading the gospel of Yeshua HaMashiach through languages never before spoken by them. As I stated, salvation came to the Jew first. As the Gentiles became one with God, the same Godly power and authority was demonstrated through them as was done through Yeshua and His Jewish disciples. Just as with His disciples, Yeshua will work with and through us as we preach the gospel wherever He sends us (Mark 16:20).

Adam was a prototype of Yeshua, but without the glory of God. Adam never attained that level of perfection because of his sin. However, the death, burial and resurrection of Yeshua will allow for Adam and his chosen descendants, whose names remain written in the Book of Life, to receive their incorruptible bodies, the glory of God, and the ability to be 100 percent God and 100 percent man, thereby making us, through loving obedience, one with God and friends of Yeshua (John 15:10-15). This type of friendship is closer than any imaginable.

The more we experience this degree of oneness with God, the more empowered we become, just as the saints at the Pentecost were empowered. At that time, the Holy Spirit was sent into the world to indwell the elect of God. He will continue to indwell every person who is spiritually reborn until our glorified perfection upon Yeshua's return. During these last days of the so-called "church age," the Gentile elect of God are beginning to comprehend that true oneness with God will only be realized when Jew and Gentile believers are individually and collectively one with each other and with God through Yeshua HaMashiach.

Can any of us truly say that we fully comprehend the significance of being created to be one with God? This wonderful eventuality has not been the topic of many sermons. Nor has it been the prolific subject of biblical literature. However, its absence from the lips and pages of professing believers does not detract from the reality of its truth. Indeed, Jewish and Gentile believers have long recognized this truth. It is the fundamental truth of our creative purpose that answers the questions of why our loving obedience to God was tested in the Garden of Eden, why Satan continually seeks to destroy us and why God has chosen to redeem us. We have eternal life because Yeshua is eternal life and we live in Him and He in us. His eternal life becomes our eternal life when we become one with Him. Upon our perfection, each of us shall approach the very throne of God and gaze into His eyes and reverently say, "Oh, Father God, with all of my substance I give You thanks and praise because You are, **I am**, and You and I are one." This truth is confirmed in the Holy Scriptures (Genesis 3: 13-14, John 14:19, 17:22: 18:5-8).

If this does not cause you to spiritually, if not physically, jump out of your seat and do a victorious praise dance, then you have yet to be spiritually reborn. Should this be the case with you, I pray that you take this opportunity to accept the death, burial and resurrection of Yeshua for the forgiveness of your sins and be spiritually re-born as a child of God. Eternal salvation and oneness with God is available to any "one" who seeks to be all that he or she was created to be.

CHAPTER THREE

THE FALL OF MAN

The overriding lesson to be gleaned from the Holy Scriptures is that love of God can only be demonstrated through obedience to God. God is 100 percent true, pure, uncompromising and unconditional love. Love is as much a part of God as we are human. Love is who and what God is. As previously stated, we have to be compatible with God in every way in order to become one with Him.

Therefore, it is essential that we possess this Godly characteristic of love. Before perfecting oneness with Adam and Eve, God wanted them to demonstrate uncompromising and unconditional love for Him by placing obedience to Him above everything else, including their own desires. God knew that they would fail this test and would require a personal demonstration of His limitless love. Only then would Adam and Eve, and their progeny, appreciate the fact that unconditional, selfless love is the essence of God and, therefore, must be the essence of Mankind, God's highest creation, if we are to become one with our Creator God.

This chapter focuses on Adam and Eve's failure of God's obedience test. It begins with the creation of the angelic hosts who witnessed the test. We then discuss how Satan's sin of pride caused him to become a rebellious, deceptive player in this test. We examine the details of the test, why Adam and Eve failed God's obedience test, the catastrophic consequences of their disobedience and God's covenant of redemption.

Praise be to God for not letting the story of Mankind end with Adam and Eve's sin of disobedience. God promised to redeem both Adam and Eve, and their progeny, and set in motion a plan to personally demonstrate His uncompromising and unconditional love for Mankind by having His Spoken Word become His only begotten Son and fulfill that promise by lovingly shedding every drop of His eternal, sinless, Godly blood for the remission of all the sins of the world.

The Creation of the Angels

We know from the Word of God that the angels were created to worship and praise God and to be ministering servants. The hosts of heaven have no other function. We also know that the physical realm was created for the sole purpose of providing a physical means through which God may manifestly demonstrate His awesome power, magnificently perfect love and limitless grace.

All things created exist and consist by and through God and they honor and glorify Him by the perfect order of their ways. Every living creature was made in its own image and after its own kind, except for Mankind, who was created in the image and after the likeness of God. There is no greater way to honor and glorify God than to be what we were created to be. This is no less true for the angels.

The Word of God tells us something about these spiritual beings called angels, who were created to live in the timeless existence with God that we call heaven and whom the apostle

Paul cautions us not to worship (Colossians 2:18). One order of these angelic beings is the Cherubim. The word "cherubim" is the plural form of the word "cherub" and is derived from the Hebrew word *kărūbh*. According to Ezekiel 1:5-25 and 10:13-22, each of these beings has four faces and four wings, with the hands of a man under their wings. They have the faces of a man, the highest creature created with intelligence; of a lion, the greatest animal of prey; of an ox, the strongest beast of burden; and of an eagle, the king of the air. The cherubim, therefore, apparently possess intelligence, ferocity, strength and regality, characteristics often symbolized by these four creatures. The soles of the cherubim's feet are described as the soles of calves' feet and these beings sparkle like the color of burnished brass. They come and go like flashes of lightning. They are obviously formidable and splendid creations. Yet, with all their power and splendor, they were not created in the image or after the likeness of God.

The Holy Scriptures describe yet another form of heavenly being that appears to be related to and inseparable from the cherubim. They are sometimes referred to as the Ophanim. The prophet Ezekiel describes them as having the appearance of a beryl stone. Each one of these magnificent creatures looked the same—a wheel in the middle of a wheel. They each had eyes all over their bodies. Each of the Ophanim was paired with a cherub. Whatever and wherever the cherub did or went, so did and so went the wheels, because the spirit of the cherub was in the Ophanim (Ezekiel 1:15-21, 10:9-17). Despite the wonder and purpose of these spiritual beings, they also were not created in the image or after the likeness of God.

Isaiah 6:2-3 describe a third form of angelic being created by God: the Seraphim. Each of these beings has six wings: two cover their faces, two their feet, and with two they fly. The word "seraphim" is also the plural form of the word "seraph" and was taken from the Hebrew word *sārāph,* which means "burners or burning ones." Despite the unique beauty and majesty of these angelic beings, they too were not made in the image or after the likeness of God.

These angelic creatures were made to be ministering servants (Psalm 104:4, Hebrews 1:14). Though mighty, they were sometimes charged with error (Job 4:18) and considered unclean in the sight of God (Job 15:15). Thus, the angels are capable of sinning before God. Yet, as we shall see, even the unclean angels were allowed by God to perform ministerial services. Angels are referred to as the sons of God (Job 1:6, 2:1). Being spirits, they, therefore, must be spiritual sons of God.

Though asexual (Matthew 22:30), they are always referred to in the masculine sense. They are to be distinguished from Mankind in that Mankind is both male and female and can, therefore procreate, and is destined to be the physical and spiritual children of God. Scripture tells us that thousands upon thousands of angels were created (Revelation 5:11). In fact, they are innumerable (Hebrews 12:22). If Yeshua had but asked, His Father would have given Him more than twelve legions of angels (Matthew 26:53), all of whom witnessed His earthly ministry (1 Timothy 3:16).

The scriptural descriptions of angels suggest that there are categories of angels that may have specialized functions. There is Michael the Archangel (Jude 9), the highest order of the angels, who leads God's angels into combat (Daniel 10:13, 21; 12:1; Revelation 12:7), there are angelic messengers, such as Gabriel, who deliver messages from God (Daniel 8:16; Luke 1:19, 26) and there are angels of destruction sent by God to execute His wrath (Psalm 78:49). Matthew 18:10 suggests that each child of God has an assigned angel who has direct access to God in heaven.

The cherubim are apparently guardian and covering angels. They were responsible for keeping Adam and Eve out of the Garden of Eden after their expulsion (Genesis 3:24). The cherubim covered the mercy seat of God (Exodus 25:18-20) and are constantly in the presence of the Glory of God (Ezekiel 10:1-22). Perhaps, the cherubim were created to cover God's judgment. This would explain why Satan, a fallen cherub (Ezekiel 28:14-16), accuses us daily before the throne of God, requesting that God render unto us the judgment we so rightly deserve (Revelation 12:10), instead of seeking to cover our judgment as he was created to do.

The seraphim continually fly in the presence of God, the Father, declaring His Holiness, praising and worshiping Him (Isaiah 6:1-3). They are associated with sacrificing and cleansing (Isaiah 6:5-7).

According to Hebrews 1:13-14, all angels are ministering spirits sent forth to minister, not just to God, but also to all of us who shall be heirs of salvation. Those same verses also tell us that none of the angels will sit at God, the Father's, right hand, nor will God make their enemies their footstool. This He gives only to Yeshua. Indeed, Isaiah 45:23 and Philippians 2:4-11 tell us that every knee shall bow before our Lord and Savior, Yeshua HaMashiach, and shall proclaim Him Lord to the glory of God. This will include the angels.

Satan's Rebellion Against God

Of course, the most infamous angelic being who witnessed creation week is Lucifer, who, before he sinned against God from the beginning (1 John 3:8), was described in Ezekiel 28:14 as "the anointed cherub." Being a cherub, Lucifer (later known as Satan) was also created to have four faces: one of a man, one of a lion, one of an ox and one of an eagle. He is therefore intelligent, ferocious, powerful and regal. As all other cherubim, he has four wings, with the hands of a man under his wings. The soles of his feet are like calves' feet that sparkle like burnished brass, and he goes and comes as a flash of lightning. Satan would also have an Ophanim, who possesses his spirit, by his side wherever he goes. Very seldom will you see Satan depicted as he truly is.

It is of some significance that Satan was created to be a covering cherub. As previously stated, two cherubim covered the mercy seat with their wings (Exodus 25:18-20). The Hebrew words from which we get the phrase "mercy seat" have been translated to mean "place or object of covering, concealment, redemption, ransom and atonement." This place of covering (i.e., "mercy seat") was where the Jewish high priest would sprinkle the blood of sacrificed animals for the temporary forgiveness of the sins of the nation. Apparently, one of the creative functions of the cherubim was to cover this place of atonement where God sometimes dwelt (Psalm 80:1).

Upon the ultimate sacrifice of Yeshua, there is no longer any need for the continuing covering of the sins of the world because they were forever forgiven by the death, burial and resurrection of Yeshua HaMashiach. Because of his sin of pride, Satan lost his desire to cover. Now, he not only seeks the execution of God's judgment upon Mankind but also consistently seeks to persuade Mankind to reject the sacrificial, salvational death of Yeshua HaMashiach on their behalf.

Satan is one of the most astounding spiritual beings created by God and, like all cherubim, has always been associated with the judgment of God. According to Ezekiel 28, Satan was present in the Garden of Eden and had every precious stone as his covering, which included the sardius, topaz, diamond, beryl, onyx, jasper, sapphire, emerald, carbuncle, and gold.

It is of interest to note that every one of the precious stones that covered Lucifer were required to be included in the four rows of stones set in gold in the breastplate of judgment worn by Aaron, the first Jewish high priest (Exodus 28:15-21), and his successors. Also included in the breastplate were jacinth, agate, and amethyst. Aaron and his seed were to continually bear the symbolic judgment of Israel upon their hearts by wearing this breastplate whenever they came before the Lord. Perhaps, this was done as a constant testimony to God that Mankind's continual state of sin, and consequently any judgment thereof, must be rendered in the context of the deception of one of His highest covering cherubs.

Many of these precious stones also appear in the Holy Scriptures as adornments to the foundations of the new Jerusalem, which shall be made of pure gold and shall be the habitation of all whose names remain written in the Lamb's Book of Life (Revelation 21:9-27). God, in His eternal wisdom, uses the same types of precious stones—which initially covered Lucifer, before he became Satan, and which covered the breastplate of judgment worn by the high priest of the twelve tribes of Israel until their redemption through Yeshua HaMashiach—to cover the twelve foundations of the Holy City that will eternally house the people of God. Because God is perfect in all His ways, we must assume that His use of these stones in these ways has a significance that we, as yet, do not fully understand.

We have already discussed how Ezekiel 28:11-19 describe the beauty and magnificence of Satan before his fall. Ezekiel 28:13 indicates that, before his sin of pride, Satan possessed wonderful timbrels and pipes with which he provided tremendous musical worship of God. According to verses 14 and 16, he had access to the holy mountain of God and walked up and down in the midst of the stones of fire. Yet, even Satan was never made in the image and after the likeness of God.

It appears from these same passages that, given his awesome power and splendor (Ezekiel 28:17), Satan was unable to remain a ministering servant who sought to cover God's judgment of Mankind. Isaiah 14:12-33 vividly describe the fall of Satan when iniquity was found in him. According to these verses, Satan was sinless before God at some point during his existence. 1 John 3:8 tells us that the devil sinned from the beginning. The Greek word for "from" is *apo*. This word has been interpreted to also mean "in" or "since." Thus, it can be inferred that Satan's first sin occurred sometime during the beginning, not before the beginning.

John 8:44 tells us that Satan was a murderer from the beginning. Something happened, either during or immediately after creation week, that caused pride to swell up in his heart and caused Satan to rebel against God and seek to usurp, through deception, God's plan for Mankind by murdering us, physically and spiritually, through the commission of sin. Satan's tremendous self-pride prevented him from accepting his creative covering purpose in God's master plan.

The Holy Scriptures further reveal that, just like Adam and Eve, Satan did not know good or evil before he sinned. His sin of pride was the source of his knowledge of evil, which he clearly possessed by the time he tempted Eve. There is no indication in the Holy Word of God that Satan ever came to know good. He possesses only an evil nature. There is no truth in him (John 8:44). Satan can therefore do only what he knows how to do, and that is evil. To know evil necessitates the commission of sin. Just like a man biblically knows a woman when he has sexual intercourse with her, one cannot know sin unless he engages in it. When Satan sinned against God, he became one with sin, taking on a sin nature.

There is no greater deceiver or liar than Satan, for it is written that he is the "father of lies" (John 8:44) and could appear as an angle of light (2 Corinthians 11:13-14). As a result of his deception of Adam and Eve, Satan was cursed. God prophesied that Satan would ultimately be destroyed by Yeshua HaMashiach, the seed of the woman (Genesis 3:14-15). Satan will be bound for 1,000 years, loosed for a while, and then eternally removed from the presence of God, God's children, and all creation (Revelation 20:1-15).

Satan purposed to overcome this curse by causing Yeshua to sin and thereby bring into condemnation the souls of a sinful Mankind. For Adam and Eve, their sin was in disobeying God and obeying Satan. Their obedience to Satan caused them, and their offspring, to take on Satan's sin nature and to become one with him as his children. Thus, it is written of those who choose Satan over God:

> Ye are of your father the devil, and the lusts of your father ye will do. He was a murderer from the beginning, and abode not in the truth, because there is no truth in him. When he speaketh a lie, he speaketh of his own: for he is a liar, and the father of it. (John 8:44)

Because Adam and Eve ate from the Tree of the Knowledge of Good and Evil, they knew both good and evil. Anyone with free will who possesses such dual knowledge, through sin, cannot coexist with God because, invariably, evil will be chosen despite having the knowledge of good, especially if one has a sin nature. Once sin is chosen, we can no longer be one with God because a person cannot be one with both Satan and God (Matthew 6:24). For the unsaved, the penalty for sin is a form of eternal death that can be described as the complete physical and spiritual separation from God. Unlike Adam and Eve, Satan understood all too well the wages of his sin. He nonetheless believed that he could be separate but equal to God if he could become one with

Mankind, through sin, and use us to assist him in his physical and spiritual rebellion against God.

Satan lost his desire to serve God as a covering cherub when iniquity was found in his heart, but he continues to have access to the throne of God. For instance, in Job 1:6-7, well after the creation of all things, Satan presented himself before God along with the other angelic sons of God to discuss his goings and comings and God's servant Job. God often uses His enemies to effectuate His holy will. He did so with the heathen kings during the post exilic era of the Israelites. God permits Satan to continually test Mankind, His highest creation, to determine whether our love of God supersedes our love of self.

Psalm 33:6 tells us that God spoke all of creation, including the angels, into existence. Nehemiah 9:6 provides some guidance as to the order of that creative process:

> Thou, even thou, art LORD alone; thou hast made heaven, the heaven of heavens, with all their host, the earth, and all things that are therein, the seas, and all that is therein, and thou preservest them all; and the host of heaven worshipeth thee.

This verse confirms that God created the celestial heavens, His spiritual Kingdom, the earth and all that is in it. With respect to the earth, God created the planet, formed the lands and seas, created its animal inhabitants and created Mankind to exercise dominion over all the earth. After God created Mankind, He rested, confirming that the entire creative process had been completed. Clearly, the creation of the spiritual realm occurred prior to the creation of the physical realm that included Mankind.

Since God's spiritual Kingdom and its angelic citizens were created before God created the physical realm (Genesis 1:1, Nehemiah 9:6, Job 38:4-7, Psalm 104:4-5), the angels, who reside in His presence, witnessed every phase of the creation of the physical realm (Job 38:4-7). The angelic hosts were firsthand witnesses to the supernatural creation of the world and would have heard every verbal command of God. They would have seen God's creative will wonderfully, majestically and miraculously realized day by day as each command was uttered. As the order of creation was revealed to them, they no doubt realized the fullness of God's creative design, their role in it and, eventually, Mankind's role in it. The angels would have understood that the order in which all seen and unseen things were lovingly and faithfully realized spoke volumes about the ever-increasing significance and level of importance attributed to each ensuing phase of the creation process according to God's Holy will.

Just like all the other angels, Satan would have been present during creation week and would have observed the order of God's creative process. With access to the throne of God, he would have had a front row perspective of the awesome power, authority and faithfulness of God being demonstrated as each verbal creative command was effectuated by the Living Word of God, including the last and most important creative utterance of God: "Let us make man in our image, after our likeness."

Satan understood the significance of this statement and knew that Mankind, though made a little lower than the angels (Psalm 8:3-9, Hebrews 2: 6-11), was purposed to mirror God in appearance, mannerisms, attributes and characteristics and, ultimately, be above all of God's creations, including the angels. He had to know that God intended to become one with Mankind so that He could manifest Himself in and through Mankind. One of the definitions given for the word "manifestation" in the *Webster's New World Dictionary* could not be more on point: "a form in which a being manifests itself or is thought to manifest itself, especially the material or bodily form of a spirit." Satan realized that his creative role, as well as that of the other angels, was to be that of ministering servants to God and eventually to every human being in whom God resides.

Satan was so proud of his beauty, splendor and power that he thought himself greater than Mankind and equal to God. It is apparent that he could not bring himself to serve either. According to Isaiah 14:14, Satan blasphemed in his heart that he will be *like* the Most High, not *greater than* the Most High. Indeed, Paul used Satan to teach saints not to blaspheme (1 Timothy 1:20). Even Satan recognized, in his moment of sin, that no creature can be greater than the Most High.

Satan, obviously, had enough faith in his abilities that he believed that he could attain a status equal to God. Satan apparently understood, by observing the power of God's faith being demonstrated during creation week, what could be obtained through faith. However, Satan's faith, as we discussed earlier, is vain in that it is not of God. By that I mean Satan's faith is not based upon love which is God. It is Godly love that believes and hopes for all things (1 Corinthians 13:7). It is faith that brings these hoped for things into realization (Hebrews 11:1). It all begins and ends with Godly love. Because there is no Godly love in Satan, he will never be able to attain his desired results.

Satan also knew that only Mankind was made in the image and after the likeness of the Most High. We were given the privilege of being what Satan wanted to be. Satan was not content with his position in God's ordered creation, having angelic attributes after his own kind. Satan's pride prevented him from accepting the fact that another created being would become so much one with God that it would be impossible to distinguish between the creation and his God. Essentially, this creation of God would be God in the flesh. Satan could not accept the fact that he would have to be subservient to, in his opinion, a lessor created being.

Satan, therefore, purposed in his heart that, in order for him to be like the Most High, he had to become one with Mankind before God perfected His oneness with His highest creation.

Satan correctly reasoned that, should Adam and Eve sin, they and their progeny would have to suffer death in the form of eternal physical and spiritual separation from God. I say "and their progeny" for two reasons. First, since all Mankind descended from Adam and Eve, every one of us received the sin nature they possessed upon their fall. They could not pass on anything other than who they were. Second, though many would deny it, every descendant of Adam and Eve would have chosen the same sin of disobedience if faced with the same test. Adam and Eve were the best of Mankind and, yet, they sinned before God. There is every reason to believe that, even at our best, we would have committed the same sin. Thus, but for the sacrificial death, burial and resurrection of Yeshua, we would all be doomed to suffer eternal physical and spiritual separation from God.

This would make all of Mankind available for Satan to become one with them through sin. Satan wanted to be worshiped by all creation. Since all creation revolves around Mankind, Satan reasoned that, once he became master of Mankind through sin, he would consequentially be master of all creation. Satan has always sought to have what God has, nothing more, because there is nothing more, but nothing less.

Knowing all things, God was aware of Satan's rebellious plan before Adam and Eve's obedience test. Yet, God decided not to permanently address Satan's sin at the moment of his sin. Instead, He allowed Satan to become an active participant in the test of Adam and Eve's love of God through obedience. Apparently, God wanted Satan to perform his creative function as a ministering servant by assisting in the administration of

God's obedience test of Adam and Eve despite his sin of pride. If this is true, then Satan had to be aware that his attempt to deceive Adam and Eve was done with God's permission.

If Adam and Eve had obeyed God despite Satan's deception, Mankind would have been perfected in God and Satan's damnation would have been swift, immediate and eternal. Should Adam and Eve give in to sin by eating from the forbidden Tree of the Knowledge of Good and Evil, Satan would then be permitted to prove to God that every one of their offspring, given the free will to do so, would invariably choose evil over good.

Satan sought to present to God irrefutable evidence that dominion, power and authority cannot be effectively exercised by God through a creature who, when given the choice, would never place love of others above love of self. Satan contended that Mankind would fail to reciprocate the degree of selfless love that God exhibits toward them.

Having determined within himself to challenge God's authority by seeking to raise himself above his created estate to a status equal to God, Satan welcomed this ministerial task and, indeed, may have requested it. He set about to cause Adam and Eve to sin against God just as he later set about to cause Job to curse God to His face. Satan knew that the wages of Adam and Eve's sin would cause them to die through eternal physical and spiritual separation from God. They would then no longer possess the characteristics and attributes of God. They would be in the image and after the likeness of themselves (Genesis 5:3), becoming one with Satan in sin. God would not be able to become one with Adam and Eve while they were in this sinful state.

If Mankind could be turned into an enemy of God, Satan's rebellion against God would take place in the physical realm over which he now has dominion and authority and the spiritual realm where he had the support of a third of the angels (2 Peter

2:4; Jude 6; Revelation 12:4, 7-9). He mistakenly believed that he would then have the advantage over God. In reality, while Satan may have thought that he was successful in throwing the proverbial wrench into God's creative process, it was anticipated and permitted by God Who knew that a demonstration of His perfect love was necessary for Mankind to fully appreciate His creative purpose. Eventually, all will be restored to its original perfection and every person who chooses God's way over Satan's way will be restored to his/her rightful place as God's greatest creation and will become one with God. With his service complete, Satan will then be tossed into the eternal lake of fire.

By bringing about the fall of Adam and Eve, Satan temporarily usurped their authority and dominion over the earth to do with as they pleased (Luke 4:5-7). When Satan succeeded in deceiving Adam and Eve, they became Satan's captive, being one with him through sin and forced to do his bidding (2 Timothy 2:26). Satan was then able to work his rebellion against God through Adam and Eve and their offspring (Ephesians 2:2). Mankind was originally intended to be inhabited by God. Instead, we are inhabited by Satan. Satan's misuse of us has caused us all to sin and will result in our physical and spiritual deaths unless we are freed from these death sentences by accepting, in faith, the sacrificial death of Yeshua the Messiah in our stead. Upon doing so, we are spiritually reborn as new creatures. Satan no longer lives in us. Instead, God lives in us.

Unless or until we are spiritually reborn in and through Yeshua, our sin natures will cause us to invariably sin. Any sin, whether great or small, significant or insignificant, requires the same physical and spiritual death penalty. That is why it is impossible for any offspring of Adam and Eve to enter the Kingdom of Heaven if they do not accept God's sacrifice for the propitiation of their sins. No amount of obedience or good works can offset the death penalty required for just one sin, let alone many. It is unfortunate that many people believe that they will not suffer eternal damnation and separation from God because, for the most part, they have led decent and upstanding lives. They cannot fathom the fact that, even if they committed the most insignificant sin only once over their entire lifetime, they would still be deserving of eternal physical and spiritual death because that one sin would make it impossible for them to coexist with a sinless, Holy God, let alone enjoy a mutual inhabitation with Him.

It is for this reason that we needed, and received, a Messiah, a Savior, Who delivered us from our death penalties by physically and spiritually dying in our place thereby giving us the victory over death and Satan (John 12:31, 19:30). Yeshua, in Hebrew, means salvation or to rescue, to deliver. Yeshua, of course, physically died. It could be argued that Yeshua suffered spiritual death, at least for the time that He bore the sins of the world on the cross, because, in that condition, He was unable to be one with God, the Father, Who is a Spirit and cannot know sin (Mark 15:34).

The Holy Scriptures appear to indicate that Pilate fully understood that Yeshua was called HaMashiach ("the Messiah") and what that title meant to the Jews (Matthew 27:17-18, 22). He marveled greatly at Yeshua's humility and submissive attitude even though Yeshua answered affirmatively when asked by Pilate if He was, in fact, the King of the Jews (Matthew 27:11-14). This troubled Pilate so much that he attempted to avoid responsibility for this crucifixion by washing his hands (Matthew 27: 24-26).

Satan's service to God will end when he initiates a war against God in heaven. God's holy angels, possibly led by Michael the archangel, will prevail against Satan and his fallen angels. God will cast them out of heaven into the earth (Revelation 12:7-9). When Yeshua said, in Luke 10:18, that he "beheld Satan as lightning fall from heaven," one must keep in mind that Satan is a cherub and therefore he moves as a flash of lightning. Also, as previously discussed, Yeshua HaMashiach, the literal Word of God, is God and, therefore, the Alpha and the Omega, as stated in Revelation 1:8,11. Consequently, not being confined to this world's temporal existence, He can speak in past tense about seeing Satan being cast out of heaven even though, according to this world's time, it has not yet happened.

Shortly after his permanent ouster from heaven, Satan will continue his war against God on the Earth. Yeshua will prevail against Satan's earthly forces as well (Revelation 19:19-21). Satan's judgment occurred when Yeshua sacrificed His sinless life on the cross, was buried, resurrected by God and ascended into heaven (John 12:31, 16:7-11). That judgment will be enforced when Yeshua returns at the end of the tribulation period. At that time, all the enemies of God will be placed under the feet of our Messiah (1 Corinthians 15:27, Hebrews 2:8). Since all of God's children compose the Spiritual Body of Yeshua, Satan and his demons will be placed under our feet (Romans 16:20).

In the Gospel of John, footnote 16:8-11 of the *Thomas Nelson Study Bible* inform us that, in the original Greek text, the word *kekritai* means "has been judged." Yeshua's innocent death for sins He did not commit paid the price for all the sins of Mankind (1 John 2:2) and resulted in Satan's judgment approximately 2,000 years ago. Satan initially succeeded in causing us to fall from grace and to come under his authority, but the great love of God, the Father, was demonstrated by allowing His living Word, which is a part of Himself, to become one of us in and through the person of Yeshua HaMashiach and to suffer our death penalties in our stead. Yeshua's sacrificial death forever frees us from the clutches of Satan. We need only accept, in faith, this sacrifice on our behalf.

Satan's Deception of Adam and Eve

With direct access to the very throne of God, Satan observed God in all His splendor and glory and had to know that any power and magnificence he possessed as an angel paled in comparison to that of God. Yet, he obviously was not awed into submission by God's glory and power because he determined to establish his own agenda when permitted to intervene into God's obedience test of man by attempting to deceive Adam and Eve into believing that they could obtain, through sin, what God had already intended to freely give them through selfless, loving obedience.

Satan's deception of Adam and Eve was actually comprised of several deceptions. He initially deceived Adam and Eve into believing that it was God's creative intent that they would never be more than what they were. Satan then provided them a way to be more than they were created to be. Had Adam and Eve known that they were made to be one with God, a level of existence far greater than what they were, they may never have believed the serpent's lie that they had to eat of the forbidden fruit to be like God. They must have thought that they were made after their own kind just like every other created thing.

These deceptions were crucial to Satan's plan for their submission to him through the sin of disobedience. They formed the basis for Adam and Eve's desire to be more than what they believed they were. Once Adam and Eve fell for these deceptions, Satan succeeded in further deceiving them into believing that God lied to them to keep them from being like God. This second deception was made possible because of the success of the first deception. Adam and Eve were willing to believe that God would lie to them because of their desire to improve their status quo in God's ordered creation. In other words, Adam and Eve were willing to choose love of self over love of God. Adam and Eve's desire was the same as Satan's desire as they all sought to improve their status in God's ordered creation.

As mentioned, Adam and Eve's willingness to believe that God would lie to them strongly suggests that they were unaware that they were created in the image and after the likeness of God, thereby possessing an imperfect form of God's characteristics and mannerisms. Since God cannot lie (Titus 1:2), Adam and Eve, before their fall, also could not lie. Had they known that this personality trait was from and of God, they would have known that the serpent, not God, was the liar. They must have seen the similarities between their character and that of God, but there is no indication in the Scriptures that they were ever told that they mirrored the image and likeness of God in every way or that they were created to become one with God.

In order for them to pass the obedience test, Adam and Eve would have to obey God for no other reason than because they loved God more than they loved themselves. They were not given the option to obey God because of what they could gain as a reward. It was to be obedient out of love or no obedience at all. Adam and Eve, by their choice of disobedience, established that their love of self was greater than any love they had for God.

As a result of Adam and Eve's love of self, it was easy for Satan to accomplish the final deception even though God told Adam and Eve that the only way for them to ever suffer death was to disobey His edict not to eat of the forbidden fruit. Satan succeeded in his complete deception of Adam and Eve because he convinced them that they would not only continue to live but would also know the difference between good and evil, knowledge reserved only unto God. They were deceived into believing that such knowledge would be a positive change in their status in God's ordered creation when, in fact, it would destroy their heightened status. Acting upon this deception, Adam and Eve partook of the forbidden fruit in direct, intentional disobedience to God.

These deceptions brought about the fall of Mankind who was created to be one with God by the grace of God. Their fall from grace, through sin, resulted in Satan, the father of sin, becoming one with them and their progeny, all having a sin nature just like Satan. Their sin should have ensured their permanent separation from God through physical and spiritual death, which is the result of sin. But God, through His infinite love and mercy, decided to spare them and their descendants from the death sentences they so rightly deserved.

Mankind was created to be inseparable from God, to be one with God. Eternal separation from God would be the antithesis of God's plan for man. This is because our eternal souls have always been a part of the Word of God, the second personage of our triune Godhead Who is the eternal *I AM*. The life that was breathed into the nostrils of Adam was the Word of God. Adam, thereby, became a living soul. Adam's sin caused God to end His spiritual relationship with him, albeit allowing Adam to continue as a living soul until his physical death. This separation would have been an eternal one but for the unconditional love of God.

Therefore, God initiated a plan for our salvation. This redemptive plan required the Word of God to take on flesh and pay the death penalty for every one born of Adam and Eve. It can be argued that Yeshua's Spiritual Body is not a created thing. Instead, it is eternal in nature. Thus, it can be further argued that every saved soul, who is a member of the Spiritual Body of Messiah, spiritually died with Him at Calvary and was also spiritually raised with Him unto salvation and ultimate glorification.

Therefore we are buried with him by baptism into death: that like as HaMashiach was raised up from the dead by the glory of the Father, even so we also should walk in the newness of life (Romans 6:4).

God's plan was effectuated by the death, burial and resurrection of Yeshua HaMashiach for sins He did not commit. As a result, only those of Mankind who would reject God's free offer of eternal salvation and succumb to the same deception as did Adam and Eve, by choosing their own way over God's way, would be eternally physically and spiritually separated from God. Satan, as well as all the angels who followed his lead, were defeated by Yeshua's obedience unto death and were, thereby, brought under the feet of Yeshua. It is their fate to suffer eternal damnation, along with the unsaved, because of their collective and individual decisions to sin against God.

In Matthew 3:12, the wicked among Mankind is depicted as the chaff, the righteous is referred to as the wheat. Instead of immediately destroying Satan and his fallen angels, God uses them to continually identify the spiritual chaff among Mankind so that, in the end, God need only separate the wheat from the chaff. God will execute His judgment upon the chaff and become one with the wheat (Matthew 13:24-30).

God's Obedience Test

It bears repeating that, upon their creation, Adam and Eve had the appearance and characteristics of God, yet they did not possess the knowledge of God. Obviously, the degree of Adam and Eve's oneness with God, which they enjoyed prior to their fall from grace, was not perfected and, indeed, was unknown to them. The Holy Scriptures tell us that they could only achieve this knowledge through unconditional, loving obedience that would be eternally perfected when they ate from the Tree of Life. Their lack of such knowledge made Adam and Eve susceptible to Satan's deceptions. Their lust to fulfill their personal desires led to their willful disobedience of God and embracement of Satan's temptations.

The entire Garden of Eden experience was set up to determine whether they would obey God until they ate from the Tree of Life or disobey God by eating from the Tree of the Knowledge of Good and Evil (Genesis 2:15-17). The test was to determine whether or not Adam and Eve were willing to demonstrate to God their God-like characteristic which is pure, unadulterated, unconditional, selfless love. They would have to demonstrate this degree of love without knowing that it is the greatest characteristic, attribute and mannerism of God. Indeed, they would have to do so without knowing that God is 100% love. This degree of love would make it impossible for them to do anything but please God. They would be subsumed with an innate desire to lovingly and obediently serve their God.

God knew, however, that Adam and Eve, once given the gift of free will, would fail to demonstrate this Godly characteristic. Consequently, through this test, God wanted Mankind to learn a very painful lesson. When given the gift of free will, Mankind will become the servant of his own will even if it meant giving up the greatest relationship a creature can have with his God. The lesson having been learned, God then prophetically demonstrated to Adam and Eve how pure, unconditional love of others is greater than any love we could have for ourselves.

God's loving obedience test did not stop with Adam and Eve. Every one of their descendants must undergo the same test. If Adam and Eve had passed this initial test, there would have been no need for any of their offspring to be tested. Unfortunately, because they did not, their offspring must be similarly tested. The Holy Scriptures contain several instances in which descendants of Adam and Eve have been tested by God. For instance, in Genesis 22:1-14 Abraham was tested when he was asked to offer up his son Isaac. In Deuteronomy 8:2, 16, the Holy Scriptures tell us that the Israelites were tested in the wilderness to prove their commitment to the Lord. Job was tested in Job 1:7-12.

However, Christians are armed with the knowledge of the magnitude of God's love. Our test, therefore, is determined by the extent of our faith in that knowledge. In fact, the faith of every child of God is continually tested so that, when proven, we may obtain praise, honor and glory upon Yeshua's return (1 Peter 1:7). This was the same prize that awaited Adam and Eve had they passed their test. However, by the grace of God, what Adam and Eve could not acquire through lack of loving obedience, was obtained through the sacrificial death, burial and resurrection of our Lord and Savior, Yeshua HaMashiach.

The dictates of Adam and Eve's test required that they be created with bodies that were perfect but capable of corruption, depending on their performance on the test. They were created with free will because the test required them to choose to be obedient out of love for God or to choose disobedience out of love of self. With multiple options, free will is a necessity. God knew that Adam and Eve would not place obedience to Him above their own selfish desires. Adam and Eve had to learn, through the painful lesson of physical and spiritual death, that love of self is always set aside when the opportunity to express Godly love of others is presented.

When they chose to satisfy their own desires instead of the desire of God, they demonstrated the extent of their hatred of God. This is because their sin of disobedience made them servants of sin (John 8:34). Matthew 6:24 and Luke 16:13 tell us that we cannot serve two masters because we will hate the one and love the other. As the servants of sin, Adam and Eve became lovers of sin and haters of God. When we love anything other than God, we become the enemy of God (James 4:4). Their sin against God caused them to fall from grace and to be deserving of both physical and spiritual death, i.e., separation from God. But God, the Father, so loved the world that He gave His only begotten Son so that all who believe are resurrected unto everlasting life never to be separated from God again (John 3:16). Our triune Godhead had to demonstrate to Mankind what perfect love is. The greatest exposition of God's perfect love is set forth in the NIV version of 1 Corinthians 13:4-8.

Love is patient, love is kind. It does not envy, it does not boast, It is not proud.

It does not dishonor others, it is not self-seeking, it is not easily angered, it keeps no record of wrongs.
Love does not delight in evil but rejoices with the truth.
It always protects, always trusts, always hopes, always perseveres.
Love never fails...

This perfect love is the very essence of our triune Godhead. As creatures made in the image and likeness of God, love was always intended to be the core of our existence. God wants every human being to fully appreciate what it means to be perfect love. How best to teach this most valuable lesson than through personal application. The Holy Scriptures are replete with examples of our God demonstrating the love that He is. We have but to follow His example.

Only God knows how Adam and Eve would have responded to this test absent Satan's deception. Satan was unable to discern the thoughts and intents of the hearts of Adam and Eve. The answer to that question was, however, irrelevant to Satan. Satan fully understood that, if Adam and Eve were to sin at all, it had to be in servile partnership with his sin. Therefore, he was more than willing to take part in this test because his desire to become one with man through sin depended entirely upon their disobedience of God in servitude to Satan, indeed, at his bequest.

Adam and Eve were more willing to obey Satan to fulfill their own lusts than to obey God Who freely and lovingly gave them everything. From Satan's perspective, it was imperative that his sin of rebellion against God be merged as one with Adam and Eve's sin of disobedience against God. Once this was accomplished, Satan knew that Adam and Eve, and their progeny, were now under his authority through sin and could no longer enjoy any form of oneness with God.

Satan's deception of Adam and Eve was achieved, in part, because Adam and Eve also were unable to discern the thoughts and intents of the hearts of others, including Satan. Satan knew that Adam and Eve, having yet to eat from the Tree of the Knowledge of Good and Evil, could not tell the difference between good and evil. Satan was, therefore, assured that Adam and Eve would never be able to perceive his true evil intentions. Satan was able to deceive them into believing that the obtainment of this knowledge would make them that much closer to being like God, but only by eating of the forbidden tree in direct disobedience to God and in obedience to Satan.

Genesis 3:1-13 tell us the story of man's failure of God's obedience test. To tempt Adam and Eve, Satan deceptively possessed a serpent. His possession of the serpent was not done outside of the knowledge of God. God knew of Satan's deceptive intentions and allowed him to proceed with his plan. After all, there can be no greater measure of Adam and Eve's unconditional and uncompromising love of God than to test their free will through temptation from a source other than God.

According to Genesis 1:26, Adam and Eve were given dominion over all the earth, which included every creeping thing, including serpents. For Adam and Eve to effectively exercise their dominion over the world, they had to possess enough power and authority to ensure the submission of the earth and everything in it. In our current fallen state, it is difficult for us to fully comprehend the awesome power and authority wielded by Adam and Eve before their fall. Though they may not have fully appreciated their role in God's creative process, they possessed the attributes and characteristics of God and were a legitimate force to be reckoned with. They were quite capable of exercising the dominion given to them by God over the earth.

But we need not stretch our imaginations too far to envision these two spectacular beings. Yeshua is the last Adam (1 Corinthians 15:45), who possesses all the attributes, glory and knowledge of God. When we look at the power and authority exercised by Yeshua during His earthly life, as set forth in the Holy Scriptures, we can get a glimpse of the power and authority that Adam, and perhaps Eve, possessed before their fall, absent God's glory and knowledge. For instance, Yeshua calmed the seas by command (Mark 4:35-41), walked on water (Matthew 14:22-33), withered a fig tree by a curse (Matthew 21:17-20), and commanded fish to seek the fishermen's nets (Luke 5:1-11).

When questioned by the band of men and officers from the chief priests and Pharisees as to whether He was Yeshua of Nazareth, as set forth in John 18:1-6, Yeshua answered and said, "I am." These words spoken by Yeshua threw the men backward and onto the ground. This passage clearly demonstrates that Yeshua is the same I AM as is God, the Father, Who identified Himself by that name when asked by Moses in Exodus 3:14.

It also demonstrates the complete control Yeshua has over His limitless power. Yeshua did exactly what His Father wanted Him to do to His accusers and nothing more.

Adam and Eve were not all that Yeshua was during His earthly life because Yeshua, being God, also possesses the glory and knowledge of God. He can discern the thoughts and intents of the hearts of men. These are Godly qualities that Adam and Eve could only attain through loving obedience. Nonetheless, they most likely exercised significant power and authority over nature and the animal Kingdom. Clearly, they were powerful creatures and more than capable of ruling the world. Nothing on earth would dare challenge Adam and Eve's God-given authority over them.

This may explain why Adam and Eve chose to believe one of God's creations under their God-given dominion, power and authority. The Holy Scriptures tell us that, of all the creatures under their dominion, the serpent was the most subtle (Genesis 3:1). The Thomas Nelson Study Bible, in footnote 3:1 of the Book of Genesis, explains that, in the Books of Proverbs, Job and Matthew, the word "subtle" has been used to mean prudent on the one hand and cunning or crafty on the other. *Webster's New World Dictionary* defines the word "prudent" as "capable of exercising sound judgment in practical matters, especially as concerns one's own interests."

Not being able to discern the difference between good and evil, Adam and Eve would not have contemplated any of the creatures under their authority as being evil-minded toward them seeking to advance its own interests. Therefore, they would have innocently, and perhaps naively, viewed the serpent as one who is prudent and wise. The question as to whether the serpent was providing sound judgment or deceitful advice would never have entered their minds. Who better to inform them about the ability to discern between good and evil than the one creature under their dominion they knew to be renowned for its ability to exercise sound judgment in practical matters, especially since Adam and Eve viewed the serpent's interests as their own interests?

Nor did Adam or Eve think it strange or in any way unusual for a serpent to talk to them. They had no reason to be suspicious about the identity of the speaker or his intentions (Genesis 3:1-6). Either both were quite familiar with this form of communication with the creatures over which they exercised dominion or they were acquainted with the practice of angels speaking to them through these subordinate creatures. The former is the more likely scenario because deception is involved. Satan could have approached them directly and attempted to convince them to disobey God, much like what he did with Yeshua in the wilderness. It was unsuccessful with Yeshua and probably would have been unsuccessful with Adam and Eve. This is primarily because Adam and Eve were not yet given authority and dominion over the angels. Without this authority, they may have questioned the veracity of the statements of Satan if spoken to them directly.

In addition, the order of God's creation was perfect and good (Genesis 1:31). Before Mankind's fall, there very well may have been this form of communication between Adam and Eve and the creatures of the earth. Again, the Thomas Nelson Study Bible, in footnotes 1:24 and 2:1-3 of the Book of Genesis, informs us that all animal life on earth is referred to as *nepesh chayah* ("living creatures"), which is the same Hebrew phrase used for Mankind in Genesis 2:7. The main distinction between the two is that the animals were each made after its own kind, whereas Mankind was made in the image and after the likeness of God.

There is nothing in the Holy Scriptures to indicate one way or the other that all living creatures under Adam and Eve's dominion could communicate with them. However, there are three scriptural references to occasions in which living or spiritual creatures speak and where people see spiritual beings. The first is in Numbers 22:1-35. The colloquy between Balaam and his donkey was made possible because God "opened the mouth of the ass." It is important to note that these verses indicate that the donkey was a female (Numbers 22:28, 33) who spoke to Balaam from a first-person perspective (Numbers 22:28-30). No spiritual being possessed the donkey and spoke through it because, as previously noted, the angels are always referred to in the masculine sense. Not only was the animal able to hold its own conversation with Balaam, it could also see the angel without having to have its eyes opened (Numbers 22:27, 33).

Balaam, however, had to have his eyes opened to see the angel (Numbers 22:31). Nothing is said as to whether the two servants, who accompanied Balaam, were able to see the angel or hear the conversation between the ass and Balaam or the angel and Balaam.

The second reference is found in 2 Kings 6:8-17 where the king of Syria warred against Israel and sought to take the prophet Elisha captive by surrounding the city in which he resided. When the servant of Elisha rose early in the morning and saw the vast army, he inquired of his master as to what they should do. The prophet prayed to God that his servant's eyes be opened and God complied. The servant saw a mountain full of spiritual beings on spiritual horses and chariots of fire. The fact that this servant's eyes had to be opened implies that they were closed by God.

The third instance is contained in Revelation 5:13. In this verse, the Apostle John describes a scene in which every creature in heaven, on earth, under the earth, and in the sea speak blessings, honor and glorification to God the Father and God the

Son. Clearly, every creature who has God's breath of life in them was created to praise and honor their Creator.

I submit these incidents confirm that Adam and Eve were initially able to both see spiritual angels and converse with the creatures under their dominion. They lost the ability to do these things apparently upon their fall from grace. If this were true, Adam and Eve would have been able to see God and the hosts of heaven, including Satan, before their fall. This would also explain why Adam and Eve could commune with God in the garden before their fall. The only way for Satan to conceal his presence was to possess the serpent. It also implies that the mouths of all animals were initially open to commune with Mankind but were closed at some point in time, again, most likely, upon Mankind's fall. Adam and Eve's sin caused the physical realm to lose some measure of its perfection and caused Adam and Eve to lose most of their spiritual and physical abilities, which included their abilities to see and commune with God and to directly communicate with the creatures over which they exercised dominion.

Nothing can be opened unless it was first closed. Nothing can be closed unless it was first open. If animals were indeed able to speak to us, they would be able to express their own thoughts, opinions, and feelings just as the donkey did to Balaam. Nothing in these passages suggests that Balaam was the least bit surprised upon hearing his donkey speak. He immediately answered it and held a brief conversation with it. Further Scriptural evidence of creatures verbally communicating is found in Revelation 5:13 which is a description of every creature in heaven and on earth praising God, the Father and God, the Son.

If all living creatures on the earth were initially capable of communicating with each other, this would more than explain why Adam and Eve did not find it peculiar that a serpent was conversing with them. Clearly, the serpent's ability to converse with Adam and Eve was within its creative abilities.

When faced with the apparent contradiction between God's word and the word of the serpent, Adam and Eve chose the latter. They did not recognize the fact that one of their subservient creatures was possessed by Satan, one of the greatest angels created by God, who purposed tremendous ill will toward them. Adam and Eve, in their innocence, could not contemplate a creature under their dominion disrespecting their authority and dominion by deceitfully lying to them. Adam and Eve had every reason to believe the serpent because, without Satan's instigation, the serpent would never have sought to deceive them into disobeying God. Imagine Eve's shock when she exclaimed in response to the Lord God's inquiry, "The serpent beguiled me, and I did eat." (Genesis 3:13). The Scriptures are silent as to when Adam and Eve became aware that Satan was behind the serpent's deception.

Satan was, indeed, cunning in his deception of Adam and Eve. By inferring that God had lied to them, Satan caused Adam and Eve to be hesitant or, perhaps, unwilling to seek counsel from God on this matter before taking action in disobedience of God. The Scriptures suggest that Adam and Eve enjoyed a wonderful relationship with God before their sin. There is no indication that they kept anything from God. Yet, when faced with the Satanic proposition that God had kept the knowledge of good and evil from them for selfish reasons, Adam and Eve decided to immediately act in, what they thought were, their best interests without consulting their God.

Upon hearing Satan's deceiving words through the serpent, Eve focused on the Tree of the Knowledge of Good and Evil. She saw that the tree was good for food, pleasant to the eyes, and to be desired to make one wise (Genesis 3:6). The Holy Spirit's description of Eve's perception of this tree gives us insight into what led to her and Adam's sin and, ultimately, the sins of all Mankind.

The Thomas Nelson Study Bible's footnote 2:16 of 1 John 2 informs us that all sinful temptation can be categorized into three general but fundamental areas of life: (1) the lust of the flesh, (2) the lust of the eyes, and (3) the pride of life (1 John 2:15-16). The lust of the flesh includes all physical desires. The lust of the eyes relates to all personal desires. The pride of life concerns all manner of self-interests. When we give in to any of these three forms of temptation, whether overtly or secretly in our hearts, our actions or thoughts give birth to sin, and when sin is full-grown, it gives birth to death (James 1:14-15).

Interestingly, when God created the Garden of Eden on earth, He made every tree in the Garden to be good for food and pleasant to the sight (Genesis 2:9). This included the Tree of Life and the Tree of the Knowledge of Good and Evil. As Adam and Eve were allowed to eat from every tree in the Garden, except the Tree of the Knowledge of Good and Evil (Genesis 2:16-17, 3:2-3), it was not sin for them to fulfill their physical and personal desires in this manner. Indeed, it is reasonable to conclude that Adam and Eve ate from various trees in the Garden except these two trees, constantly yielding to the lusts of their flesh and eyes on numerous occasions prior to Satan's deception.

Since God allowed them to indulge these two lusts, to fill their stomachs and please their eyes, Adam and Eve may not have considered it deserving of death to satisfy these lusts by eating from the Tree of the Knowledge of Good and Evil, despite God's warning to the contrary. They were obviously mistaken because the test was for them to demonstrate their uncompromising love for God. This kind of love does not need to be justified or earned. It is the same kind of love that Yeshua obediently demonstrated to His Father and to every one of us by giving up His life so that we may be saved while we were yet sinners (Romans 5:8).

Any attempt by Adam and Eve to justify their actions would indicate that they missed the point of God's commandment not to eat from the forbidden tree. In any event, they couldn't blame their actions on ignorance because they gave in to the forbidden third form of lust, namely, the pride of life. Up to this point in their earthly existence, Adam and Eve had never attempted to satisfy their pride of life. If there was any credence to the argument that their eating the fruit of the Tree of the Knowledge of Good and Evil to fill their stomachs and to please their eyes, though forbidden, should not be deserving of death because they did not fully comprehend the reason for the prohibition and because they had been satisfying these lusts all along, that argument becomes moot when they ate from this forbidden tree to satisfy their pride of life.

Adam and Eve were never permitted by God to satisfy this form of lust. To do so, Adam and Eve had to knowingly and intentionally place their love of self over their love of God. Their pride in who they were and what they could become through disobedience overwhelmed any love they had for the God Who created them. According to Proverbs 16:18, pride goes before destruction and a haughty spirit before a fall. Satan's sin of pride is an excellent illustration of this adage (Isaiah 14:12-13). The same fate befell Adam and Eve.

Satan, through the serpent, tempted Adam and Eve in all three of these ways. Adam and Eve did not have to disobey God and eat from the Tree of the Knowledge of Good and Evil to satisfy the first two types of lustful desires because they could have satisfied these two lusts by eating from any of the other trees in the Garden. However, their decision to satisfy these two lusts by partaking of the Tree of the Knowledge of Good and

Evil, knowing that it was against the commandment of God, was a clear statement of their willingness to defy God, and that statement, combined with their decision to satisfy their pride of life, served to be their physical and spiritual death knell.

When Eve saw that the fruit of the Tree of the Knowledge of Good and Evil was to be desired to make one wise, she was overcome by her desire to have that Godly attribute she believed would make her more like God, even though God forbade her from eating of the fruit of this tree. Eve's covetousness caused her to give in to her desire to satisfy her self-interests, and she ate of the forbidden fruit not so much to feed herself or to satisfy the lust of her eyes, but to have what she knew she couldn't have—to satisfy her pride of life.

It appears, from a literal reading of Genesis 3:6, that Adam was nearby at the time of Satan's deception of Eve because the verse states "she took of the fruit thereof, and did eat, and gave also unto her husband with her, and he did eat." This verse implies that, while Eve was the only one of the two deceived by Satan (Genesis 3:13; 1 Timothy 2:14), Adam, through Eve, was also the indirect recipient of all three temptations and ate for the same reasons that Eve ate of the fruit of the forbidden tree (Genesis 3:17). Adam, therefore, must have also seen that the Tree of the Knowledge of Good and Evil was good for food, pleasing to the eyes and to be desired to make one wise. Like Eve, Adam also must have knowingly decided to choose love of self over love of God, life without God instead of life in and through God.

Upon observing Eve's willingness to engage in the sin of disobedience, Adam was faced with three courses of action. First, he could have prevented Eve from eating of the tree. He could have been adamant about it, leaving her no other option but to disobey her husband as well as God if she wanted to eat from the tree. Eve, being created from the rib of Adam (Genesis 2:21-22), was extremely devoted to her husband, perhaps more so than to God. It is doubtful that she would have rebelled against her husband and God to satisfy her self-interests.

Second, if unsuccessful in preventing Eve's sin, Adam could have refused to give in to the temptations despite Eve's sinful actions, much like what Yeshua did when He was similarly tempted by Satan in the wilderness (Luke 4:1-12). Had Adam withstood these temptations, he could have interceded on Eve's behalf before God and, if necessary, died in her stead. His sinless death would have been an atonement for her sins, restoring her to her original estate with God. God would have surely resurrected Adam just like He resurrected Yeshua, Who was later required to offer His divine sinless life for the sins of not only Adam and Eve but all Mankind.

Finally, Adam could have chosen to join Eve in the satiation of their lusts. Unfortunately for all of us, he chose the latter of the three options before him.

The Holy Scriptures suggest that Adam and Eve knew of the existence of the Tree of Life in the Garden of Eden. Genesis 2:8-17 state that Adam was placed in the garden that was planted by God in the eastern portion of Eden. Adam then witnessed God causing to grow every tree that was pleasant to the sight and good for food, including the Tree of Life and the Tree of the Knowledge of Good and Evil. Indeed, Adam was instructed by God to tend and maintain these trees. Thus, Adam, and subsequently Eve, had to fully understand the peculiar natures of both the Tree of Life and the Tree of the Knowledge of Good and Evil.

They had to know that eating from the Tree of Life would cause the partaker thereof to live forever (Genesis 3:22). They also had to know that the fruit of the Tree of Life gave the partaker thereof wisdom and understanding/discretion (Proverbs 3:13-26). They had to further know that eating from the Tree of the Knowledge of Good and Evil would cause the partaker thereof to be able to know the difference between good and evil (Genesis 3:6; 22). They had to fully appreciate everything relating to the power of these two trees because the Garden of Eden was located on the earth and, thus, came under their authority and dominion.

Assuming this to be true, it must be concluded that Adam and Eve wanted more than wisdom, understanding and eternal life that was freely available to them in the form of the Tree of Life. They wanted to know both good and evil and, thereby, be like God. Perhaps, they reasoned that eternal life, without this missing Godly attribute, would leave them eternally that much less than their Creator. They sought to unilaterally improve their position in God's order of things by eating of the forbidden fruit and then securing forever their newly obtained Godly attribute by eating of the fruit from the Tree of Life.

By choosing to disobey God, Adam and Eve intentionally chose their own way to be like God over God's way. The Holy Scriptures tell us that God protected Adam and Eve from themselves. God prevented them from eating from the Tree of Life which would have caused them to live forever in their sinful state. God drove them out of paradise and placed angelic guards at the East gate of the Garden of Eden, and a flaming sword, that turned in every direction, to deny them access to the Tree of Life (Genesis 3:22-24).

Essentially, Adam and Eve made a choice between life and death: life through loving obedience or death through disobedience. In the end, every human being will have to choose between life (in and through God, through unconditional and uncompromising obedient love) or death (separate and apart from God, through selfish disobedience). One illustration of the choice of physical death through disobedience is the story of Lot's wife, who suffered a horrible death because she missed her worldly life so much that, in direct disobedience of God, she looked back upon the destruction of Sodom and Gomorrah. An illustration of the choice of spiritual death through disobedience is that of the rich man who, upon his death, went to hell while the poor man, Lazarus, went to Abraham's bosom.

Praise be to God, Adam and Eve were denied the perfection of their ill-gotten evil ways. However, their God-given power and authority left them upon their separation from Him through sin. When this occurred, they realized that they could never truly wield any power and authority independent of God. This same power and authority was later given to Yeshua upon His sacrificial death, burial and resurrection (Matthew 28:18). As a result, all who accept, in faith, the death, burial and resurrection of Yeshua HaMashiach for the forgiveness of their sins will have this power and authority not only restored unto them but also perfected.

Satan deceived Adam and Eve into believing that if they disobeyed God and ate of the Tree of the Knowledge of Good and Evil, they would be as God, implying an existence that is equal to but separate from God yet under Satan's lordship. Little did Adam and Eve know that they were created, not to be equal and yet apart from God, but to become God in the flesh by being one with God. They were made in God's image and after His likeness so that God could abide in them and they in God.

Had they eaten of the Tree of Life prior to Satan's deception and their sin, their oneness with God would have been perfected to the same extent that Yeshua is one with His Father (John 17:11, 21-22). Their oneness with God would have meant that Adam and Eve would fully possess the attributes, characteristics and mannerisms of God, including wisdom and discretion. Evil would have no place in their new perfected state of oneness with God.

What greater deception could Satan have used but to convince Adam and Eve into obtaining, through disobedience, so much less than what they would have been freely given through obedience? They did not know that what they sought to become on their own, against God's will, could not be compared to what God had intended them to be in His will. Adam and Eve sought to be separate but equal to God. God wanted them to be one with Him. They wanted to be like God. God wanted to abide in and through them and for them to abide in and through Him, a condition so much better than being like God. Adam and Eve treasured love of self. God wanted them to treasure love of their Creator. They did not know that they were destined to receive the power, glory and wisdom of God, which is now available to all of us who are called by God (1 Corinthians 1:24). Having learned this very costly lesson, God immediately explained to Adam and Eve the consequences of their sin and His plan for Adam and Eve's, and our, reconciliation.

The Consequences of the Sin of Adam and Eve

Adam and Eve willingly sinned in every way a person can sin. They gave in to the three basic forms of human temptations. The extent of their sin has set the standard for the sins of all their descendants throughout time. The sin nature of all Mankind, which is not of God and permeates the world, causes all of us to consistently give in to these three types of temptations (1 John 2:16). Jeremiah 17:9 tells us that the heart is deceitful above all things, and desperately wicked, who can know it? The Apostle Paul tells us that we cannot resist our sin nature (Romans 7:15-23).

When we begin to understand that every person, born into this world, inherits an irresistible sin nature, we may also begin to understand why God is willing to forgive a repentant heart to the extent that our sins are removed from us as far as the East is from the West (Psalm 103:12). The lusts of the flesh and of the eyes and the pride of life will result in the commission of innumerable sins by everybody. We cannot judge lest we be judged (Matthew 7:2, 18:21-35, Luke 6:37). We must forgive so that we will be forgiven (Luke 6:37). It is our nature to sin. Prior to our spiritual rebirths, we cannot control our sin nature. We are like predatory animals whose nature it is to kill to eat. Upon our acceptance of Yeshua's eternal sin offering, our sins are forgiven. It is for this reason that Yeshua admonishes us to continually forgive those who sin against us (Matthew 18:21-22, Luke 17:3-4).

With sin comes its consequences of death (Romans 6:23) and all that is associated with it. The Scriptures also make it very clear that the consequences of the sins of one generation will be visited upon generations to come (Exodus 20:5, Numbers 14:18, Deuteronomy 5:9). The undeniable causal relationship between sin, sickness and death can best be exemplified by the words of Yeshua when He unequivocally healed the sick by forgiving their sins (Luke 5:15-26, John 5:14) and when He associates conversion from a life of sin with healing (Matthew 13:13-15). James 5:14-15 confirm the association between healing of the sick and the forgiveness of sins.

Is anyone among you sick? Let him call for the elders of the church, and let them pray over him, anointing him with oil in the name of the Lord; and the prayer offered in faith will restore the one who is sick, and the Lord will raise him up, and if he has committed sins, they will be forgiven him.

This makes perfect sense since, without sin, there would be no sickness or death. These passages confirm that the authority given to Yeshua by God (John 5:26-27) is greater than the earthly authority Satan temporarily possesses. This world, and all the horrors of it, have been under the authority and control of Satan (Luke 4:5-7, 13:16) until Yeshua obtained the victory (1 Corinthians 15:54-57).

Eventually, sin brings about the wrath of God (Revelation 6:12-17). For instance, the sin of unnatural sex brought down the wrath of God on the cities of Sodom and Gomorrah (Genesis 18:20-21, 19:4-15). The men of these cities sought unnatural sex with the angels of God who were in the form of men. Having no desire to have natural intercourse with the opposite sex is not a sin because Yeshua tells us that some are born that way, some are made that way by other men and some choose to be that way (Matthew 19:12). If, being in that state, they, nonetheless, choose to obey God's ways, they will receive eternal rewards (Isaiah 56:4-5).

However, if any person chooses to engage in unnatural sex, they will come under the judgment of God and shall not inherit the Kingdom of God (Romans 1:21-2:3, 1 Corinthians 6:9-10). Just as with Sodom and Gomorrah, any society, which legalizes such acts, engages in "mischief by a law" and faces similar condemnation from God (Psalm 94:20-23). God's wrath is not reserved for this type of sin. It is revealed from heaven against all ungodliness and unrighteousness of men (Romans 1:18). Nonetheless, this sin of unnatural sex has taken front stage with its recent legalization by the Supreme Court of the United States.

The Bible defines sin as "the transgression of the law" (1 John 3:4), presumably God's law. According to the Book of James, sin occurs when a person is drawn away of his own lust and is enticed (James 1:14-15). The wages of sin is death (Romans

6:23). The death referred to here is both physical and spiritual in that the offending soul will suffer physical death and will be eternally spiritually separated from a Holy God.

So, what is the law of God as it relates to marriage? Genesis 2:24-32 and Matthew 19:4-6 tell us that marriage is the union between a man and a woman so much so that they become one flesh. A man and a woman become one flesh through procreation. It is, therefore, impossible for two people to become one flesh in marriage unless they are joined as husband and wife. This is the law of God.

So, when a man lusts for another man or a woman for another woman, such acts are considered by God to be unclean, vile, unnatural and of a reprobate mind (Romans 1:24-32) and in violation of His law. Hence, they are sinful in nature. Indeed, they are an abomination to God deserving of death (Leviticus 18:22-30; 20:13). Such was the fate of the citizens of Sodom who were judged by God to be guilty of this sin (Genesis 18:20; 19:1-11; 24-25). Just as with any sin, anyone who engages in such acts must repented of his/her sin and accept Yeshua as his/her savior. They shall then inherit the Kingdom of God (1 Corinthians 6:9-10).

State legislatures have enacted laws which seek to legalize this transgression of the clear law of God. Unfortunately, this is not simply a state issue. Our Supreme Court has recently made it the official law of the land by opining that gay marriage is a constitutional right. However, homosexuality is a sin in any form, even under the guise of protected civil liberties.

It is important to note that state legislatures, our political leaders and the U.S. Supreme Court are well aware of God's law as it relates to gay marriage and the attendant consequences should God's law be transgressed. Numerous spiritual leaders have proclaimed the applicability of God's law to the issue at hand. Our Supreme Court acknowledged that the traditional definition of marriage has existed for "millennia."

So, the legalization of gay marriage is an intentional act. What does the Bible say about intentional sin? It tells us that, should we sin willfully, knowing the truth, we can only look forward to judgment and fiery indignation, having performed a contemptuous act against the Holy Spirit (Hebrews 10:26-29). The Book of Numbers tells us that such souls shall be cut off from among their people (Numbers 15:30). Once again, Biblical scholars will confirm that this passage speaks of both physical and spiritual death.

Every human being has sinned (Romans 3:23; 5:12) and, unless saved by the blood of Yeshua HaMashiach, each is subject to both physical and spiritual death. All sin bears the same death penalty. Mankind cannot arbitrarily and unilaterally change the laws of God. Nor can Mankind alter the consequences of sin. Legalizing sin will not somehow pardon the sin or its consequences. By legalizing sin, isn't this country directly rebelling against God Himself? Is this nation so willing to defiantly shake its proverbial fist in the face of God? If it is so willing, let there be no misunderstanding, the consequences are severe and eternal in nature.

Far from legalizing same-sex marriage, every effort should be undertaken to lovingly and forgivingly condemn the sin as we should for any sin yet love the sinner because we are also sinners. Civil liberties should be afforded to every citizen. However, no government should, through the enactment of a law, formally endorse the freedom to sin. While there are many in this country who refuse to acknowledge God's hand in the birth of this great nation, it will be abundantly clear that God is involved in the downfall of this country should we openly declare war against Him by legalizing sin.

In 1973, the U.S. Supreme Court legalized abortion, the sin which brought me to repentant knees seeking forgiveness from my Lord and Savior resulting in myspiritual rebirth. Abortion is a deadly example of choosing selfish desires over the life of the unborn, unless, of course, death of the unborn or the mother or both may result if the birth is allowed to take place.

Jonathan Cahn, a Messianic rabbi, has preached that every seven years since the legalization of the sin of abortion, this country has experienced ever-increasing financial setbacks. He notes the oil embargo and recession in 1973, the 1980 S&L crisis, the 1987 "Black Monday" stock market crash, the 1994 bond market crash, the 9/11 event in 2001 with its ensuing recession, the 2008 stock market crash creating the worst recession since the Great Depression, the economic crisis of 2015 and, in 2022, the worst, stock market crash since 2008. In 2022, the U.S. Congress passed the Respect for Marriage Act that legalizes same-sex marriage among other things. We wait to see God's response. Rabbi Cahn refers to these seven-year cycles as the Shemitah ("Shmita"), a Jewish term referring to the Sabbath year as it relates to the seventh year of a seven-year agricultural cycle mandated in the Torah. Rabbi Cahn - describes how this relates to the United States in his book entitled *The Mystery of the Shemitah*. With the legalization of same-sex marriage in June 2015, should we expect anything other than God's wrath? Praise be to God that the U.S. Supreme Court has recently decided that an abortion is no longer a constitutional right.

The consequences of Adam and Eve's sin progressively moves Mankind farther and farther from being one with God.

Adam and Eve's choice was either eternal life in and through God or knowledge of good and evil through an existence separate and apart from God. Had they chosen the former, they would have lived as temples of their Holy God whose life would have become their life. No one can have life independent of God's life. If they had eaten from the Tree of Life before sinning, their sinless nature would have been perfected and they would never have known sin, just as Yeshua never knew sin (2 Corinthians 5:21).

A person cannot be one with God and know sin. To commit sin requires the absence of love. By choosing to eat from the Tree of the Knowledge of Good and Evil, Adam and Eve demonstrated their rejection of the kind of love that is God. Instead, they coldheartedly chose an existence apart from God wherein they could choose to do good or evil as the lusts of their hearts so determined. They would experience both good and evil and, hence, know them. The ramifications of their sin of disobedience meant that they would have no life at all.

Satan succeeded in persuading Adam and Eve to yield to their lusts and eat of the fruit from the forbidden tree. His participation in God's obedience test of Adam and Eve was allowed by God to demonstrate their lack of Godly love. This test unfortunately evidenced the fact that every one of us, if given the choice in an innocent state, would succumb to our own lusts instead of lovingly obeying God. The Edenic test of Adam and Eve also made clear that Mankind needs a Savior Who can, through His sacrificial death, burial and resurrection, usher us into the oneness with God that we were created to experience.

Before their fall, there was no sin in Adam and Eve. God told them that disobeying His commandment to refrain from eating of the Tree of the Knowledge of Good and Evil is the only way they could suffer death (Genesis 2:16-17). Specifically, God said: "For in the day that thou eatest thereof thou shalt surely die" (Genesis 2:17). By disobeying God, Adam and Eve were, therefore, condemned to death. We know that death can be both physical and spiritual. Physical death is the separation of the spirit from the body (James 2:26). Spiritual death is the eternal separation of the individual spirit from God, resulting in eternal damnation in the lake of fire (Revelation 20:14; 21:8). We needed a Savior.

God instituted a practice of sacrificing the innocent blood of animals as a temporary atonement for the sins of Adam and Eve and, later, the Jewish nation. However, only the sacrifice of Yeshua's eternal sinless blood permanently atoned for the sins of the whole world.

Chapter 3 of the Book of Genesis indicates that Adam and Eve's spiritual relationship with God was immediately impacted by their sin. It also establishes that neither Adam nor Eve immediately suffered physical death after their sin. God does not lie, and He didn't lie here. God's choice of words in this warning is telling. He said "in the day," not "on the day." The use of the preposition "in" here denotes "at some point during a period of time." As we discussed earlier, from God's perspective, a day is as a thousand years, and a thousand years is as one day (Psalm 90:4, 2 Peter 3:8). We saw that this statement could be interpreted to mean that a day is as infinity and infinity is as a day. However, this statement could also mean exactly what it says: a day is as a thousand years. Assuming this interpretation, it is interesting to note that no man has ever lived for more than 999 years which would be a day from God's eternal perspective. It is reasonable to believe that God's Word can be taken both literally and figuratively at the same time.

The oldest person identified in the Bible is Methuselah, who lived 969 years (Genesis 5:27). Genesis 5:5 tells us that Adam lived 930 years. According to God's time, Adam did not live for more than one day and did indeed die "at some point during the day" that he ate of the forbidden fruit. God's word is true. The Bible is silent as to when Eve died, and so there is every reason to believe that she also did not live for more than one day (according to God's perspective of time) and died "in the day" that she ate of the forbidden fruit.

Both Adam and Eve suffered physical and spiritual death because their spirits, once separated from their bodies because of physical death, were not allowed to be with God. They were kept in Abraham's bosom (Luke 16:22) until Yeshua's ascension, when He led captivity captive (Ephesians 4:8-10) and sacrificially reconciled their spirits with the Spirit of God. The physical and spiritual death sentence promised by God not only applied to Adam and Eve but also to their descendants. Praise be to God because Yeshua is the propitiation for the sins of the whole world (1 John 2:2). All human beings have the breath of life in them (Genesis 2:7; 6:17; 7:15, 22). Everyone is but a breath (Psalm 39:5, 11). In Yeshua is life and His life is in every man (John 1:4). Therefore, the sacrificial offering of Yeshua's eternal life, through the shedding of every drop of His blood, covers the sins of everyone because all have the breath of life in them.

God's Covenant with Adam and Eve

There is an inseparable connection between Mankind and all temporal creation. This can be gleaned from the Word of God because the earth and everything in it lost its perfection with the fall of Adam and Eve (Genesis 3:17-18; Romans 8:19, 22). Before Mankind's fall, all earthly creatures lived in harmony feeding on the land instead of each other. There will come a time when all creatures shall once again return to this state of perfect harmony (Isaiah 65:17-25).

It is interesting to note that Satan's sin, and the sins of the fallen angels, did not adversely affect anything in the physical realm. Only the fall of Mankind, to whom God gave dominion over every living thing on the earth, directly affected the entire creation. Our redemption, through Yeshua HaMashiach, is critical to the restoration of the earth and, indeed, the entire universe to its original state of perfection. As promised by God, all dominion, power and authority have been given to Yeshua, Who is the last Adam. As members of the Spiritual Body of Mashiach, we can exercise that dominion, power and authority in and through Him.

Our triune Godhead created Mankind in Their image and likeness so that They could physically manifest all that They are in and through man, a feat that could not be accomplished through spiritual angels, who were created to be ministering spirits (Hebrews 1:14). For God to achieve His intended creative purpose for Mankind and all of creation, we had to be redeemed.

Yeshua's death, burial and resurrection has permanently resolved all the consequences of our sins and has enabled us to be restored to our original state of perfection should we embrace His sin sacrifice on our behalf. Once this restoration is complete, a new heaven and earth shall replace the old ones that shall pass away (2 Peter 3:7, 10-13; Revelation 21:1-6). Yeshua, who is the Living Word of God in the flesh, sustains the universe (Colossians 1:17). We, who are one with Yeshua, have God in us, and we are in God. However, we are yet to be perfected mirror images of Them.

Upon our perfected oneness with our triune Godhead, we shall share in the responsibility of sustaining the universe as we were originally created to do. Until we are resurrected in glory, we may never fully understand and appreciate the responsibilities we share as the children of God through Yeshua HaMashiach which includes the exercising of our dominion, power and authority, in and through Yeshua HaMashiach, over all of God's creation.

The Thomas Nelson Study Bible, in footnotes 3:15 and 3:20, 21 of the Book of Genesis, discusses how God, in His infinite mercy, offered Adam and Eve, in Genesis 3:15, a promise of complete atonement for their sin in the first Messianic prophecy of the Bible. God promised that they would be physically and spiritually restored to their original estate and reconciled with their God. These footnotes further state that, in verse 20 of that same chapter, Adam takes his first act of faith in furtherance of God's promise of salvation unto eternal life by naming his wife "Eve," which comes from the verb "to live" and, in Genesis 3:21, God acknowledged Adam's act of faith by covering their sin symbolically through the shedding of blood and physically covering their nakedness with coats of skin or tunics.

God had to shed the innocent blood of one of His creatures to cover Adam and Eve temporarily, physically and spiritually. The Word of God doesn't indicate what kind of animal lost its life, but the innocent animal certainly did not deserve death because of the commission of Adam and Eve's sin. This is the first recorded death in the Holy Scriptures and it was at the hands of God. We do not know if Adam and Eve fully understood the prophetic significance of this symbolic covering by the shedding of innocent and unblemished blood. God would continue to require the periodic shedding of innocent, unblemished animal blood for the temporary atonement of Mankind's sins until Yeshua Messiah shed His own eternal, innocent, sinless and unblemished Godly blood so that all the sins of the world may be forever forgiven.

Every descendant of Adam and Eve, who believes that God, the Father, in furtherance of His covenant with Adam and Eve, allowed a part of Himself, His Living Word, to become flesh and to be innocently sacrificed on the cross for the forgiveness of all of our sins, thereby redeeming us to the fulfillment of our creative purpose in His image and after His likeness, will be saved (1 John 5:4-5, Romans 8:29-30). The same is true for all those who may never hear the gospel of salvation through Yeshua HaMashiach because their salvation is secured by their belief in God based upon their observance of all of creation that surrounds them (Romans 1:20). 1 John 3:2 tells us that when Yeshua reappears, every saved person shall be like Him, for we shall be transformed into His image and likeness through our belief in Him.

Though husband and wife in Eden, Adam and Eve never conceived before the completion of their test. If they had, any offspring born before their fall may not have inherited their parents' fallen sin nature acquired because of their sin of disobedience. Being without sin, any pre-fall offspring of Adam and Eve may have been free to partake of the Tree of Life and to become immediately and forever perfectly one with their Creator God. Any one of these pre-fall children of God may then have been available to be sacrificed for the redemption of Adam and Eve and their fallen progeny.

However, God, knowing that Adam and Eve would fail the test of loving obedience, wanted to openly demonstrate His perfect, unconditional and uncompromising love for His highest creation by sacrificing the second personage of our triune Godhead to redeem Mankind. It was preordained that the Word of God take on flesh and redeem the members of its Spiritual Body. Yeshua considers every member of His Spiritual Body to be His friend (John 15:13-15). There is no greater demonstration of love than for a man to lay down his life for his friends (John 15:13).

Before their expulsion out of the Garden of Eden, God told Eve that she would conceive in pain (Genesis 3:16). In addition, when Mankind began to multiply on the earth, they were begotten in the image of man, after his own kind and not after

God, much like all of God's other earthly creations (Genesis 1:21, 2425; 5:1-3). Specifically, in Genesis 5:3 we are told that Adam "begat a son in his own likeness, after his image, and called his name Seth."

1 Corinthians 15:45-49 tell us that, just as we have borne the image of man, we shall also bear the image of the heavenly. In other words, we were born in Adam's fallen image, but God's promise to us is that we shall once again bear God's image and be able to fulfill our original creative purpose to be physically and spiritually one with our triune Godhead.

Despite Satan's initial successes in the enlistment of Mankind in his rebellion against God, we can collect on the redemptive promises of God by individually passing the eternal test of loving obedience through faith. Are you willing to dedicate the rest of your earthly life to a loving obedience to God in return for an eternity of oneness with Him?

When compared to eternity, our earthly lives are brief moments in time (Psalm 78:39, James 4:14). They are but whispers in the wind, briefly heard and then remembered at best. However, our brief lives provide more than enough time for us to embrace God's free gift of eternal salvation through His Son, Yeshua HaMashiach. The question each of us must now answer is whether, armed with the knowledge of our true creative purpose, we will choose to demonstrate our unconditional and uncompromising love for God or whether we will choose to demonstrate our hatred of Him by continuing to blatantly disobey Him.

CHAPTER FOUR

THE REDEMPTION OF MAN

In the previous chapters, we have examined the creative process, generally, and, specifically, as it applies to Mankind being made in the image and after the likeness of God. We have also looked at the reason for Satan's rebellion against God, the lesson of love taught through God's obedience test of Adam and Eve and Satan's deceptive role in that test. We have further considered the consequences of Adam and Eve's disobedience to God and God's promise of salvation to Adam and Eve and every one of their descendants who would accept it.

We shall now examine God's redemption of His highest creation and why God chose not to redeem the fallen angels. We shall see how God induced Satan, the father of deception, into believing that he could destroy God's redemptive plan for Mankind by persuading Yeshua, through extreme persecution, to sin in His heart and, thereby, become one with Satan through sin. Satan's efforts to do so resulted in him performing the very acts that provided for our redemption. Satan, who was directly responsible for the enslavement of Mankind through sin, was also indirectly responsible for Mankind's salvation by personally orchestrating the sacrificial shedding of the innocent blood of Yeshua HaMashiach for the remission of the sins of the world.

God's Redemptive Plan for Mankind

Mankind lost the ability to become one with God through sin. However, the redeemed sons and daughters of God are one with God as members of the Spiritual Body of the second personage of God. Through Yeshua HaMashiach, all reborn children of God are now a part of the triune Godhead. Yeshua is the head of the Body (Colossians 1:18). Wherever the head goes, the body must follow.

Perhaps, this partly explains why Yeshua could say that all who overcome will sit with Him on His throne just as He overcame and sits on His Father's throne (Revelation 3:21). Luke 1:32 tells us that Yeshua shall be given King David's throne. God's throne is in heaven (Acts 7:49, Hebrews 8:1, Revelation 4:2). Since every child of God is a member of the Spiritual Body of the Messiah, we get to spiritually sit, through Yeshua, on His earthly and heavenly thrones. Ephesians 2:6 supports this extent of our oneness with God in that it states that God has raised the saved to sit together in heavenly places in Messiah.

In subsequent chapters, I will delve into those Biblical passages that appear to describe, in more detail, the magnitude of this oneness man was created to share with his triune Godhead. Suffice to say that, as glorified members of the Spiritual Body of the Messiah, reigning in and through Yeshua forever will be nothing short of an eternal experience of being the physical manifestations of God. It is Mankind's creative purpose to become one with God to this unimaginable extent.

The Garden of Eden experience provided an opportunity for Mankind to perfect his predestined oneness with God. Had Adam and Eve eaten from the Tree of Life, instead of the Tree of the Knowledge of Good and Evil, they and their progeny would have perfected, through their demonstration of unconditional, uncompromising and loving obedience, this oneness with God forever.

Unconditional and uncompromising appropriately describe the kind of love that God is and that we must become before we can be one with Him. No deeds or thoughts can stop, or in any way lessen, this kind of love. This kind of love forever seeks to love to the fullest extent possible, even at the expense of self-interests. It was this kind of love God was seeking from Adam and Eve in the Garden of Eden. This type of loving obedience required them to be content to glorify God by being that which they were created to be, even if their obedience was not based upon a complete understanding of their creative purpose.

It required them to give up all self-interests and desires to the extent that they contradicted God's will. Adam and Eve had to trust that whatever God had in store for them would allow them to function at their maximum creative potential. When we lovingly place obedience to God above our own personal interests and desires, God's interests and desires become the only reason for our existence. We must give up any desire to have a life independent from God in order for us to gain eternal life in and through God.

Unfortunately, when given the choice between (1) giving up self-identity and allowing God to live in and through them and (2) existing separate from God but constantly seeking to be like God, Adam and Eve chose the latter. As a result, this desire to be like, but separate from, God has been ingrained in Mankind's nature since his fall from grace.

Having succumbed to Satan's temptation to disobey God's command not to eat from the Tree of the Knowledge of Good and Evil, Adam and Eve deserved and were destined for physical and spiritual death. If this were to happen, God would have to abandon His plan of becoming one with, and physically manifesting Himself through, His greatest creation.

Satan's deception resulted in every human being becoming one with him in sin, instead of one with God in love, and, thereby, doomed every human being to share in Satan's eternal damnation and separation from God. Satan assumed that, because of Adam's sin, Mankind would be forever removed from his first estate just like Satan was removed from his first estate because of his sin of pride. Obviously, Satan did not fully appreciate the limitless extent of God's unconditional love and God's willingness to personally demonstrate this love.

Satan was correct that Adam and Eve's fall from grace demanded their condemnation. However, God's love for Mankind would not allow Satan to profit, at Mankind's expense, from his sin of rebellious pride. God allowed the Garden of Eden experience because God knew that Mankind needed a first-hand demonstration of exactly what Godly love is. God knew, before creation week, that, if Mankind was to be spared the consequences of their sins, someone would have to die in their place.

The creation of Mankind was the climatic event of creation week. No other creature held an estate equal to or higher than man, much to the consternation of Satan. If all of Mankind were to be pardoned from our death sentences, there was but one entity who could die in our place and that would be God, through the second personage of our triune Godhead in and through Whom the redeemed of Mankind exist. So, God purposed to have His Living Word, through Whom He spoke into existence the universe (Hebrews 1:2) and through Whom all creation consists (Colossians 1:16-17), to become flesh (John 1:14) and die in Mankind's place.

As a sin offering, Yeshua's unblemished, spotless, Godly blood had to be sacrificially shed unto death for the remission of the sins of the world (1 Peter 1:18-19, 1 John 2:2). To accomplish this sacrificial death for the remission of sins, Yeshua purposefully spoke in parables so that the hearers would not be able to perceive and understand His Gospel, repent, and be saved (Mark 4:11-12). Nor did Yeshua want unclean spirits to proclaim His identity (Mark 1:34, 3:11-12).

Yeshua's accusers falsely charged Him with sins against their religion and against Rome. They had no intentions of participating in a sin offering. They simply wanted Yeshua dead. Having committed no sin, Yeshua would have lived forever. Yeshua allowed His accusers to succeed in killing Him so that He could voluntarily offer His innocent blood for the remission of the sins of the world (John 10:15-18). They were unwitting participants in the greatest sin offering of all time. God, in the form of Yeshua, the High Priest, offered Himself as the ultimate sin offering.

Through the death of Yeshua HaMashiach, Who knew no sin and Who was undeserving of death, we, who embrace His sacrificial death unto the salvation of our souls, are relieved of our death sentences. Is not this the ultimate demonstration of unconditional and uncompromising love?

In 1 John 2:12, it is written:

I write unto you, little children, because your sins are forgiven *you* for his name's sake. (Emphasis added)

The apostle John implies in this passage that the sins of every believer have been forgiven to the glorification of God's name. It further implies that no believer will be required to pay the price for the forgiveness of his sins. That is why it says "your sins are forgiven you" instead of "your sins are forgiven." The addition of the word "you" in this verse signifies that someone will have to pay the price for the forgiveness of your sins. It just will not be you. Another person will be held accountable for the sins of the world in our place. However, that person must be blameless because, otherwise, he/she would shed blood for the forgiveness of that person's own sins. We are forgiven of our sins and thereby released from our death penalties because Yeshua was that blameless person Who satisfied God's requirement that the consequences of our sins be fulfilled.

Since the life of the flesh is in the blood, and the wages of sin is death, our redemption and restoration could only be achieved if there was a shedding of blood unto physical and spiritual death. For it is written:

> And almost all things are by the law purged with blood; and without shedding of blood is no remission (Hebrews 9:22).

It had to be the shedding unto death of blood from a sinless person because the death of a sinful person cannot pay for the sins of others, since his death would be the consequence of his own sins. More importantly, it also had to be the shedding unto death of blood that contained eternal life, so that the sins of the entire world could be forgiven. Only Yeshua, Whose very essence is pure, perfect, unconditional and uncompromising love, could make His eternal life-giving blood available to pay the death penalties for all the sins of Mankind. Yeshua's sacrificial, sinless death was endured, not only for believers, but also for the sins of the whole world (Luke 2:32, John 1:29, 1 Timothy 4:10). In 1 John 2:2, it is written:

> And he is the propitiation for our sins: and not for ours only, but also for the sins of the whole world.

Consequently, every human being born of Adam and Eve had his or her death penalty paid by the death, burial and resurrection of Yeshua the Messiah. However, you can provide water. You can lead the horse to the water, but you can't force the horse to drink the water. The shedding of Yeshua's eternal, life-giving blood unto death was sufficient for the propitiation of the sins of any person who accepts this sacrifice, in faith, being reconciled unto God (2 Corinthians 5:19).

This begs an interesting question. Can some of the souls, facing the great white throne judgment, be capable of repentance and salvation, thereby avoiding eternal judgment in the lake of fire? The answer is, unfortunately, no, even though it is the will of God that all men be saved (1Timothy 2:4, 2 Peter 3:9).

There are some who will tell you that, since Yeshua paid the price for the sins of the whole world (1 John 2:2), all are saved. They may say that there will come a time when every knee shall bow, see the salvation of God and confess that Yeshua is Lord, implying submission unto salvation (Isaiah 45:23, Luke 3:6, Philippians 2:9-11).

They would have you imagine a scene in which those resurrected souls, who died in their sins, are facing the great white throne judgment. The saints of God, who are enjoying a glorified and perfected oneness with their triune Godhead, are in attendance. Unconditional love sits in judgment through Yeshua. They would then have you conclude that these condemned souls would be forgiven and granted eternal life.

However, nowhere in the Holy Scriptures is there any support for this proposition. In fact, the Holy Scriptures are quite clear as to the fate of these condemned souls. Revelation 20:15 tells us that all of Mankind whose names are not found written in the Book of Life will be cast into the lake of fire. Yeshua specifically states as much in Matthew 7:22-23; 25:41.

Upon repentance, Yeshua tells us, in Matthew 12:31-32, that all manner of sin and blasphemy shall be forgiven, except blasphemies against the Holy Ghost. Individuals who engage in this type of sin are in danger of eternal damnation (Mark 3:29). Clearly, blasphemers of the Holy Ghost are in danger of eternal condemnation. In addition, those who attempt to explain or defend their sins are similarly condemned (Matthew 8:21-23). While it is true that, through Adam, all Mankind must die and, through the Messiah, all Mankind will be risen from the dead (Acts 24:15, 1 Corinthians 15:22), not all will be saved.

Salvation is available for the living, not those who die in their sins. Salvation is available even up to the point of our last breath. Yeshua tells us, in Matthew 20:1-16, that such souls, not only can be saved, but will receive an equal portion of the Kingdom despite their late salvation. An excellent illustration of the equality among the members of the Spiritual Body of the Messiah is contained in the parable of the workers in the vineyard (Matthew 20:1-16). In this parable, Yeshua describes the Kingdom of heaven as being full of workers who, at the end of the day, are paid the same wages regardless of whether they worked the entire day, three-quarters, half, one-quarter, or the last hour of the day. Yeshua ends this parable by stating that "… the last shall be first and the first last: for many be called, but few chosen." The important point to take from this parable is, whenever chosen, the reward is the same.

Every spirit, who confesses that Yeshua HaMashiach, is come in the flesh, is of God (1 John 4:2, 15). Similarly, every soul who confesses his sins shall be forgiven and cleansed of all unrighteousness (1 John 1:9). You see, "with the mouth confession is made unto salvation" (Romans 10:9-10). All Mankind has sinned. Yet, through Yeshua, all can be saved. We simply must accept and confess our salvation through Yeshua the Messiah while we have the breath of life in us because it is written in Hebrews 9:27: "And it is appointed unto men once to die, but after this the judgment."

For God's blood to be shed for the sins of Mankind, He had to have a human body. This was accomplished by the Holy Spirit impregnating Mary, whose sinful flesh gave birth to Yeshua, her first-born son (Luke 2:7). Yeshua is the only person who is capable of redeeming Mankind because, though He was born with the sinful nature of Adam and Eve through His mother, Mary, He was also born of God and, therefore, born with a sinless Godly nature. He is human and yet impeccable.

Just as God permitted Satan to tempt Adam and Eve in the Garden of Eden, He also permitted Yeshua to be similarly tempted by Satan in the wilderness where Yeshua fasted for forty days and forty nights (Matthew 4:2, Luke 4:2). Anyone who has ever fasted from food for spiritual reasons knows that during the fast you are continually tempted to give in to one or more of the three fundamental areas of sin (1 John 2:15-16). You will be tempted to break your fast by satisfying (1) your lust of the flesh (i.e., hunger), (2) your lust of your eyes (i.e., delectable food); or (3) your pride of life (i.e., putting your self-interests before the purpose of the fast). Anyone who has fasted also knows that forty days of eating nothing will test one's resolve against these temptations to the absolute maximum. *The Thomas Nelson Study Bible* identifies two cross-references to Luke 4:2 where individuals fasted for forty days and forty nights. Moses did so on Mount Sinai (Exodus 24:18, 34:28; Deuteronomy 9:9-25), and Elijah did so on Mount Horeb (1 Kings 19:8).

Luke 4:1-2 tell us that Yeshua, being full of the Holy Spirit, was led by the Spirit into the wilderness where He fasted forty days. The Holy Spirit isolated Yeshua so that He could focus on the supreme test of loving obedience to God, just as Adam and Eve were isolated in the Garden of Eden when they were similarly tested. These verses also state that, throughout the entire forty-day fast, Yeshua was continually tested by the devil.

These tests involved each of the three areas of temptation in which Adam and Eve were tested and the intensities of these tests no doubt increased as the fast progressed. After the forty-day fast had ended, but before Yeshua had an opportunity to replenish Himself, Satan tempted Yeshua one last time in each of the three aforementioned areas of temptation. Satan specifically tested Yeshua's hunger, visions of worldly power and glory, and sense of self-pride. Yeshua's successful resistance of these three fundamental forms of temptation, on this occasion and, indeed, throughout His earthly life until His sacrificial death, burial and resurrection, has placed Him in a position to aid all who are similarly tempted (Hebrews 2:18).

Satan knew that Yeshua was another form of Adam, a progenitor of the spiritually reborn children of God, much like Adam was the forefather of Mankind. Through the wilderness temptations, Satan sought to entice Yeshua into sinning against God, thereby removing any apparent hope for our spiritual rebirths. Despite Satan's best efforts, Yeshua never sinned.

By lovingly choosing God's interests and desires over His own, Yeshua was given authority over heaven and earth and the right to grant eternal life to anyone who would choose to do the same thing on the faith of Yeshua's promises. Had Yeshua given in to any of these three forms of temptation, He would have placed Himself above the will of God and would have shown that His love of God was conditional and secondary to His love of self. He would have, therefore, sinned against God. But praise be to God, unlike Adam and Eve, Yeshua demonstrated that He loved God more than anything else, including His own interests (Luke 4:1-13).

To have undergone forty days of this type of intense temptation while depriving the body of its essential needs, and yet never sinning, is a testament to the limitless faith of Yeshua and the complete and total freedom from sin that we can enjoy if we allow God to abide in us to the extent God abides in Yeshua. The sacrificial death of Yeshua, the Word of God Who became the sinless Son of God and Whose blood contained eternal life, brought about the redemption of all sinful flesh who are spiritually reborn into this sinless state. There are three Greek words used in the New Testament to describe the redemption of the children of God. *The Thomas Nelson Study Bible*, in footnote 1:18,19 of the Book of 1 Peter, explains that one such word is *agorazo*, which means "to purchase in the market" (Revelation 5:9; 14:3-4). Another is *exagorazo*, which means "to purchase and take home" (Galatians 3:13). The last word is *lutroo*, which means "to purchase and give freedom" (Luke 24:21, 1 Peter 1:18). Through the blood of Yeshua the Messiah, all of Mankind were purchased, brought home and set free from their captivity to sin and its accompanying death sentence.

However, our redemption would not be imposed on us, just as the eternal union with God in Eden was never imposed on Adam and Eve. When they elected to become like God through disobedience, Adam and Eve chose not to accept anything that God had to offer. In their defense, Adam and Eve were unaware of the magnitude of what God had in store for them if they obeyed His commandment. No person, who has heard the Gospel of Yeshua HaMashiach, has that excuse. Unlike Adam and Eve, we have an informed choice. Now that same eternal gift is, again, freely available to every person who will knowingly accept it.

We are all familiar with the story of the prodigal son as set forth in Luke 15:11-32. I once heard a radio message, given by a preacher whose name I cannot now recall, that enlightened my understanding of this parable. The parable begins by the younger of two sons demanding his inheritance before his father has died. According to the radio message, it was the custom of those times that the father would seriously rebuke any child who prematurely sought his inheritance in this fashion because it would be interpreted to be a statement that the child could not wait for his father to die to get what would then be his rightful inheritance. If the father neglected to rebuke the son, the eldest son would have surely stepped in to do what the father failed to do.

However, in this story, the father divided up the inheritance and gave it to both sons. The father exhibited a tremendous degree of unconditional and uncompromising love to both sons. He allowed his youngest son to disrespect him and leave his presence with his portion of the inheritance, and his oldest son to quietly take his portion of the inheritance though the father had not yet died. By their actions, both sons demonstrated that they were lost because they placed their own self-interests above the interests of their father.

The radio message further explained that, when the youngest son repented and made his way back home, he had to know that the custom of the times also required him to be stoned to death for his disrespectful actions upon his return. He had every reason to believe that he was coming home to a death sentence. Thus, he was willing to give up any claims to heirship and live as a servant with no rights or privileges.

However, his father, even though his son was a great way off, ran to him and welcomed him back into his arms before his son could utter a request for forgiveness. In fact, the father does not respond to his son's confession of sin. Instead, he commands that his son be restored to his former position, with the rights and benefits of an heir, and that a feast be prepared. The oldest son protests but appears to have been similarly forgiven. The father's unconditional and uncompromising love for both sons is an excellent example of the degree of love God has for each one of us despite our continuing disrespect for Him through our commission of sin. God welcomes back all who are repentant. God forgives and completely restores (Ezekiel 18:25-32). Our restoration, however, came at a price. God had to take His love for us to a level higher than that of the father of the prodigal sons. He had to become man and pay the death penalties reserved for us because of our sins.

The oneness with God that Adam and Eve enjoyed before their fall was but a precursor to the indivisibility we shall experience when we become one with Him in glory (Philippians 3:21, Colossians 3:4). Yeshua is the personification of Mankind being one with God in glory. The children of God will be conformed into the glorious image of Yeshua HaMashiach (Romans 8:29-30, 2 Corinthians 3:18), who is the express image of the heavenly God (Hebrews 1:3). God's ultimate plan to become forever one in glory with His highest creation could never be permanently thwarted by Satan.

If we will accept, in faith, God's death on our behalf for the propitiation of our sins, we will be spiritually reborn and physically resurrected unto eternal life just as God, the Father, resurrected Yeshua. This eternal resurrection is for everyone. In John 1:12 it is written:

> But as many as received him, to them gave he power to become the sons of God, even to them that believe on his name.

When Yeshua returns, all believers of Yeshua's day and those who have and continue to believe, in faith, on His name, will be given incorruptible bodies. When this happens, our oneness with God will be perfected, in answer to Yeshua's prayer (John 17:21), and God's chosen of Mankind, Jew and Gentile alike, will abide in Him and He in them. It is impossible for us to fully envision just what it will be like to be one with God, yet this is exactly what the Word of God tells us we will become if we are the children of God.

God's Eternal Perspective of Man's Redemption

From God's perspective, everything happens at once. God is not restricted by any temporal limitations. He is the beginning and the end, both at the same time (Psalm 90:2; Revelation 1:8, 11; 21:6; 22:13). All eternity occurs simultaneously from God's perspective. Thus, when God, the Father, speaks, His words transcend all eternity and time, simultaneously. This would explain how Yeshua, the Messiah, Who is God, can be the same and will remain the same forever (Hebrews 13:8). There is no opportunity for change because He covers the beginning and the end at the same time. Time is a subset of eternity. Eternity existed before and after time. This helps us better understand how Yeshua could be slain from the foundation of the world (Revelation 13:8) from an eternal perspective, and yet, from our temporal perspective, undergo that fate 2,000 years ago.

Knowing the hearts of men, God looked out over time and identified all of Mankind who would be receptive to His free offer of salvation and kept their names in the Book of Life which was written from the foundation of the world (Revelation 17:8). Consequently, it is reasonable to conclude that the names of all Mankind were written in the Book of Life from the foundation of the world. Names are blotted out if they die in their sins.

For instance, in Exodus 32:32-33, Moses affirms the existence of a Book containing the names of all people who are to be given the gift of eternal life. Moses prayed for God's forgiveness of His people's sins and offered to have his name removed from this Book in return for God's grace. God responded by saying that only those who have sinned against Him shall have their names blotted out of this Book. Should anyone have the misfortune of having his or her name removed from God's Book of Life, that person will be judged, found wanting and cast into the lake of fire. (Revelation 3:5; 20:12, 15; 22:19). These individuals are not entitled to enter into God's Kingdom. I say "entitled" because every person must have the title of "child of God" to have his name remain in the Book of Life (Philippians 4:3; Revelation 21:27). After all, they take on the name of God through Yeshua, their Messiah.

From God, the Father's, eternal, timeless and everything-in-the-present perspective, He continually experiences a perfect, complete and total oneness with every one of His children who were spared from the wages of their sins by the death, burial and resurrection of Yeshua HaMashiach even though that reality has yet to be fully experienced by us. We shall one day be able to experience the simultaneity of God. In that state of coexistence with God, all that will happen from the beginning to the end of all things will be simultaneously experienced by God and us. From that point on, nothing will be unknown to us. We shall possess all the fullness of God (Ephesians 3:19).

From our current temporal standpoint, we can take confidence in the fact that we are sealed by the Holy Spirit unto the day of redemption at the very moment of our salvation and spiritual rebirths through acceptance of our Lord Yeshua as our Savior (Ephesians 4:30). Our temporal existence will not allow for us to experience the past or the future while we experience the present. We live in the faith and the hope that God's perspective will become our perspective. We should have unwavering faith in what the future holds for us because, from God's eternal perspective, it is already occurring.

God's master plan to redeem us, through the sacrificial blood of Yeshua HaMashiach, Who came to seek and to save that which was lost (Luke 19:10), was therefore completed by God from the foundation of the world (Hebrews 4:3). However, to us, it is being carried out over the span of millennia.

This interrelationship between the eternal and the temporal is demonstrated when our prayers are answered. Our prayers, which are made over time, are heard and answered from God's eternal perspective. From His perspective, a name can remain written in the Book of Life before the foundation of the world as a direct result of the fervent prayer of a child of God today or at any time since the foundation of the world because, from His perspective, it all happens at once.

One of the first multimillion-dollar verdicts I was involved with occurred relatively early in my legal career in 1992. I was one of three attorneys from our firm who were assigned a group of three plaintiffs, each allegedly suffering from an asbestos-related cancer, two lung and one laryngeal. Their cases were to be tried in Washington, D.C. Superior Court and so we secured living arrangements nearby. As God would have it, I was assigned the laryngeal case, which was the most difficult to prove given the sparsity of the state of the art (medical and scientific literature) at that time associating a causal link between exposure to asbestos and laryngeal cancer. According to this same state of the art, a strong association between smoking and laryngeal cancer was established and my client was about to testify that he continues to smoke through the hole in his neck.

The defendants in my case filed a motion to have my client's case dismissed pursuant to a D.C. statute that they argued required dismissal of a products liability action where the plaintiff waits more than one year from the date he first misses work, due to a work-related injury, to sue an entity whose negligence was alleged to have caused the injury. My client's case was filed more than one year after he first missed work due to the development of laryngeal cancer allegedly caused by his occupational exposure to asbestos. He had missed six months from work due to his cancer. The court set a deadline for me to establish why my client's case should not be dismissed. We had every reason to believe that the statute was applicable.

The D.C. statute was derived from a California statute. I attended law school in Los Angeles. I researched the California statute but was unable to get a copy of that research until the morning of the deadline.

The morning of the court hearing, I arose from bed, got on my knees, and asked God, Who knows the hearts of everyone involved, to take this matter from me and let His will be done. I had yet to receive the results of my research. Almost immediately, I was overcome with a sense of joy and relief. There was no stress. It was no longer my concern. It was God's to do with as He pleased. Keep in mind that I was but a few hours away from having my client's case dismissed, and I knew of no legal reason why that should not be my client's fate. Yet, I had this indescribable inner peace.

About an hour later, I was moved to call the home office. Upon doing so, I was informed that they were faxing a copy of my research to the copy center across the street from where I was staying. I immediately picked it up. It was a copy of the annotated code of the California statute that established that the one-year statute of limitations does not begin to run unless or until the worker was unable to return to work. As my client returned to work after a six-month recovery period, his case could not be dismissed. I could hardly contain my excitement.

132 Oneness With God

Upon receipt of this research, the court denied the motion and my client went on to win a $9 million verdict, millions more than the other two plaintiffs, who received verdicts of $4 and $2.5 million, respectively.

What took days to unfold from my perspective occurred simultaneously from God's eternal perspective. The Holy Spirit, Who dwells in me, allowed me to experience the joy of victory before it actually occurred from my perspective because it had already happened from His perspective.

Once our eternal lives are perfected with and in God through our Messiah, Yeshua, God's timeless existence will be our timeless existence. Each day will be like an infinity and infinity will be as a day to us. Upon our glorification in and through Yeshua, the Word of God Who stands forever (Isaiah 40:8), we shall also be both the beginning and the end, the Alpha and the Omega.

No Salvation for the Fallen Angels

The Holy Scriptures are clear that both angels and men are referred to as the sons of God (Genesis 6:2-4; Job 1:6, 2:1, 38:7, John 1:12; Romans 8:14-19; 1 John 3:1-2). Yet, Hebrews 2:16 tells us that Yeshua sought not to help the angels, but the seed of Abraham. From this verse, it must be concluded that God chose to redeem Adam and Eve and those of their descendants, who are called by God to Himself, but not the fallen angels (2 Peter 2:4).

Why weren't the fallen angels also offered the gift of eternal salvation? Perhaps, it was because Adam and Eve sinned before they fully understood and appreciated the benefits and responsibilities associated with their first estate, whereas the fallen angels fully understood all these things and yet sinned nonetheless.

Adam and Eve, in their innocent state, had yet to experience oneness with God with incorruptible bodies that could not sin, a position for which they were created. Unaware of this fact, they chose to attain this eternal God-like status through disobedience. They were never able to fully appreciate all that they were created to be because they sinned before they were glorified by becoming eternally one with God. *The Thomas Nelson Study Bible*, in footnote 4:1-35 of the Book of Leviticus, states atonement can be had for sins done in ignorance (*bish-gagah*). In fact, Yeshua said shortly before He died on the cross: "Father, forgive them; for they know not what they do" (Luke 23:34).

Satan and his angels fully understood that they were all they were going to be and sinned presumptuously because they wanted to be more. In Numbers 15:30, it is written:

> But the soul that doeth aught presumptuously, whether he be born in the land, or a stranger, the same reproacheth the LORD; and that soul shall be cut off from among his people.

Again, the *Thomas Nelson Study Bible*, in footnote 15:30,31 of the Book of Numbers, tells us that the word "presumptuously" in this verse literally means "with a high hand"; in other words, raising one's hands in defiance of and against God. If a person would not be forgiven should he defiantly blaspheme the Lord (Hebrews 10:26-28), surely an angel who takes up arms against the Holy Spirit would not be forgiven. Satan and his angels, being spiritual entities, engaged in a spiritual rebellion against the Spirit of God. God, in His mercy, will forgive a sin against Him but not a sin against His Holy Spirit (Isaiah 63:10; Matthew 12:31-32; Mark 3:29; Luke 12:10; Acts 5:3-4, 9; 7:51; Hebrews 10:29). God will also forgive a sin done in ignorance or unbelief (1 Timothy 1:13). Such was not the case with the rebellious angels who sinned against God intentionally though they believed (James 2:19).

It could also have been that Adam and Eve ate from the Tree of the Knowledge of Good and Evil, and thus they knew both good and evil. Should our evil nature be redeemed, we would know only good and have only a good nature. The fallen angels, however, never ate from this tree and therefore only knew evil because of their sin. Since they did not know good, there were no redeeming qualities in the fallen angels. Salvation was not an option.

Finally, the souls of Mankind were always a part of the eternal, ever-present Spiritual Body of Yeshua, the breath of life. These eternal souls became living souls once they were breathed into the nostrils of Adam. This life of God was in the blood of Adam enabling every one of his descendants to have this same life. The salvation of these living souls was the responsibility of the ever-present I AM in Whom they abide.

Thus, God, the Father, in His infinite mercy was willing to allow His Holy Word to become flesh through Mary and, though sinless, take on the sins of the world and satisfy the death penalties associated with them. God, the Father, was thereby able to separate Himself from His only begotten Son, for a time, for the salvation of Mankind because Yeshua, as man, possessed His own body and soul that could be separated from God.

The angels do not possess physical bodies, nor are they members of the eternal, Spiritual Body of the Messiah. Thus, the salvation of the angels would have required the purely spiritual separation of God from Himself unto spiritual death. God cannot spiritually die for He is Holy and without sin. Because God cannot spiritually die for them, the fallen angels are destined to be eternally spiritually separated from God. For it is written,

Every Kingdom divided against itself is brought to desolation; and every city or house divided against itself shall not stand: And if Satan cast out Satan, he is divided against himself; how shall then his Kingdom stand (Matthew 12:25-26)?

For whatever reasons, God decided not to redeem the fallen angels including those who left their estate to sleep with the daughters of men (Genesis 6:1-4; Jude 6). The fallen angels continually tempt us to be our own god instead of allowing God to exist in and through us. It could be argued that each of these fallen angels are cherubim because their ministerial service to God involves the judgment of Mankind. This may also be true because there are no scriptural references that depict seraphim leaving the presence of God in heaven.

Those angels, who kept their first estate, are allowed by God to perform the ministerial functions for which they were created including separating the chosen (the wheat) from the condemned (the chaff) on the day of judgment.

Overcoming the temptations of life, through Yeshua, draws those called by God closer to Him. It is our demonstration of loving obedience to God during these tests that allows us to be separated as wheat from the chaff.

Satan's Self-Deception

As previously discussed, the only way for our sinless God to die in our place was for God to become man. The Living Word of God was made flesh, and we beheld His glory (John 1:14). He is the every utterance of God, and He became God's only begotten Son (John 1:18, 1 John 4:9). Footnote 1:18 of the Gospel of John in the *Thomas Nelson Study Bible* informs us that some manuscripts interpret the phrase "only begotten Son" as "only begotten God." In fact, footnote 9:6,7 in the Book of Isaiah in the same study bible states that the child, who is given unto us, as referenced in Isaiah 9:6, is called *El Gib-bohr* meaning "The Mighty God" or "God Hero."

Yeshua became both God and man from the moment of His conception (Matthew 22:41-46). Thus, He is the express image of God (2 Corinthians 4:4; Hebrews 1:2-3) because the Spirit of God abides in Him. Yet, Yeshua was susceptible to the sins of the flesh; of the eyes and of pride of life because He was made in the likeness of man (Romans 8:3-4, Philippians 2:7). As God, He was nonetheless able to remain sinless throughout His entire life.

Lest anyone think that it was easy for Yeshua to live a sinless life for thirty-three years in this sinful world, the author of Hebrews tells us that in every way, shape, or fashion, Yeshua's temptations were the same as ours:

> For we have not a high priest which cannot be touched with the feeling of our infirmities, but was in all points tempted like as we are, yet without sin (Hebrews 4:15).
>
> Who in the days of his flesh, when he had offered up prayers and supplications with strong crying and tears unto him that was able to save him from death, and was heard in that he feared; Though he were a Son, yet learned he obedience by the things which he suffered; And being made perfect, he became the author of eternal salvation unto all them that obey him (Hebrews 5:7-9).

The fact that Yeshua was able to live in the flesh for thirty-three years without sinning begs the question: Why would Satan, being an intelligent creature, cause Yeshua to experience a sinless death knowing that, as a result thereof, souls would be saved and not suffer condemnation? Perhaps, Satan reasoned that no man could endure the suffering Yeshua went through without sinning by cursing God orally or in his heart. Any sin on Yeshua's part would have rendered His death the wages of His own sin and thus could not serve as a propitiation for the sins of anyone else, let alone the whole world. Assuming this was, in fact, Satan's reasoning, it was woefully inaccurate. However, there are scriptural references that suggest that Satan may have been induced, through selfish pride, into a form of self-deception.

The story of Job is illustrative. Job lived in the land of Uz (Job 1:1) hundreds, if not thousands, of years before the birth of Yeshua. Job is described as a man who was blameless before God and who shunned evil (Job 1:8, 2:3). From this, we must conclude that, up to this point in Job's life, he was sinless before God. Of crucial import is Job 1:5 because it explains one of the main purposes of the entire Book of Job. This verse tells us that Job completely understood that Mankind can sin and curse God in their hearts and so he offered burnt offerings on behalf of his sons continually for the remission of this type of sin. The fact that this particular sin is identified at the very beginning of the Book of Job suggests an importance that will be revealed in the Book. In other words, there is a purpose for it being in the opening verses of this Book. Of note is the fact that Satan focused only on Job orally cursing God to His face. Satan doesn't mention Job cursing God in his heart.

A literal translation of ensuing verses, specifically Job 1:22 and 2:10, strongly suggests that Job, himself, fell victim to this same sin. What Satan may have taken away from his Job experience is that a sin in the heart against God has the same physical and spiritual death sentence as any overt sin against God. Satan's immense pride in his complete and total control over the sin nature of Mankind would not allow him to believe that he could not cause Yeshua to sin either orally or in His heart. This unfounded pride may have been the deciding factor in convincing Satan to persecute Yeshua unto death reasoning that all he needed to achieve was to have Yeshua sin in His heart against God, a result Satan was able to achieve as to Job. Satan's pride preceded his destruction and his haughty spirit preceded his fall (Proverbs 16:18).

As the story of Job goes, despite his sin of pride, Satan had a ministerial service to perform and thus was permitted to accompany other angelic beings when they presented themselves before God during Job's time (Job 1:6, 2:1). On two of these occasions, God asked Satan from whence he came, and Satan responded that he came from going to and fro in the earth and walking up and down in it (Job 1:7, 2:2). The Scriptures are silent as to the nature of Satan's activities while traversing the globe, but the nature of the service he was performing for God up to this point suggests that he was busy tempting Mankind with the permission of God. On each of these two occasions, God brought the subject of Job to Satan's attention. God, Who knows all things, knew that Satan, who does not know all things, would rely on his experience with Job when he encountered a later blameless man before God who shunned evil, namely Yeshua, HaMashiach.

During the first angelic presentation before God, Satan told God that Job was blameless before Him only because God protected him. Satan proposed that Job would curse God to His face if that protection was removed and requested that he be allowed to fill Job's life with great tragedy. So, Satan was given permission by God to destroy all that Job had, including his children, but he could not touch the person of Job (Job 1:12). The test was to see if Job would sin by cursing God to His face.

Job was a wealthy and well-respected man with a wife, seven sons, three daughters, and many possessions (Job 1:2-3). Satan took the lives of his ten children and his earthly possessions through human, natural, and supernatural means (Job 1:13-22). This was possible because Satan possesses supernatural abilities and, through the sin of Adam and Eve, had become one with sinful Mankind, had usurped Mankind's dominion and authority over the earth and had continued access to heaven seeking the judgment of Mankind.

Interestingly, Satan did not take the life of Job's wife. By leaving Job's wife alive, Satan had a living soul, who has sinned, available to tempt Job to sin just as Satan had Eve to tempt Adam to sin. Yet, despite this great string of tragedies in his life, Job never sinned (Job 1:20-22).

On the occasion of the second angelic presentation before God, Job was again brought to Satan's attention by God. Satan further proposed that Job would yet curse God to His face if God would remove His protection of Job and allow Satan to attack the body of Job. Therefore, Satan was given permission to inflict great physical and emotional pain and suffering upon the person of Job. It is unclear whether Job's sinless death would have paid the death penalty for the sins of others. Obviously, it was not God's intention for Job to sacrifice his life in this manner because God told Satan that he could not take Job's life (Job 2:6).

At this time in Mankind's history, there appears to have been a general acknowledgement that an association exists between personal affliction and sin. If it was indeed commonly believed at that time that a person could not suffer illness, tragedy or death unless or until he had sinned, this would partially explain why Job's three friends considered his sufferings the result of previous sins.

Again, Satan's attack on the person of Job was to see if this would cause Job to sin by cursing God to His face. Job's wife, being a witness to Job's supposed fall from grace, told Job to curse God and die (Job 2:9). This statement by Job's wife is telling because it implies that (1) Satan inspired her to make the statement because it was the exact sin Satan sought Job to commit and (2) she believed that, for Job to die, he had to first overtly sin. In this case, cursing God would be the means of his sin.

Job certainly considered cursing God in one's heart to be a sin because he offered burnt sacrifices daily for his ten children, before their untimely deaths, to sanctify them just in case they may have sinned by cursing God in their hearts (Job 1:5). Satan and Job's wife wanted Job to overtly curse God. Job was aware that a person could also curse God in his heart. At this stage of the test, Satan doesn't appear to fully appreciate the existence of, let alone the magnitude and resulting consequences of, the covert sin of cursing God in one's heart.

Job refused his wife's suggestion that he curse God and die at least with his lips (Job 2:10). This scriptural qualification infers that Job sinned in his heart while subjected to Satan's intense persecution. There can be no other justification for this qualifying phrase, especially since we are introduced to Mankind's ability to sin in one's heart at the very beginning of the Book of Job before Job was brought to Satan's attention by God.

The Word of God makes a clear distinction between Job's response to each test. When Satan took everything from Job but did not touch Job, Job simply never sinned nor charged God foolishly (Job 1:22). However, when Satan subjected Job to incredible persecution, Job never sinned with his lips (Job 2:10). The significance of this distinction is critical to our appreciation of what was going on during these tests between God and Satan.

We know that Job obviously sinned at some point because the Holy Scriptures tell all have sinned and gone astray (Psalms 14:1-3, 53:1-3; Ecclesiastes 7:20, Isaiah 53:6, Romans 3:10), because Job tells God that he despises himself and repents in dust and ashes (Job 42:6) and because Job ultimately died (Job 42:17).

Satan would not have known, during his persecution of Job, whether Job had sinned in his heart because he cannot discern the thoughts and intents of the hearts of men, only God can do that. Satan told God that Job would fail the tests by cursing God to His face, suggesting an oral overt act. Job never did that. However, when Satan observed God's chastisement of Job and the death of Job, he undoubtedly realized that Job must have sinned in his heart as a direct consequence of the intense suffering Job had to endure at Satan's hands.

This realization may have led Satan to further believe that, given enough suffering, every man will sin, at the least in his heart, and should he do so, he will suffer physical and spiritual death for that sin just as surely as if he had sinned overtly. Satan clearly understood that, once any man sinned, his death would be for his own sin and therefore could not be for the sins of anyone else.

From his experience with Job, Satan may have mistakenly and pridefully concluded that no man could endure the degree of suffering that he can put upon him and never sin overtly or in his heart. The Bible gives us a glimpse of the extent of the suffering Satan put upon Job. His oxen, asses, and camels were stolen from him (Job 1:14-15,17); his servants were killed (Job 1:15-17); his sheep were burned by a fire from heaven (Job 1:16); his seven sons and three daughters were killed when the home of one of them collapsed (Job 1:19); he was smitten with sore boils from head to foot (Job 2:7); he was the greatest of all the men of the east (Job 1:3) and received much respect (Job 29:7-25), but was left so poor that he resided among the ashes (Job 2:8); his flesh was caked with worms and clouds of dust; his skin was cracked and broke out afresh (Job 7:5); he suffered terrible dreams and visions (Job 7:14); he was mocked by his friends (Job 12:4, 16:20); he wept unto God (Job 16:16,20); he saw his condition as hopeless (Job 19:10); all of his family and friends abandoned him (Job 19:13-19); his wife was repulsed by his breath (Job 19:17); he was literally skin and bones (Job 19:20); he had enjoyed a personal relationship with God but now felt abandoned (Job 23:8-17, 29:2-5); his bones gave him piercing pain at night and he suffered constant gnawing pain (Job 30:17) and his skin turned black and fell off of him and his bones burned with fever (Job 30:30).

Upon Job's successful completion of the tests by not overtly cursing God, God blessed Job with more than he had before the tests. Job did eventually die, and the Scriptures are silent as to whether Job sinned at any time after the tests.

Satan took this knowledge into his experience with Yeshua. Satan had to know that Job was all man, with his attendant sin nature as a descendant of Adam, whereas Yeshua had a human mother but God as His Father. Satan understood that Yeshua, therefore, had both man's sinful nature and God's sinless nature. Satan knew that Adam also did not have a sin nature, and yet Satan was able to induce him to overtly sin against God. So, when presented with the opportunity to test the blameless life of Yeshua years later, Satan's Job experience may have deluded him into believing that Yeshua would also sin against God openly or in His heart if the suffering was great enough, thereby eliminating any hope of success for Yeshua's Messianic mission.

Satan convinced himself of Yeshua's susceptibility to sin because of Yeshua's inherent sin nature given to Him by Satan through His mother, Mary. Satan was very aware of Scripture which says that the heart of man is deceitful above all things and desperately wicked (Jeremiah 17:9). Satan knew that every descendant of Adam and Eve was born with his sin nature and, therefore, would inevitably sin and die. Finally, Satan knew Yeshua to be the promised Messiah Who came to take all earthly authority from him and usher in a new eternal Kingdom.

However, Satan had tremendous confidence in the dominating power of his sin nature and was willing to put it to the test when Yeshua came to lay down His sinless life for the sins of the world. Satan knew that his sin nature was engrained in Yeshua since it is a part of every human being due to Adam's sin. However, Satan also knew that Yeshua possessed God's holy, loving nature as being one with God. Had Satan understood that it was impossible to cause Yeshua to sin and that He would succeed in paying the death penalty for all Mankind, he and his demonic angels would not have crucified him (1 Corinthians 2:8).

Satan's persecutions of Job would not have been possible unless God removed His hedge of protection from around him. Yeshua permitted His persecution by Satan (Job 1:10; 2:4-6; Luke 22:53; John 7:30; 8:20). Satan was not allowed to kill Job, only to persecute him. Yeshua allowed Satan to persecute Him and take His life knowing that Satan's actions were according to the will of God, His Father. Because Satan knew that Yeshua was fully man (John 1:14, Hebrews 2:14) and fully God (John 1:1), he left nothing untried in his bag of tricks when it came to his attempt to cause Yeshua to sin either overtly or in His heart.

Satan understood that the deciding battle for the souls of Mankind was to be played out through the persecution unto death of Yeshua. Should Yeshua suffer at his hands unto death without sinning, all would be lost for Satan and God's prophecy, contained in Genesis 3:15, would be fulfilled. If Yeshua sinned overtly or in His heart before death, the victory would be Satan's and Mankind would continue to be subjected to his dominion and control. Satan may have thought that causing Yeshua to sin would be a demonstration that his power and authority would be equal to that of God.

So, Satan risked everything on his misplaced confidence in the overpowering strength of Yeshua's sin nature and engaged in the ultimate battle between good and evil for the souls of Mankind. Satan was convinced that his sin nature was so dominant in Yeshua that it would easily win out over God's holy, loving nature and Yeshua would sin. He grossly underestimated the power of God.

With so much at stake, Satan's persecution of Yeshua subjected Him to a degree of suffering worse than anything Job experienced. In fact, it was more suffering than any man will ever live to endure. In Isaiah 52:14, it is written:

> As many were astonished at thee; his visage was so marred more than any man, and his form more than the sons of men.

This verse tells us that the beatings and scourging that Yeshua suffered at the hands of Satan, through sinful man, was worse than any human being will ever have to endure. The New Living Translation of Isaiah 52:14 is as follows:

> Many were amazed when they saw him—beaten and bloodied, so disfigured one would scarcely know he was a person.

This verse tells us that Yeshua's disfigurement was so horrible that it was barely possible to tell that He was a human being. It is one thing for Yeshua not to be recognized as Yeshua because of the beatings, but this was far worse. He could barely be recognized as a person. In his best-selling book, *The Case For Christ*, Lee Strobel interviews Alexander Metherell, MD, PhD, a world-renown medical doctor and research scientist who has "extensively studied the historical, archaeological, and medical data concerning the death of Jesus of Nazareth." Mr. Metherell posits that Roman floggings similar to what Yeshua underwent would sometimes cut so deep into a person's back that parts of the spine would be exposed. Citing Eusebius, a third-century historian, Dr. Metherell described such floggings as "The sufferer's veins were laid bare, and the very muscles, sinews, and bowels of the victim were open to exposure."

Isaiah 50:6 tells us that Yeshua's beard was literally plucked out of His cheeks. Yeshua underwent torture so extreme that no man will ever be called upon to suffer similar or greater suffering. Satan put Yeshua through a degree of physical, emotional, and spiritual suffering that has never been nor ever will be experienced by Mankind.

Yeshua was fully aware of the degree and extent of suffering He was to endure for our sakes. In Matthew 26, Yeshua prayed three times to His Father that, if it be His Father's will, this cup be passed from Him. According to Luke 22:44, Yeshua agonized over His impending persecution so much so that His "sweat was as it were great drops of blood falling down to the ground."

It is important that we fully grasp the true nature and extent of Yeshua's suffering for our sakes. It is extremely unfortunate that practically every depiction of the persecution and suffering Yeshua lovingly endured fails to accurately reflect the totality of its gruesome details. Perhaps, if we saw His suffering as it truly was, we would have a far greater appreciation for the tremendous price God had to pay for the salvation of our souls, and the limitless love He has for every one of us. Revelation 5:6 tells us that we will one day see Yeshua as He was slain.

Satan's insatiable desire to put unconscionable pain upon Yeshua, the human manifestation of God, to cause Him to sin, blinded Satan from the repercussions of his actions. Had Satan fully understood the wisdom behind God's sacrificial offering of His Son, he may never have crucified Yeshua (1 Corinthians 2:8). Job received twice as much as he possessed before the tests, and Yeshua brought about the salvation of the world. It is ironic that the father of deception, through his experience with Job, deceived himself into performing the very acts upon the Son of God, which undid the consequences of his initial deception of Adam and Eve. Praise be to God because Yeshua, despite Satan's horrific persecution, remained sinless to the end.

Every child of God should be constantly praising, thanking and glorifying our God Who caused Satan to use his own deceptive nature against himself to the end that Yeshua would suffer a most agonizing death for such undeserving creatures as us.

The Atoning Power of Yeshua's Ultimate Sacrifice

Since death can only occur by the commission of sin, a sinless man will never know death. The death of such a man could pay the penalties of condemned souls. The Bible cites an incidence when the life of a sinless person was about to be offered. The Scriptures tell us it was to test the obedience of Abraham (Genesis 22:12).

It is found in Genesis 22:1-19. This is, of course, the account of God's request that Isaac, the supernaturally born son of Abraham and Sarah, be offered as a sacrifice to God which may have been at, or near, the location where the supernaturally born Yeshua would later be slain for the sins of the world (Genesis 22:2). Footnote 22:1-14 of the *Book of Genesis* in the Thomas

Nelson Study Bible states that Moriah is also in the vicinity where Solomon built his holy temple (2 Chronicles 3:1). It is of note that it took three days for Abraham and his son to arrive at Moriah. In addition, Isaac carried the wood for his sacrifice to the altar much like Yeshua carrying His cross to the place of His sacrifice.

The prophetic significance of these facts clearly suggests that the location and details of Isaac's intended sacrifice was meant to be a symbolic precursor of Yeshua's ultimate sacrifice for the remission of the sins of the world.

God halted the sacrifice of Isaac at the last minute and provided a ram in his stead (Genesis 22:13). The ram was used in Old Testament times for consecration (Exodus 29:22, 27, 31; Leviticus 8:22, 29), for atonement as a trespass offering (Leviticus 5:16-18; Numbers 5:8), and for a peace offering (Leviticus 9:4, 18; Numbers 6:14-17). Since this was the animal sacrificed in Isaac's stead, it is reasonable to conclude that the ram was to be offered (1) to consecrate the place where Yeshua would later give His life for the sins of the world and where the house of God was later to be built, (2) to temporarily atone for the sins of Abraham and his people, and (3) to serve as a peace offering to confirm Abraham and Isaac's relationship with God.

We know that anything sacrificed unto God had to be free of any blemish (Deuteronomy 15:21). Indeed, each of the above-referenced passages concerning the sacrifice of a ram required the ram to be without blemish. Thus, we can infer that Isaac was blameless as of the time he was to be offered as a sacrifice, and Abraham had to be aware of this fact. If so, Abraham knew that, even if Isaac was sacrificed, God would resurrect him. Footnote 22:1-14 of the *Thomas Nelson Study*

Bible confirms this inference by citing to Hebrews 11:17-19 as support for the premise that Abraham expected Isaac to be resurrected.

God wanted to see if Abraham was willing to demonstrate his uncompromising and unconditional love for God by obediently sacrificing his son, Isaac. God blessed Abraham for his willingness to obey God to this extent.

The nature and extent of his relationship with God would suggest that Abraham understood all too well the importance of what he was asked to do. The Holy Scriptures state that Abraham saw the redemption of Mankind through Yeshua, HaMashiach and was glad (John 8:56). Ultimately, Abraham and God offered their offspring to be sacrificed for the sins of the world because Yeshua is Abraham's descendant (Luke 3:23-38) and the Son of God (John 3:16).

Yeshua is a sinless progenitor, Who gives eternal life. The atoning power contained in His sinless, Godly blood, which was shed for the sins of Mankind, was more than sufficient to pay the death penalties for all the sins of the world. Yeshua is the Alpha and the Omega, the beginning and the end (Revelation 1:8,11; 21:6; 22:13) outside of time. The beginning and the end happen at the same time in His eternal existence. Thus, His eternal blood, at the moment of its sacrifice, covered all sins from the beginning to the end.

The Scriptures tell us that Yeshua is the Way the Truth, and the Life (John 14:6), that eternal life is in Him (John 1:4; 1 John 5:11), and that He is the Bread of Life (John 6:35, 48) Whose words are Spirit and Life (John 6:63). The life discussed in these scriptural passages is spiritual and eternal. However, Yeshua knew that the life of the flesh is in the blood (Leviticus 17:11, 14). For us to be redeemed, the eternal, blemish-free, life-filled blood of the Son of Man, which is powerful enough to permanently cover the sins of Adam and Eve and every one of their descendants, must be shed unto death.

Death is the absence of physical life, spiritual separation from God, and the wages of sin. As a result of Yeshua's sinless sacrifice, death would have no victory over God's chosen people. The eternal life-giving power contained in every drop of Yeshua's blood was extracted from His body in the most excruciating fashion. He was pierced through, utterly crushed and beaten with blows that cut in (Isaiah 53:5).

It is of note that the resurrected Yeshua described His resurrected body as flesh and bones as opposed to flesh and blood (Luke 24:39). The Apostle Paul also acknowledges the absence of blood in the resurrected body of Yeshua when he refers to all saints as members of the Spiritual Body of the Messiah which Paul describes as flesh and bones (Ephesians 5:30). These passages confirm the fact that every drop of Yeshua's precious sinless blood was shed for the remission of the sins of the world. A literal interpretation of these verses also suggests that the resurrected, incorruptible and eternal bodies of the saints of God will resemble the Body of Yeshua and be bloodless. We will be flesh and bones. The Apostle Paul adds credence to this interpretation when he tells us that flesh and blood cannot enter the Kingdom of God (1 Corinthians 15:50).

Bishop Clifford M. Johnson, Jr., in a sermon at Mount Pleasant Church and Ministries in Baltimore, Maryland, referred us to Romans 6:6 for the proposition that sinful man was crucified with Yeshua. Citing Galatians 2:20, he posits that we were crucified with the Messiah and, therefore, we no longer live but Yeshua now lives in us. We are now flesh of His flesh and bones of His bones (Ephesians 6:6). We have become one with Him just as a man becomes one with his wife through marriage (Ephesians 5:30-31).

During our earthly lives, the life of the flesh is in the blood (Genesis 9:4; Leviticus 17:11, 14). During our eternal lives, we shall eat of the Tree of Life and drink the water of life (Revelation 22:14, 17). The Word of God tells us that life, therefore, will no longer be in the blood. Life will be in us through Yeshua. In Revelation 22:19, the world is warned not to take away from the words of that Book lest God take away their part out of the Book of Life, the Holy City, and from the things which are written in that prophetic book.

Footnote 22:18,19 of the Thomas Nelson Study Bible's Book of Revelation suggests that this warning would appear to apply as well to all inspired Scripture which is the Word of God (Deuteronomy 4:2, Proverbs 30:6, Galatians 1:6-7). The footnote further informs us that almost all Greek manuscripts concerning this passage in Revelation 22 read "tree of life" instead of "book of life." Both phrases refer to Yeshua, who is "the life" (John 11:25). Yeshua, therefore, is the Tree of Life, the Book of Life, the Holy Scriptures and, indeed, life itself. Yeshua is the source of all life, temporal or eternal.

The Holy Scriptures tell us that Yeshua's sacrificial death released all Mankind from Satan's bondage, literally and figuratively. For instance, upon His death, Yeshua led captivity captive (Ephesians 4:8). This verse has been interpreted to mean that Yeshua, during the three days His body was in the tomb, gathered all the souls in Abraham's bosom and led them to paradise.

In addition, Yeshua's self-sacrifice also caused the veil, separating man from the presence of God in the Holy temple in Jerusalem, to be rent in half thereby reconciling man with God (Matthew 27:51). This was a symbolic statement that man no longer needed a human high priest to intercede on his behalf before God. Anyone can now come before God at any time in and through Yeshua HaMashiach.

Finally, one of the sinners crucified with Yeshua was taken to paradise the very day of his repentance (Luke 23:43). Salvation is immediately available to everyone after the eternal once-for-all sin offering had been paid.

The magnitude of the atoning power attendant to Yeshua's sacrificial death and resurrection was further demonstrated by the resurrection of the bodies of saints who went into Jerusalem and appeared unto many immediately after His resurrection (Matthew 27:52-53). It is reasonable to assume that these resurrected saints never died again and were taken to His eternal Kingdom with every other soul who occupied the bosom of Abraham (Luke 16:22-23, Ephesians 4:8). Upon His resurrection, all authority, that is in heaven and on earth, was given to Yeshua (Matthew 28:18). The children of God, who before had not obtained mercy, now have obtained mercy (1 Peter 2:9-10).

But we have obtained so much more than mercy. Matthew 28:18 must be fully appreciated for its meaning and the implications. Since *all* authority in heaven and on earth has been given to Yeshua, there is no longer any authority exercised by the principalities, powers, rulers of the darkness of this age, thrones and dominions identified in Ephesians 6:12 and Colossians 1:16. All means all. There is no authority left for Satan and his demons. They have been rendered powerless, lacking as they do any authority. As members of the Spiritual Body of Yeshua, we live in Him and He in us. Therefore, all the authority Yeshua possesses and exercises, we now possess and can exercise. This is because we and the Messiah are one in answer to Yeshua's prayer in John 17. Yeshua walked this earth humbly, yet with all the power and authority of God. No demon could resist His will.

If our faith is strong enough, we can similarly walk this earth now. Upon our perfection, every member of the Spiritual Body of Yeshua shall humbly and lovingly exercise all authority in heaven and on earth. How awesome is that!

No other creature in or under heaven could pay the death penalty for sinful man. We had to die for our sins. By one man's offense and disobedience all men became sinners and were condemned, but by the righteousness and obedience of Yeshua, the Messiah, the only begotten Son of God, many will be made righteous and justified (Romans 5:17-19, 1 John 4:9). The sacrificial shedding of the innocent, life-filled blood of God, through Yeshua HaMashiach, paid the physical and spiritual death penalties of all those who are willing to accept, in faith, this sacrifice on their behalf. Yeshua's resurrection unto eternal life ensures that all of God's spiritually born offspring will be similarly resurrected and will never know eternal death. They shall be resurrected unto eternal life, in and through Yeshua, because their eternal physical and spiritual death penalties have been paid by Him. They are in Him and He is in them and, together, They shall reign forever.

We have redemption through the shedding unto death of the life-filled blood of Yeshua HaMashiach, Who is the image of the invisible God (Colossians 1:14-15). By accepting God's sacrifice, through faith, for the forgiveness of our sins (Romans 3:25), we are indeed forgiven and receive an inheritance among the sanctified by faith, which is in Yeshua, the Messiah (Acts 26:18). "Inherit" means that it will be our birthright as the children of God to be His heirs and to possess the rights and privileges of being one with our Father. It is the power of our God-inspired faith in Yeshua that brings about our salvation. By this faith, we are spiritually begotten of God with the word of truth (James 1:18). We are God's creation in Yeshua, HaMashiach, unto good works (Ephesians 2:10), and we keep ourselves unspotted from this world (1 John 5:18-19).

We then put on the "new man, which after God is created" (Ephesians 4:23-24). This new man is spiritual and bears the image of the heavenly (1 Corinthians 11:7, 15:42-49, 2 Corinthians 3:18, Colossians 3:10). Our heavenly Father gives the Holy Spirit to all who asks (Luke 11:13). From then on, the Holy Spirit dwells in us and we become the temples of God (1 Corinthians 3:17, 6:19). We now have received the Spirit of God, and we speak spiritual words He teaches us (1 Corinthians 2:12-14). As the redeemed of the Lord, we are heirs of all the promises of God. We are His children, and He is our God and Father (Romans 8:15). We dwell in Him and He in us. Upon our glorification, we will be one with Him to the same extent Yeshua is one with God, His Father.

However, during this life we can also attain a measure of oneness with our God. I am sure you have heard the phrase "walking in the Spirit." The degree of our earthly oneness with God depends on the degree of our walk with Him. We experience that walk daily as we observe how God orders our steps. I remember many occasions when the court scheduled a hearing on a day and time that conflicted with a previously made commitment. During my early walk with God, I would immediately cancel the previous commitment. However, the Holy Spirit stayed my hand and I watched Him manipulate events in such a way that one of the commitments would be rescheduled without my intervention. All I had to do was sit back and watch my Father in Heaven order my steps.

There were also countless occasions where I did not have the means to pay a bill or the funds to afford daily provisions. Yet, the bills were paid and my needs were met. I cannot tell you how many times the Lord delayed me, whether it be for a few seconds, days or years, only to find out that it kept me out of harm's way or was somehow for my good. Being one with God means that we should never worry or stress about anything. God controls every aspect of our lives. God is so intimately involved with every breath we take that nothing is left to chance. We are truly free and can rest in His Peace while He handles everything for us.

Those who walk in the Spirit receive His daily inspirations. The more we recognize them as coming from the Holy Spirit, the more we are likely to act upon them. We must be sensitive to these inspirations. For instance, we receive inspirations to pray, to give, to assist the helpless and to fast. Over time, our walk with the Holy Spirit will develop into a close and intimate relationship that we will deeply cherish.

As much as I try, I cannot find the words to adequately describe all that is entailed in being one with God in and through our Lord and Savior, Yeshua HaMashiach. However, in his book, *My Utmost for His Highest*, Oswald Chambers delves into the length, breath, width and depth of what it means to be one with God in and through Yeshua. He tells us that our sanctification makes us one with Yeshua. Being one with Yeshua means that we must give all that we are over to Him until we literally become Him. Since Yeshua is the personification of the will of God, a true right-standing relationship with God means that we become the will of God in and through Yeshua. We never have to ask God to show us His will because we are His will. Our total purpose in life is to effectuate His will as it is laid out for us by the Holy Spirit. Nothing else matters. No one nor any thing can take precedence over this oneness with God. To fully appreciate all that is meant by being one with God, we must let the law of the Spirit of Life completely fill us with Its righteousness (Romans 8:1-17). The Holy Spirit will take over our lives, influencing us to obey God and to do good works (Mark 14:7, 2 Corinthians 10:5-6, 1 Peter 1:2).

There is a tendency for some of the lost or the less mature children of God to be apprehensive about the prospect of being filled with the Holy Spirit to the extent that He influences them to obey God and to do good works. They envision being possessed to the point that God takes over their bodies and they are relegated to a shell-like existence, while God takes away their free will.

In truth, we never lose control over our bodies or our lives. The Holy Spirit we receive does not take these away from us. Instead, the Holy Spirit brings about our adoption to sonship whereby God becomes our Father (Romans 8:15). Not only do we keep our bodies and our lives, but we do so unto eternity, for it is written:

He that loveth his life shall lose it; and he that hateth his life in this world shall keep it unto life eternal (John 12:25).

When we are filled with the Holy Spirit, our sin natures are replaced with God's Holy nature. Even though our carnal natures cause us to sin even if we do not want to (Romans 7:13-22), our Spirit-filled natures cause us to obey because we want to. If we give up our quest to be separate but equal to God, we gain oneness with God without losing our individuality. We get to experience God from a first-person perspective, and we get to collectively experience God with every other child of God. When we become the children of God and joint heirs of God with Yeshua, we shall be glorified together with Yeshua (Romans 8:17) and become 100 percent God and 100 percent human, just like Yeshua because we shall be in Yeshua.

Until Yeshua returns and we actually experience the fullness of being one with God, we may never fully grasp the totality of what it means to be one with our triune Godhead. However, even with our limited imaginations, we can envision a oneness with God that excites us beyond measure and fills us with so much joy that we cannot contain it.

As members of the Spiritual Body of the Messiah, Who is God in the flesh, we shall also be God in the flesh. By claiming to be the Son of God, Yeshua thought it not robbery to be equal to God (John 5:18, Philippians 2:6). Indeed, according to Yeshua, He and His father are physically and spiritually one (John 10:30, 14:10-11, 17:21-22). Likewise, we also call God our Father (Romans 8:15) and are the sons of God by faith in Yeshua (Galatians 3:26). We are predestined to be conformed to the image of Yeshua (Romans 8:29). Our bodies are the physical temples of God (1 Corinthians 6:19). We shall have the mind of the Messiah (1 Corinthians 2:16). We shall look upon all of creation with the eyes of God. The love of God will be so much a part of us that its power shall permeate the environment around us. Everyone and everything in our presence shall be overwhelmed by the love that exudes from us.

Just as Yeshua , being the incarnate Word of God, could do or say nothing that was not commanded of Him by the Father (John 5:30, 8:28; 12:49, 14:10), we shall also be unable to do or say anything that is not commanded of us by God through Yeshua. The Almighty, All-Knowing, All-Loving and Ever-Present God shall be so much one with us that we shall experience His existence (John 17:21), His glory (John 17:22) and His love (John 17:26). In and through Yeshua HaMashiach, we shall also be God in the flesh. Take a moment to fully comprehend exactly what that means.

However, Satan will not stand idly by and watch our transformation into oneness with our Creator God. We shall see in the next chapter that, as members of the Spiritual Body of Messiah, we will have to individually and collectively suffer as Yeshua suffered (Romans 8:17, 2 Corinthians 4:8-14, Philippians 1:29, 2 Titus 2:12, 3:12, 1 Peter 2:21). Nonetheless, despite Satan's best efforts, just as Yeshua was raised from the dead by the Spirit of God, so shall the members of the Spiritual Body of the Messiah be raised from our physical deaths by the Spirit Who dwells in us (Romans 6:4, 8:11).

We have an opportunity, through Yeshua, to demonstrate our unconditional and uncompromising love for our Creator God through obedience. Are you willing to make good use of this benevolent opportunity? With what is at stake, can we afford to disregard it?

CHAPTER FIVE

OUR SPIRITUAL REBIRTHS AS THE CHILDREN OF GOD

God cannot become one with Mankind unless His and our characteristics, attributes and mannerisms are compatible; indeed, are one. This type of compatibility is best demonstrated through the person of Yeshua HaMashiach. In this chapter, we shall discuss how every reborn child of God is transformed into the image and likeness of Yeshua. How they begin to exhibit His characteristics, mannerisms, and attributes. We shall compare these yet to be perfected Godly traits of the saved with those of the unsaved whose characteristics, mannerisms, and attributes resemble and therefore are compatible with those of Satan. We shall discuss how the life, death, burial, and resurrection of Yeshua, the Messiah, provide us with the means to claim victory over death and to be adopted as sons and daughters of God. Each child of God is reborn with a measure of spiritual gifts as determined by the will of God. Finally, we shall delve into the Holy Scriptures to better understand the requirement that every member of the Spiritual Body of Messiah must suffer just as Yeshua suffered to an extent and degree as, again, determined by the Holy will of God.

The Reborn Children of God

As we have repeatedly stated, when Adam and Eve were first created, they were created in the image and after the likeness of God. Upon their fall from grace, all of Adam and Eve's descendants were born in their image and after their likeness. Yeshua was called upon to pay the ultimate price for the redemption of Adam and Eve and their progeny. Thus, anyone who accepts Yeshua's sacrifice for the remission of his sins, in faith, will be restored to the original position of Adam and Eve, in the image and after the likeness of God, as a child of God. We become children of God only because we are in Yeshua Who is God's Son (Galatians 3:26-29). God confirms this glorious fact on numerous occasions throughout the Holy Scriptures. Colossians 3:10 and 1 John 3:2 tell us that we have become new individuals renewed in knowledge after the image of Him that created us.

John 4:24 tells us that God is a Spirit and we who worship Him must worship Him in spirit. To do this, we must become the children of God by being spiritually reborn in Yeshua. James 1:18 tells us that God, the Father, begot us with the word of truth (i.e., Yeshua Messiah) to be a kind of first fruits of His creatures. This verse appears to make an analogy to the Old Testament tithing of first fruits found in the Book of Genesis.

The *Thomas Nelson Study Bible's* footnote 1:18 of the Book of James tells us that the reborn children of God are the first form of offering to God in the redemptive process of all creation. When this occurs, 2 Corinthians 5:17 tells us that we become new creatures, that old things are passed away and that all things are become new. Ephesians 4:23-24 tell us that we will then be renewed in the spirit of our mind. We will put on the "new man, which after God is created in righteousness and true holiness."

1 Corinthians 3:13-15 and 2 Corinthians 5:10 tell us that we shall be refined by fire at the judgment seat of the Messiah and rewarded for our earthly works. Even if Satan could witness the perfection of the Spiritual Body of Messiah, he will be totally unable to do anything about it.

God, the Father, who foreknew His chosen children prior to their earthly existence, predestined us to be conformed to the image of His Son, which is His image (Jeremiah 1:5; Romans 8:29). Philippians 1:6 tells us that He who began a good work in us will complete it. As we grow spiritually, our spiritual Father, Who loves us beyond measure, will correct us and chasten us just as our earthly fathers do (Hebrews 12:3-11). We walk in the Spirit (Galatians 5:16) and, indeed, are led by the Spirit (Galatians 5:18). As we have discussed, our Father is Spirit and He dwells in our reborn spirits. Anyone who is reborn of God cannot habitually sin because God's seed is in him (1 John 3:9; 5:18-19). Through our Father's guidance, we shall develop into mature, spiritual children, and His faithfulness will cause us to realize the perfect oneness that was the originally intended relationship between the Creator and His highest creation.

Through the Holy Scriptures, God reveals to us the purpose behind the creation of the spiritual and physical realms. The Holy Spirit enlightens the spiritually reborn children of God about the nature, attributes and characteristics of our triune Godhead by opening our spiritual eyes to who we are and why we were created. Unless we are spiritually born again, we will not see these things. We will see and hear physically but not spiritually. You see, the spiritual senses of the unsaved are and will continue to be dead. They will be oblivious to God's master plan for His children that was established before the foundation of the world. Without this rebirth and spiritual sense of direction, mankind is truly lost.

It should be pointed out that Yeshua, Who is the true light, gives His light to every person born into this world (John 1:9). That is, perhaps, why children can enter God's heavenly Kingdom should they die before reaching the age of reason (Matthew 18:3). Upon reaching the age when sin can be committed, Mankind loses this light and needs salvation (Romans 6:23). We must choose to be born again to be saved (John 3:3).

Salvation is achieved when, as lost persons, we repent of our sins, accept the sacrifice of Yeshua Messiah for the propitiation of our sins, and welcome Him into our hearts as our Lord and Savior. Salvation is free and is not based on good works. Therefore, no one can boast that he earned his salvation (Ephesians 2:8-9). When we come to that point in our lives where we realize that it is our nature to sin and that we cannot save ourselves from the consequences of our sins in this life or the next, we desperately cry out for salvation. We then become mindful of God's promise that we will be saved if we believe, in faith, that He sent His only begotten Son to die for all the sins of Mankind.

Just as we were babes when we were physically born, we are also babes when we are spiritually reborn. Thus, we start out with spiritual milk (1 Corinthians 3:1-2). As we mature as reborn children of God, we can have spiritual meat as well as drink (1 Corinthians 10:3-4). What is this spiritual milk and spiritual meat? It is none other than the Word of God: Yeshua, the Messiah. On several occasions in the Holy Scriptures, it talks about "tasting the Lord." Deuteronomy 8:3 and Matthew 4:4 tell us that man lives not by bread alone, but by every word that proceeds out of the mouth of God. Since Yeshua is the literal word of God, He is the Bread of Life (John 6:35). The verb "proceeds" is in the present tense, denoting an ongoing process. Psalms 34:8 and 119:103 tell us that, when we taste our Lord, Who is the Word of God, it is so good that it is as sweet as honey to our mouths. This can only be done spiritually (1 Peter 2:1-5). As we are spiritually fed the living Word of God, we are ultimately filled with the Holy Spirit (Ephesians 5:18-21). We are, then, not in the flesh but in the Spirit, and the Spirit in us (Romans 8:8-10).

The Holy Scriptures also say that the Word of God is pleasing to the spiritual taste buds. Jeremiah 15:16 tells us that, when we spiritually eat the Word of God, our hearts rejoice and are joyful because we are, thereby, called by the name of God. When we spiritually eat the Word of God, we spiritually live.

In John 6:22-58, Yeshua discusses the spiritually reborn child's need for spiritual nourishment. Yeshua, teaching the people at Capernaum, explained to them that they should not seek after Him because He feeds them physical food, but they should seek after Him for the food that never perishes and lasts forever so that one hungers no more. But to do so, they must believe on Him whom God hath sent. Yeshua goes on to explain that He is the Bread of Life; no man can come to Him unless the Father draws him.

By spiritually eating and drinking the Word of God, we can have eternal life. Everyone who gains this eternal life must spiritually eat the flesh of the Son of Man and spiritually drink His blood (John 6:53). Obviously, Yeshua was not discussing the eating or drinking of His physical flesh and blood. Yeshua is the Word of God, and so he who reads or hears the Word of God spiritually eats and drinks of it and will have everlasting life.

We have talked about spiritually tasting the good Word of God, but what about tasting the powers of the age to come? These powers are those of our triune Godhead that will be exercised in and through us beginning the moment of our spiritual rebirths, continuing throughout our earthly lives, into the millennium age and forevermore. When we are ultimately glorified in and through

Yeshua, God will have completed His good work in us to do His will (Philippians 1:6; Hebrews 12:23; 13:20-21). We cannot begin to imagine what it will be like to be active participants as God, the Father, demonstrates His awesome power over all of creation in and through us for all eternity. When this happens to a child of God, he will no longer utter deceit (Job 27:3-4) and he will possess each of the characteristics of Yeshua, the head of His Spiritual Body.

The Characteristics of the Children of God

In Matthew 5:3-12, Yeshua describes, through the Beatitudes, what the personality traits are of every reborn child of God. We do not possess one or some of these traits. We possess all of them, just as Yeshua does. Once spiritually reborn, we are transformed into the image of Yeshua. We resemble Him in spiritual appearance but, more importantly, we resemble Him in His ways and characteristics. We are poor in spirit, mourners, meek, hungry and thirsty for righteousness, merciful, pure in heart, peacemakers, and persecuted for righteousness' and for Yeshua's sake. As possessors of these personality traits, we shall receive the blessings that are set forth in these verses. We shall, therefore, inherit the Kingdom of heaven, be comforted, inherit the earth, be completely satisfied, obtain mercy, see God, and receive a great reward in heaven. These traits and resultant blessings go hand-in-hand. They are mutually inclusive.

At the end of each of the messages to the seven churches in the Book of Revelation, Yeshua promises additional rewards to every child of God who overcomes. For instance, in Revelation 2:7, Yeshua promises to give each of us the right to eat from the tree of life, which is in the paradise of God. This promise confirms that our redemption, achieved by our faith and belief in the death, burial and resurrection of our Savior, Yeshua HaMashiach, we have been brought full circle back to the Garden and are allowed to do what Adam and Eve could not do because of their disobedience.

In Revelation 2:11, the children of God who overcome shall not be hurt by the second death, that is, by eternal damnation and separation from God. Yeshua also promises to give to every victorious child of God the hidden manna to eat and a white stone with a new name written on it that no one knows except the child to whom it is given (Revelation 2:17).

To every child of God who remains obedient to the end, Yeshua, citing Psalm 2:8-9 and, perhaps, Revelation 12:5 and 19:15, further promises that they shall reign with him over the nations with a rod of iron. He will also give them the Morning Star (Revelation 2:26-28). We know the Morning Star is Yeshua by His own words (Revelation 22:16).

Every child of God who overcomes, Yeshua will clothe in white raiment, will not have his name blotted out of the Book of Life and Yeshua will confess his name before His father and the angels (Revelation 3:5).

The promised rewards get even more amazing. In Revelation 3:12, Yeshua states that every child of God who overcomes shall be made a pillar in the temple of God and shall go out no more. Yeshua shall write upon him or her the name of His God, the name of the city of His God, which is the new Jerusalem that will come out of heaven from His God, and His new name. The *Thomas Wilson Study Bible*, in Footnote 3:11-13, tells us the name of His God shows ownership, the name of the city shows heavenly citizenship, and His new name indicates co-heirship with Yeshua.

Finally, Yeshua promises to every child of God who overcomes the privilege to sit with Him on His throne, just as He overcame and now sits with His Father on His throne (Revelation 3:21). As individual and collective members of the Spiritual Body of Yeshua, we shall, indeed, be wherever He is, including on His throne that is beside the very throne of God. We should take time to meditate on the significance of these rewards especially since not one of the children of God can claim that he deserves any of them. In fact, every one of us deserves the same fate as the children of Satan.

We must have the mindset of little children to enter the Kingdom of heaven (Mark 10:13-16). Just as Yeshua totally depended on God for His every need, so must we. Just as Yeshua continually sought to do God's will, so must we. Just as Yeshua loved the world more than Himself, so must we. When we love as Yeshua loves, God, Who is love, indwells us and we, thereby, become love. We are God in the flesh, just as is Yeshua (1 John 4:16) because we are in Yeshua. Such a reality is incredibly true and has always been the created purpose of Mankind.

As the children of God spiritually nurtured with the Word of God, we begin to bear the fruit of the Spirit and manifest love, joy, peace, longsuffering, gentleness, goodness, faith, meekness, temperance, tender mercies, humbleness, forbearance and charity. Above all these virtues is charity (love) that binds them all together in perfect unity. (Galatians 5:22-26; Colossians 3:12-17). Our lives are thereby completely changed and it will be self-evident to all who observe us. In fact, they will be so enthralled with who we have become, they will inquire of us how they can also obtain these Godly characteristics. This, of course, provides opportunities for us to witness and testify about our personal salvations through Yeshua the Messiah.

As maturing children of God, it becomes more and more difficult for us to sin. We will still sin, but we will sin less and less and less. For it is written, he who is born of God cannot sin

(1 John 3:9). *The Thomas Nelson Study Bible's* footnote to this verse tells us that it means that we will not give in to habitual sin. The more we are focused on Yeshua and His charge to spread His Gospel, the more productive we will be and the more we become one with Him. Indeed, the Holy Scriptures tell us that, whenever a child of God is instructed to perform a Godly service, we are to salute no man (2 Kings 4:29; Luke 10:4). In other words, we cannot allow ourselves to become distracted from the mission at hand. As the children of God, we must strive to be Godly 100 percent of the time. Ours is not a part-time relationship with our heavenly Father.

How wonderful it will be to live in God's Kingdom, which will be composed only of citizens who, being one with God, will exhibit these Godly characteristics. Imagine, if you will, billions of people who resemble Yeshua in every way. The creative energy and power of only one of these faithful children of God would be too great to fathom, let alone billions of people who can do all that Yeshua did in His earthly ministry and more. The traffic of supernatural events destined to simultaneously take place in every corner of the universe, involving dimensions yet unknown, is simply too mind-boggling for us to appreciate.

Even more exciting is the fact that all of this will be accomplished by the humblest of people, each of whom indwells God and God indwells them being individually and collectively one with Him. Because of their oneness with God, they will be all-knowing, all-powerful, and ever-present and will have as their very natures all of God's characteristics, attributes, and mannerisms the most important of which is His unconditional, uncompromising, limitless, and selfless love. All that is God is driven by love. So shall it be with each of His children. In our current temporal existence, we live in the hope of this eventuality, but our timeless eternal God is forever experiencing it.

I recently had a conversation with a dear friend who made a wonderful comment on the life of a child of God who awaits his or her ultimate glorification through Yeshua. Essentially, he said let us take each day, each moment, indeed, each breath as a gift from God. Let us live in the present, moment by moment, giving thanks to God for each moment whether it be good or bad. Let us experience each moment with a loving, obedient, and forgiving heart for we know that all things work together for the good of those who love God and who are called according to His purpose (Romans 8:28). Let us begin each new morning with compassions that are new because that is what our faithful God does (Lamentations 3:22-23). I submit to you that this is very close to how Yeshua lived His earthly life. With the help of the Holy Spirit, in and through Yeshua HaMashiach, we can live similar lives as the born-again children of God.

The Characteristics of the Children of Satan

Just as the children of God possess the personality traits of Yeshua, the children of disobedience possess the personality traits of their father, the devil. They are liars; participators in unnatural sex, filled with all unrighteousness, fornication, wickedness, covetousness, maliciousness, envy, murder, strife, deceit, evil-mindedness; whisperers; backbiters; haters of God; violent; proud; boasters; inventors of evil things; disobedient to parents; without understanding; covenant breakers; without natural affection; unforgiving; and unmerciful (Romans 1:21-31). They not only do all these terrible things but they also take pleasure in anyone who does these things (Romans 1:32).

When Satan became one with Mankind through sin, Satan's sinful nature became Mankind's sinful nature. The children of Satan sin because the devil has sinned from the beginning (1 John

3:8). Their sinful states progressively worsen as they continually deceive and are deceived (2 Timothy 3:13). Being carnally minded, they are enemies of God and cannot be subjected to His law (Romans 8:7). The children of God are spiritually fed the bread and wine of God, which is the metaphorical body and blood of Yeshua HaMashiach. The children of Satan spiritually eat the bread of wickedness and drink the wine of violence (Proverbs 4:17). They do the lusts of their father, the devil (John 8:44). According to Yeshua, the Pharisees were the children of Satan who do the lustful deeds of their father (John 8:41-44). Yeshua prohibits the preaching of the Gospel to these offspring of Satan (Matthew 7:6) mainly because it will fall on deaf ears (Matthew 13:15) and will not change their sinful behavior (2 Peter 2:20-22). They will be judged according to their works (Revelation 20:12-15).

The Holy Scriptures also tell us that certain children of Satan, including the Apostle Judas Iscariot, possessed the Godly power to cast out demons and heal the sick in Yeshua's name, yet, they will never enter the Kingdom of heaven because they are children of Satan, working iniquity (Matthew 10:1-8; Luke 23:3; Matthew 7:21-23). Contrarily, the children of God cast out devils in Yeshua's name because of their relationship with Him (Matthew 7:21-23, Mark 3:13-19, 6:7-13, 9:39-41, Luke 6:13-16, 9:1-6).

All who sin is of the devil (1 John 3:8). Therefore, Adam and Eve's sin of disobedience caused them to be under Satan's authority. Adam and Eve may not have fully understood the extent of their relationship with Satan that was established because of their sin. They thought that they could be their own boss, that they could give birth to a people and provide for their physical and spiritual needs forever without any assistance from God or Satan. In reality, they are either children of God, the Father, destined for eternal life and oneness with Him, or Satan's children destined for eternal damnation, destruction, and oneness with him. It must be one or the other. Neutrality is not an option. Yeshua said that He will vomit out of His mouth all who are lukewarm (Revelations 3:15-16).

Being lukewarm in our obedience to the Lord is probably something that every one of us has had to deal with in one form or fashion, especially in these times when tolerance and compromise is the order of the day. This is particularly true in my case as well. My family and I devoutly participated in Easter and Christmas celebrations complete with dyed eggs, decorated trees, and gift-giving. However, subsequent to my spiritual rebirth, the more I got into the Word of God, the more I began to realize that these religious holidays were a tolerant attempt to combine Godly and pagan practices.

For instance, the word Easter has its origins in the pagan worship of Ishtar, the goddess of fertility. As the bunny rabbit is a symbol of prolific fertility, it and the dyed "Easter" eggs are an integral part of Mankind's "Easter" Sunday celebrations. It was thought prudent to allow such practices to merge with the celebration of the death, burial and resurrection of Yeshua the Messiah to ensure that more pagans would willingly join the church. The church's tolerance of these pagan practices demonstrates a willingness to embrace both Satan and God, a lukewarm approach at best. In truth, we either hate God or hate Satan. We cannot serve both (Matthew 6:24). Every reborn child of God should abstain from incorporating traditions, which have their origins in pagan worship, into their celebration of God's sacrificial act of salvation.

Another example is the celebration of Yeshua's birth along with the decoration of Christmas trees and exchanging of gifts. Jeremiah 10:1-4 tell us not to go into the forest and cut down a tree, nail it so that it can stand upright and decorate it as the heathens do. These verses tell us that, as far back as Jeremiah's day, pagans worshipped tree gods and would cut them down, place them in prominent places, decorate them and place gifts beneath them. This practice is still done today by professed Christians as part of their celebration of the birth of Yeshua.

Once again, this pagan ritual was intentionally combined with a Godly celebration to lure more members into the faith. There is no Scriptural support for Yeshua being born in December. Nor is there support for the celebration of His birth. If we truly love God for what He has done, and continue to do, in our lives, individually and collectively, can we so thoughtlessly and disrespectfully participate in traditions that have their origin in pagan idol worship? Would it not be a demonstration of our love of God to completely remove any vestige of these traditions from our lives? It is the least we can do for our God Who has lovingly and graciously done so much for us.

History clearly establishes that this effort to mix pagan worship with Godly worship succeeded. But at what cost? If confronted with the decision to abstain from any inclusion of pagan practices with their Godly celebrations, how many of today's Christians would refuse to do so? Would not most of them steadfastly defend their actions as being traditional and nothing more, that they are not worshipping these false idols? While this may be true, I submit that there is a subconscious recognition of the existence of the pagan idol by our willingness to place it in our lives. Would our Lord and Savior, Yeshua, condone any conduct that has its origins in unholy pagan rituals? If I were to bring a statute of Baal into my home for use solely as a coat rack, would I not grieve the Holy Spirit by having an abomination to God in His presence since He lives in me? Given God's demonstration of His great, unconditional love for every one of us, should we dishonor that love by engaging in practices the origins of which are unholy? God forbid!

To be fair, the Holy Scriptures do say that the children of God, in their freedom in Yeshua, can be in the presence of idols and, indeed, eat meat offered to idols because we know Whose we are. Specifically, the Apostle Paul addresses this issue in his first letter to the Corinthians (1 Corinthians 8). Essentially, the Apostle informs us that, because of the freedom we have in Yeshua, the Messiah, we can sit in the idol's temple and eat meat that was offered in sacrifice to idols because we know that there is only one true God with Whom we are one. However, we are cautioned that should this practice cause those who are watching to sin because of their lack of true knowledge, we should abstain from such acts. Every child of God is a light in this world which is shown before Mankind (Matthew 5:14-16). Even if we walk in the freedom that we have in Yeshua, many of those who are constantly observing us do not possess this knowledge and may see it as a contradiction of our faith and either remain in their sin or take offence to our actions. It seems a little unrealistic that the children of God could entertain such practices and see their actions as nothing more than tradition without acknowledging, as least subliminally, their historical idolatrous origins. It would be better to abstain from such traditions altogether.

Moreover, nowhere does the Apostle Paul suggest that it is appropriate to engage in the idolatrous ritual itself whether it be for worship or tradition. Indeed, he cautions us not to be taken away by the traditions of Mankind by walking according to the basic principles of the world and not after Messiah (Colossians 2:8). We simply cannot engage in the ritualistic traditions of Mankind that have their origin in pagan worship.

As spiritually reborn children of God, we must love God with all our hearts, souls and minds. Luke 14:26 gives us a sense of the extreme nature of our expected commitment to our triune Godhead. According to this verse, our commitment to God must be such that we disdain our parents, spouses, children, siblings and, indeed, our own lives if they get in the way of our efforts to follow Yeshua. It is of a certainty, then, that traditions, grounded in pagan worship, must have no part in the life of a child of God.

In the end, we are either extremists for God or extremists for Satan. We either love God with all our hearts, souls and minds or we love Satan and the world to this extent. How many times are we instructed in the Word of God to love and serve God with all our hearts, souls and minds? All those in the middle have no place in the Kingdom of God (Revelation 3:16). We should draw comfort and strength in the knowledge that we are considered extremists for God. If this is to be our walk with God, then let all the people of God say Amen.

Unfortunately, since Adam and Eve's fall from grace, many have shied away from a walk with God to this extent. To succeed in this world, they have, instead, chosen compromise, under the guise of tolerance, over absolute, unconditional, loving obedience to God. Anything less than extremism for God is delusional. The choice between God and the ruler of this world can never be subject to compromise. Again, no one can serve both God and mammon (Matthew 6:24).

The parable of the sower of seeds is illustrative (Matthew 13:3-23). In this parable, three categories of hearers of the Word will fall away. Only those who are grounded in their faith and affirmatively act out their faith in the Word, will bear fruit. Footnote 13:20-23 of the Book of Matthew in the *Thomas Nelson Study Bible* interprets these verses to suggest that only seeds that bear some measure of fruit are saved.

Faithful extremism for God is the foundation upon which our salvation rests in and through Yeshua HaMashiach. This level of extremism is constantly put to the test as the children of God are faced with the threat of persecution for their faith. Matthew 6:24 states the saints of God will suffer persecution unto death for His name's sake. 2 Thessalonians 2 tells us many of these believers, who profess a belief in Yeshua, will fall away when faced with a choice of continued physical life or physical suffering or death in steadfast faith in Messiah. This great "falling away" will occur because only extremists for God will be willing to pay the ultimate price and give up their earthly lives in support of their faith. The Holy Scriptures tell us that they will be few in number.

It is written:

Enter ye in at the strait gate: for wide is the gate, and broad is the way, that leadeth to destruction, and many there be which go in there at: Because strait is the gate, and narrow is the way, which leadeth unto life, and few there be that find it (Matthew 7:13-14).

In the Garden of Eden, Adam, being tempted with the lust of his flesh, the lust of his eyes, and the pride of his life, could have chosen to eat from the Tree of Life and not of the Tree of the Knowledge of Good and Evil. Had he done so, he would have attained eternal life in an incorruptible body. His decision demonstrated his lack of extremism for God. We are confronted daily with the same choice Adam had. We can either choose to spiritually eat the Word of God and have eternal life, or we can choose to spiritually eat Satan's words and have eternal damnation with him. There is no middle ground. Our hearts will determine the choices we make, and our choices have eternal consequences.

Our Victory Over Satan Through Yeshua the Messiah

Yeshua came that we may have life and have it more abundantly (John 10:10). When He abides in us and we in Him, we have a degree of living that is eternal and far superior to anything we may temporarily enjoy without Him. Until we accept Him as our Lord and Savior, we are not a part of Yeshua. He does not abide in us and we truly are lifeless. How wondrous is the second personage of our triune Godhead!

To get to this state of completeness in and through Yeshua, we must be able to stand against "the wiles of the devil" (Ephesians 6:11), who comes "to steal, and to kill, and to destroy" (John 10:10). This is spiritual hand-to-hand combat, the outcome of which determines the future of our souls. This battle that we fight does not occur against Mankind.

For we wrestle not against flesh and blood, but against principalities, against powers, against the rulers of the darkness of this world, against spiritual wickedness in high places (Ephesians 6:12).

But take heart, this is a war that we cannot lose. For "if God be for us, who can be against us?" (Romans 8:31). In fact, God has already won this war. Satan and this world were judged upon the death, burial and resurrection of Yeshua HaMashiach (John 12:31). We, who are in Yeshua, now have the victory over death (1 Corinthians 15:54-57). Execution of this judgment will be effectuated when Yeshua destroys the armies of Satan and ultimately casts Satan and his fallen angels into the lake of fire (Revelation 19:17-21; 20:10,14-15). As victors, we have eternal life that cannot be taken away from us (John 10:28-30, 17:2,

Romans 2:7, 1 John 2:25). God has fulfilled the promise of redemption made to Adam and Eve.

In 2 Corinthians 12:1-10, the Apostle Paul relates to us that he was given "a thorn in the flesh," which he defines as a messenger of Satan to torment him so that he would not be exalted above measure. I interpret this phrase to mean something physical which occasionally caused Paul to sin thereby keeping him in constant need of God's grace. Paul tells us that he asked God to remove this thing from him on three occasions, but God told him that His grace is sufficient. In other words, no matter how many times we lose the ongoing battle with our sin natures, God's grace is ever present to forgive us.

Through our weakness, God demonstrates His strength. After all, it is not our ability to remain sinless that secures our salvation. That was secured by Yeshua Messiah while we were yet sinners (Romans 5:8). It is our ever-developing intimacy with God which makes it easier for us to resist our sin natures, but there will still be occasions when our sinful natures win out. In every instance, upon our repentance, God's grace is there to forgive us allowing us to maintain the same degree of intimacy with Him, through Yeshua HaMashiach, which we enjoyed before each sin.

While this war is fought on an individual soul-by-soul basis, it is also fought collectively by the entire Spiritual Body of the Messiah, of which we are members (1 Corinthians 12:12-14). The Holy Scriptures tell us that the spiritually reborn children of God compose the Spiritual Body of Messiah. They are silent, however, as to exactly how many members constitute the His Spiritual Body.

Each of us is an individual member of that Body (Ephesians 5:30-31), with Yeshua Messiah as the Head. (Colossians 1:18). Yeshua nourishes and cherishes every member of His Body (Ephesians 5:29). Just as every member of the physical body has an individual function, every member of the Spiritual Body of Messiah also has an individual purpose that must be performed for the overall function of the Body to be perfect (Ephesians 4:11-16). The Scriptures describe these individual functions as spiritual gifts, which each member of the Spiritual Body of Messiah must identify and then exercise (Romans 12:4-8, 1 Corinthians 12:1-31).

The Spiritual Gifts of the Children of God

The moment we, by faith, accept God's promise of salvation and turn our lives over to our Messiah, we are spiritually born of God. We are physically born of man but spiritually born of God just like Yeshua. The Holy Scriptures refer to every spiritually reborn person as a child of God. As such, we are destined to be heirs to all that is God's and, upon maturity and glorification, will completely coexist and be one with God. The degree to which we are spiritually mature is directly related to the extent to which we can, through faith, access the limitless power of God.

One day we will be given incorruptible bodies and will be completely both the physical and spiritual children of God. This means that our bodies shall never again be susceptible to death, illness, deterioration, or evil. We shall be immortal and Godly in every respect. Until that day, as the spiritually born children of God, the Spirit of God lives in us and is a part of us. As we grow spiritually, we begin to identify and develop the spiritual gifts bestowed upon us by the Holy Spirit at our spiritual births (2 Corinthians 12:1-6). Our joy comes in the exercising of our spiritual gifts to the glory and honor of our Father, and the fulfillment of His will.

Thus, we are encouraged to pursue charity and desire spiritual gifts because, once we identify and develop them, we can perform our necessary functions in the Spiritual Body of Messiah (1 Corinthians 14:1). Every child of God can minister his unique gifts one to another, as good stewards of the manifold grace of God (1 Peter 4:10-11).

As spiritually reborn children of God, it is essential that we begin to understand and, indeed, use our spiritual gifts. Paul tells us in 1 Corinthians 12:4-11 that there are diversities of gifts, administrations, and operations, but the same Spirit, Lord, and God, which works all in all. In these passages, Paul lists some of the spiritual gifts that are given by the Holy Spirit. They are wisdom, the word of knowledge, faith, healing, the working of miracles, prophecy, discerning of spirits, divers kinds of tongues and interpretation of tongues. In Romans 12:3-8, these gifts are further identified to include ministry, teaching, exhortation, giving, and ruling. The Holy Spirit gives these spiritual gifts to every child of God severally as He will. We are cautioned, however, to try the spirits to ensure that everyone who claims to be ministering spiritual gifts is indeed doing so (1 John 4:1-6). We are counseled to put on the whole armor of God to ward off evil spirits with evil intentions (Ephesians 6:10-18).

As stated, the extent to which we can use our spiritual gifts is directly dependent upon the extent of our spiritual growth. Our spiritual growth is measured by the extent of our faith. There is no limit to God's faithfulness. Since there is only one faith (Ephesians 4:5), our faith is God's faith. Thus, there is no limit to our faith. It necessarily follows that there is no limit to our spiritual growth and the resulting spiritual fruit generated by the exercising of our spiritual gifts. We, thereby, store up treasures in heaven which we are encouraged by the Word of God to do (Matthew 6:20). Indeed, Luke 19:11-27 suggests that our heavenly rewards will be proportionate to the levels of our spiritual production on earth. I submit that the greatest treasure to be found and secured is the treasure that is within us, the Holy Spirit, and eternal life in the Kingdom of Heaven (2 Corinthians 4:7; Matthew 13:44). "For where your treasure is, there will your heart be also" (Luke 12:34).

It is unfortunate that it takes the children of God so many years to grow enough in faith so that the Holy Spirit, who indwells them, can manifest His power through the exercising of their spiritual gifts. For instance, with respect to the spiritual gift of healing, the Holy Spirit tells us, in James 5:14, to call on the elders of the church to pray over and anoint with oil the sick in the name of the Lord. Apparently, it takes some of us decades of spiritual growth before we can recognize and effectively utilize the God-given spiritual gift of healing. Our spiritual maturation is inhibited because we allow our sin natures to hold us back. However, for others, the manifestation of their spiritual gifts is quick and forceful. We have been set free from this sin-nature bondage, but we must live in that freedom for the Holy Spirit to manifest Himself powerfully and yet lovingly in and through us by way of our spiritual gifts. It is only then that we will begin to bear spiritual fruit and fully enjoy the benefits of being children of God.

The Requirement of Suffering for the Children of God

As previously discussed, we, who were chosen by God to be His children, compose the Spiritual Body of our Messiah. It is important that we understand what the Spirit of God is telling us when He refers to all children of God as composing the Spiritual Body of Messiah. We are, literally, the collective spiritual embodiment of Yeshua, the Word of God. When Yeshua said He is the way and that no person can come to the Father unless it is by Him (John 14:6), He meant it literally. We enter the presence of God in heaven only because Yeshua is there and we are His Spiritual Body. In John 14:1-14, Yeshua is saying because He is in the Father and the Father is in Him, every believer is also in the Father as members of His Spiritual Body. The spirit of every child of God is assigned to a specific part of Messiah's Spiritual Body. 1 Corinthians 12:12-26 confirm this fact by analogizing the members of the Spiritual Body of Messiah to various parts of the human body.

We are reconciled to God because God only sees His Son Who paid the price for the sins of the members of His Spiritual Body. We have eternal life only because Yeshua is eternal life. We cannot have eternal life separate and apart from Yeshua. We are heirs as the children of God only because Yeshua is the Son of God. We shall reign with Yeshua because He is the King of Kings and the Lord of Lords. We go wherever Yeshua goes and experiences all that He is because we are His Spiritual Body. There is nothing that Yeshua does that we will not also do. We cannot be anywhere that Yeshua is not, nor can Yeshua be anywhere that we are not. Yeshua says as much in John 14:1-3. Thus, because Yeshua lives, we live.

It is important for us to keep in mind that Yeshua is the Alpha and the Omega (Revelation 1:8). He is the fulfillment of the beginning, the end and everything in between. As members of His Spiritual Body, so shall we be. That is the incredible truth that many children of God fail to fully appreciate. When God said, "Let us make man in our image, after our likeness" (Genesis 1:26), His creative intention was for us to be members of the Spiritual Body of Messiah and part of the triune Godhead through His spoken Word.

The Holy Scriptures contain several passages that state that God knew His children before our earthly lives (Romans 8:29; Ephesians 1:3-6, 11; 2 Titus 1:9; 1 Peter 1:2). Some have argued that Mankind must have had an eternal spiritual existence. It is posited that, because Yeshua's Spiritual Body has always existed, the creation of Mankind was for the specific purpose of providing physical temples to house the members of the eternal Spiritual Body of Messiah. Under this rationale, Mankind became living souls when Yeshua breathed His spiritual life into Adam who was formed from the dust of the earth. Ecclesiastes 12:7 tells us, upon death, the spirit returns to God Who gave it. Creation week would then be for the specific purpose of establishing spiritual and physical realms in which our God could manifest His glory through His Son's Spiritual Body.

It necessarily follows that, just as Yeshua physically and spiritually suffered in this world, every member of His Spiritual Body will do so physically and spiritually (Romans 8:17, Galatians 2:20, 2 Timothy 3:12), according to his or her purpose and place in the Body as determined by the Holy will of God. The faithfulness of God will preserve our souls so that our suffering will not be in vain. It is the same faithfulness of God that ensures that Messiah's suffering was not in vain.

We cannot be members of Yeshua's Spiritual Body if we do not suffer as He suffered. Every part of His body suffered for our sins, some parts more than others. After Yeshua's resurrection, while in His glorified body, He appeared to His disciples still bearing his sacrificial wounds (John 20:27-29). Revelation 5:6, as well as other passages of the Bible, describe the Lamb "as it had been slain" before the throne of God during the tribulation. Yeshua, who is that Lamb of God, continues to bear the wounds of His sacrifice at least until God's redemptive plan has been completed and, possibly, forevermore as a constant reminder to all of creation the magnitude of His sacrifice.

There is no other option for the children of God. For the Holy Spirit tells us in 2 Timothy 3:12 that all, who will live Godly in Yeshua Messiah, shall suffer persecution. He did not say that some will suffer, He said all will suffer persecution.

Therefore, Romans 12:1-2 tell us to:

present your bodies a living sacrifice, holy, acceptable unto God, which is your reasonable service. And be not conformed to this world: but be ye transformed by the renewing of your mind, that ye may prove what is that good, and acceptable, and perfect, will of God.

What is this suffering that we are expected to endure? According to Mark 10:21, we may be called upon to give up all worldly possessions. Deprivation of earthly possessions, whether self-induced or otherwise, is a form of suffering in a materialistic world. Yeshua had no earthly wealth to speak of (2 Corinthians 8:9). It is only when we do not seek or value earthly possessions that our heavenly Father gives them to us. We are then able to put them in their proper perspective, knowing as we do that they are not our possessions at all;, they are God's. It's when we intentionally decide to hold onto our earthly possessions and our lives that we end up losing both (John 12:25, Acts 5:1-11).

This is the lesson taught to us through the parable of the rich young ruler who obeyed God's commandments in every respect but was told by Yeshua that he lacked one thing, and that was to sell all he had and to take up the cross and follow Him. The young man went away sad because he was not willing to suffer financially for Yeshua's sake. He thought that his riches were his and not God's. He did not want to part with what he really did not own. He had stored up his hope and aspirations in earthly treasures. If he possessed the Godly characteristic of unconditional and uncompromising love, he would have willingly and gladly parted with the riches he possessed and followed Yeshua because he would have wanted to demonstrate his love of God by being obedient to Yeshua thereby storing up eternal treasures in heaven.

Thus, we are cautioned that it is extremely difficult and almost impossible for one, who believes that he owns the earthly riches he was blessed to possess, to enter the Kingdom of Heaven (Mark 10:23-27). In Chapter 6 of his first letter to Timothy, the Apostle Paul explains why it is so hard for the rich to keep their heart with God and how, by putting their trust in God, they can simultaneously enjoy their God-given riches and their relationship with their Creator. It is not an evil thing to be blessed with riches. Abraham, Job, David, Solomon, and other great men of God were so blessed. However, when we treasure our worldly possessions more than our intimacy with our heavenly Father, we demonstrate our lack of love for Him. Again, "For where your treasure is, there will your heart be also" (Matthew 6:21).

Obviously, our suffering is also physical since we are to take up the cross and suffer just as Yeshua physically suffered unto death for us. Indeed, God's children have suffered all manner of physical persecution since the death of Abel. Such persecutions continue to this very day.

There is an ongoing debate within the Spiritual Body of Yeshua as to when the Rapture will occur (1 Thessalonians 4:14-18). Some say it will be a pre-tribulation rapture and the children of God will not be part of the persecution foretold during the first half of that seven-year period. They reason the Children of God are not appointed to His wrath (1 Thessalonians 5:9).

However, the Holy Scriptures tell us that God's wrath is not poured out until the second half of the seven-year tribulation period (Revelation 11:18-19; 13:5; 16). It may be God's will that His children witness to the world during the first half of this tribulation period, suffer persecution and die for His name's sake. If we suffer in the flesh for the glory of Messiah, we are told that we cease from sin (1 Peter 4:1) and that we will fare better at our judgment before the Messiah (1 Peter 4:12-19).

There is arguably Biblical support for the proposition that the children of God will suffer unto death during the first half of the tribulation period. This suffering will not be put upon the saints by the outpouring of God's wrath. Instead, it will be the consequences of the war with the AntiChrist. The Ambassadors of Christ ("AOC") Network has published a series of videos that posit that the two witnesses, identified in Revelation 11:3, are two groups of people, instead of two individuals, based, in part, on Revelation 11:4 that describes these two witnesses as "Two Olive Trees" and "Two Lampstands."

These videos go on to explain that Jeremiah 11:16-17 depicts the nation of Israel as "A green olive tree." Jewish believers, therefore, a part of this olive tree. Romans 11:13-24 tells us that Gentile believers, who are their own wild olive tree, are grafted into the good olive tree, i.e., the Jewish olive tree. In other words, it is argued the two witnesses could be Jewish and Gentile believers represented as the two olive trees, one grafted into the other.

These same videos cite to Revelation 1:20 to confirm that Scripture defines Lampstands to be churches. While Chapters 2-3 of Revelation was intended for the believers of that time, they are also intended for every believer since that time. The seven churches described in these two chapters are seven types of believers, only two of which were found by Yeshua to be blameless before Him. The churches of Smyrna and Philadelphia describe two types of believers who, collectively, are persecuted, poor and who have kept His Word and has not denied His name.

Finally, these videos tell us that these two types of believers will be empowered by the Holy Spirit, as described in Revelation 11:1-14, for a period of 3 half years during which the AntiChrist will make war with them, will eventually overcome these empowered saints and leave their bodies unburied. According to AOC, just as Yeshua's body was destroyed after His 3 half year ministry, His Spiritual Body must also be destroyed after its 3 half year ministry (Romans 12:5; 1 Corinthians 12:27; Revelation 11:3). According to AOC, the end of the seven-year tribulation period will mark the end of all suffering by the Spiritual Body of Yeshua because these martyred believers will be caught up to be with Yeshua in heaven and they will immediately return with Him to begin their thousand-year reign with Yeshua.

AOC's contention assumes a mid- or post- tribulation rapture. However, most Biblical scholars disagree with this position and, instead, believe the rapture will occur pre-tribulation and it will be the 144,000 Jewish believers, identified in the Book of Revelation, who will convert new believers and, who, collectively, will war with the AntiChrist during the first 3 half years of the tribulation period. I say this because ancient Galilean weddings lasted seven days and the wedding of an ancient Galilean king lasted seven years. Therefore, it may be the marriage feast of the Lamb of God is a seven-year event. Assuming a pre-tribulation rapture, the marriage feast may take place during the seven-year tribulation period.

The support for this position is best explained in the documentary film entitled *Before the Wrath* directed by Brent Miller Jr. In this film, the uniquely specific parallels between a Galilean wedding and Yeshua's return are discussed. The film focuses on Yeshua's description of his return as contained in the

Holy Scriptures and documents how it is indistinguishable from the rituals of a Galilean wedding. Assuming the children of God is taken out of the world before the tribulation, we shall not have to endure the suffering associated with that seven-year period whether it be through persecution or God's wrath.

A third form of suffering is emotional suffering because we shall suffer false accusations (Matthew 5:11) and tribulations (Romans 5:3, 2 Thessalonians 1:4). However, we should take heart. Paul tells us, in Romans 5:3-5, that our suffering ultimately leads to our hope which triggers the outpouring of God's love into our hearts. We know, from earlier chapters, that faith is the realization of all things hoped for (Hebrews 11:1) and love always hopes (1 Corinthians 13:7). Therefore, our suffering will, in due time, bring about the hope of our salvation (Romans 8:24) and of eternal life (Titus 3:7). Yeshua and God, the Father, have promised us that They shall never leave us nor forsake us (Matthew 28:20; Hebrews 13:5). Consequently, none of these trials can separate us from the love of Yeshua (Romans 8:35). Indeed, God uses our sufferings to perfect, establish and settle us (1 Peter 5:10). In 2 Corinthians 12:10, Paul writes:

> Therefore, I take pleasure in infirmities, in reproaches, in necessities, in persecutions, in distresses for Messiah's sake: for when I am weak, then am I strong.

Finally, the Holy Scriptures speak of another form of physical suffering. In Isaiah 53:4 and Matthew 8:16-17, we are told that Yeshua heals the sick by taking the infirmities upon Himself and bearing the sicknesses of those He heals. Indeed, Isaiah 53:3-4 inform us that Yeshua was despised and forsaken by men, was a man of pains, acquainted with sickness, bore our sicknesses, carried our pains, reckoned to have been struck down by God and afflicted.

As members of the Spiritual Body of Messiah, every child of God may have to similarly endure such suffering and similarly, lovingly take on the infirmities, sicknesses, and pain of those whom Yeshua heals through us. However, we know that love beareth all things (1 Corinthians 13:7). Our reconciliation through Yeshua Messiah may mean such infirmities, sicknesses, and pain shall not be attributed to us as we are blameless and righteous before God in and through Yeshua.

Ultimately, the more we suffer for Yeshua's sake, the stronger we become because it is through our divine deliverance from these travails that we see the power of God manifested in our lives. The more intimate we become with Yeshua through these trials and tribulations, the more we see, understand, and take on the characteristics and attributes of God which shall completely replace our sinful natures upon our spiritual rebirths, glorification, and unification with God. Because we have suffered with Yeshua, we shall be glorified with Him (Romans 8:17) and will reign with Him (2 Timothy 2:12). Therefore, we must believe on Yeshua the Messiah and suffer for His sake (Philippians 1:29). It is better, if God wills it, that we suffer for good than for bad (1 Peter 3:17). Yeshua Messiah suffered leaving us an example that we should follow his steps (1 Peter 2:21).

It may very well be that every reborn child of God, depending on where in the Spiritual Body of Yeshua he or she is located, will suffer to the same extent that the corresponding part of the physical body of Yeshua suffered. Obviously, certain parts of Yeshua's body bore the brunt of His persecution. However, since He was tortured to the point that He was barely recognizable as a person, very few parts of His body were spared the shedding of blood. Nonetheless, the Holy Spirit, tells us that when one member of Yeshua's body suffers, all the other members suffer (1 Corinthians 12:26). Once our Lord can say "It is finished" with respect to the suffering of His collective Spiritual Body, the time for His, and our, glorious union with our Lord and Savior may be but a command of God away. While Yeshua knew when His earthly sacrifice would be finished (John 19:30), only God knows the day and hour when the sacrifice of the collective Spiritual Body of Messiah is finished and the Son of Man will return (Mark 13:24-37).

This requirement of suffering further explains why the road to heaven is narrow with few on it and why the road to damnation is wide and many are on it (Matthew 7:13-14). Few are willing to suffer materially, physically and emotionally for the glory of Yeshua HaMashiach even though our redemption was accomplished by the material, physical and emotional sacrifice of God Himself through Yeshua. Many are unwilling to demonstrate the same measure of love that God so passionately showed us.

As members of the Spiritual Body of Messiah, all who wish to accept this redemption must be willing to give up everything (Luke 5:11, 28; 18:28-30) and endure to the end the same sacrificial suffering Yeshua endured, each according to the manner and prescription as determined by the Holy will of God. We must be willing to give up our sin-nature and be transformed to His God-nature, which is our predestination. If we choose not to do so and remain unsaved, we will lose our lives. However, if we choose to give up our sinful lives and be transformed, we will live forever. Thus, in Matthew 10:39, Yeshua tells us: "He that findeth his life shall lose it: and he that loseth his life for my sake shall find it."

For many Christians, it is difficult to accept the teachings of Yeshua that we are members of His Spiritual Body, and, as such, must suffer as He suffered, especially since that necessarily means that some of us may suffer more than others even though we may be members of undesirable and seemingly insignificant parts of the Spiritual Body of Messiah.

The best scriptural passage that explains the relationship between the different members of the Spiritual Body of Messiah is contained in Paul's first letter to the Corinthians. In 1 Corinthians 12, Paul states that, as the physical body is one and has many members, all being members of that one body, so is the Spiritual Body of Messiah. We are baptized by one Spirit into Messiah's Spiritual Body, whether we are Jews or Gentiles, bond or free. We have all been made to drink into one Spirit. He goes on to explain that no member of the body can remove itself because it isn't as important as it would like to be, implying that some members of the Spiritual Body of Messiah may feel that their position and function in the Body is not commensurate with the degree of suffering they are asked to endure. God, the Father, has set the members the way He would have them—as it pleases Him.

Our Functions as Members of the Body of Messiah

Each member of the Spiritual Body of Messiah is assigned a function unique unto himself/herself that must be identified and lovingly exercised so that the Body can be whole (Ephesians 4:14-16). In addition, each member of the Body has need of every other member (1 Corinthians 12:12-31). The Apostle Paul informs us that we bestow on those members of the Body that we think to be less honorable more abundant honor and comeliness. Yeshua said: "He that is least among you all, the same shall be great" (Luke 9:48). When describing John the Baptist, Yeshua said that, despite his greatness, the least in the Kingdom of Heaven shall be greater than John the Baptist (Matthew 11:11).

In other words, no matter how significant our functions may be on earth as members of the Spiritual Body of Messiah, the extent of our greatness in God's Kingdom is directly proportionate to the extent to which we serve others. In other words, we must have a "servant-of-all" mentality.

According to Yeshua, the one who consigns himself to be the servant of everyone else is the greatest of all (Matthew 19:30, 20:16, 26-28, Mark 10:35-45, Luke 13:30, Philippians 2:3-4). Taking these verses literally, we must conclude that the Holy Spirit is telling us when every member of the Spiritual Body of Messiah lovingly and unconditionally seeks to serve every other member of the Body before giving any thought to serving his/her own interests, then every member is the servant of all and, by definition, is the least of all members.

Yet, because every member of the Spiritual Body of Messiah has this same servant-of-all mentality and, therefore, is the least in the Kingdom of God, each member also becomes the greatest in the Kingdom of God because every other member of the Body is committed to serve him lovingly and unconditionally. *When everyone serves all, all serves everyone.* What this means is that all members of the Spiritual Body of Messiah are the least and the greatest at the same time because all lovingly and unconditionally serve all and are, in turn, lovingly and unconditionally served by all. Imagine being completely in love with every person you meet, pouring everything you are into serving their every need without any concern or fear of vulnerability or abuse. Imagine further that every person you encounter treats you the same way. Can God's highest creation have a more wonderfully perfect oneness with each other and their Lord and Savior than this? Is not this the expected result when one considers that fact that we are talking about a Kingdom of Love since our triune Godhead is love?

This is how God has composed the Spiritual Body of Messiah, so that there would be no schism in the Body: The comely parts having no need of honor, but the uncomely parts, thought to be less honorable, needing and obtaining more abundant honor (1 Corinthians 12:23). In this way, the Spiritual Body of Messiah is whole, complete, and perfect. If one member suffers, all suffer; if one member is honored, all are honored and rejoice (1 Corinthians 12:26).

Paul concludes Chapter 12 by using the analogy of the physical body, saying that we are all the Spiritual Body of Messiah and yet individual members, each having different functions with different gifts. In his letter to the Romans, the Apostle further tells us that, ultimately, we should strive for love and not spiritual gifts or glorified functions of the Body (Romans 12:3-21). Given what we have discussed concerning the overriding importance of Godly love in God's ordered creation, we should have some measure of appreciation for and understanding about why the Apostle Paul places so much emphasis on love.

God does not honor any one member of the Spiritual Body of Messiah more than any other. When Moses exhorted Israel to love the stranger and fear the Lord because of the great things He had done for them, he emphasized that God shows no partiality nor takes bribes (Deuteronomy 10:12-22). Jehoshaphat set up judges in the land of Judah and told them to fear the Lord when they judge because there is no iniquity with the Lord, nor does He respect people. Again, we are reminded that the Lord does not take bribes (2 Chronicles 19:4-7).

When Peter preached to the Gentiles, he told them that, of a truth, God is impartial (Acts 10:34). Paul said the same thing in his letter to the Romans (Romans 2:11) and in his letter to the Galatians (Galatians 2:6). Whether we are children of parents, servants, masters, bond, or free, we are to perform our functions willingly as the servants of Messiah, doing the will of God from the heart, "knowing that [our] Master also is in heaven; neither is there respect of persons with him" (Ephesians 6:1-9).

Just as God does not show partiality to anyone, Yeshua also does not favor one part of His Spiritual Body over any other part. We are all equal partakers of the Bread of Life (1 Corinthians 10:17). Yeshua tells us that, whenever someone comes to Him, being drawn by God, He will in no way cast him out (John 6:37). In other words, once we are saved, we will always be saved. If this were not true, then the eternal life every child of God obtains by receiving the Spirit of God when spiritually reborn is not eternal at all, and the promises contained in John 3:15; 4:36; 10:28; and 17:2 are lies. John 10:28 and Ephesians 5:30 essentially say that one who has been given to Yeshua by God receives eternal life, is sealed by the Holy Ghost until the day of redemption and cannot be plucked out of the hands of our triune Godhead.

As spiritually reborn members of the Spiritual Body of Messiah, we are one with Him and are no longer of this world, as He is not of this world. We are hated by this world just as He was hated. However, though we are hated and persecuted by the powers and principalities that temporarily control this world, we are loved by God. When Yeshua returns, we will become mirror images of Him in all His glory. We shall be pure love, just as His is, having incorruptible and glorified bodies full of His every mannerism and attribute. We will then be sufficiently compatible with God to be completely inhabited by Him, enabling Him to manifest Himself in and through us forever. As His holy temples, individually and collectively, we will become active participants with our God as He lives and acts through and with us forevermore.

Just as Aaron and his descendants in the Old Testament served as a priesthood to God for the people of Israel, Yeshua and the spiritually reborn of God are a generation chosen to be a royal priesthood (1 Peter 2:9) making supplications, prayers, intercessions and thanks on behalf of all Mankind (1 Timothy 2:1). We perform our priestly function every time we go to God in prayer. As a holy priesthood, we offer up spiritual sacrifices acceptable to God (1 Peter 2:4-5). There was a time when the functions of God-appointed kings and priests were distinct and separate (1 Samuel 13:8-13). We, who are the express image of Yeshua, being members of His Spiritual Body, are made to be both kings and priests (Revelation 1:6; 5:10). We acquire our royalty and priestly status through Yeshua HaMashiach who is King of Kings (Revelation 17:14) and the high priest after the order of Melchizedek (Psalm 110:4; Hebrews 5:6, 10; 6:20; 7:11-28).

Webster's New World Dictionary defines "Order" as being "a group of persons constituting an association formed for some special purpose." In this context, then, this Order is comprised of individuals who serve the dual purpose of priests and kings in the service of God, the Father. As stated, these two functions were, for the most part, performed separately by the priests and kings of Israel and Judah. Yet, this Order does both.

Genesis 14:17-24 is our introduction to Melchizedek. According to these verses, Melchizedek was the king of Salem and, with the king of Sodom, came out to meet Abram after his victory over Chedorlaomer and the kings that were with him. Melchizedek is referred to as the king of Salem and a priest of the Most High God. Melchizedek blessed Abram and, in return, Abram gave tithes to Melchizedek of the spoils he possessed from his victory over the kings.

Hebrews 6:20-7:28 tell us more about Melchizedek, his Order and Yeshua's role as the high priest of this Order. For instance, we are told that Yeshua became a high priest forever after this Order. Melchizedek is described again as the King of Salem, the priest of the Most High God, a King of righteousness and of peace, with no parents and genealogy, eternal in nature having no beginning nor end of life and made like unto the Son of God performing his priestly duties continually. These verses also establish that Melchizedek was acknowledged by Abram to be superior to him so much so that he gave him a tenth of all the spoils he had from his victory. However, Melchizedek was not the high priest of this Order. Yeshua is the high priest.

Psalm 110:4 and Hebrews 5:6, 10; 6:20; and 7:11-28 confirm the existence of an Order of eternal priestly kings headed by Yeshua HaMashiach, its high priest Who continually intercedes on behalf of the members of His Spiritual Body. Because we are what He is, we shall also serve as priestly kings after this same Order.

Melchizedek, being eternal in nature and made like the Son of God, may be a member of this Order of priestly kings by and through Yeshua Messiah. Apparently, he is eternal because he is not a descendant of Adam and Eve as he has no father or mother. Since an Order is defined as a group of individuals formed for a special purpose, there must be additional members of this Order other than Melchizedek and Yeshua (and us through Yeshua). The only other scriptural reference to priestly kings, who are eternal in nature, having no beginning or end, is contained in the Book of Revelation.

Revelation 4:4 identifies twenty four elders who are enthroned around God, the Father's, throne in heaven and on whose heads are crowns of gold. Clearly, the inclusion of crowns in this description establishes that they are kings who have the form of men. Yet, they are spiritual beings. Revelation 5:8-10 informs us that these twenty-four kings perform the priestly function of offering up the prayers of saints and worshiping, through song, our Lord and Savior, Yeshua HaMashiach for their, and our, redemption. It is unclear why these spiritual beings would need redemption. It could be argued that each took on flesh, as did Melchizedek, and dwelt among Mankind.

There is no dispute that the Apostle John is describing a heavenly experience. Therefore, these twenty-four priestly kings must be eternal in nature. They would, thus, have no parents and no beginning or end. The fact that these kings are performing their priestly functions before Yeshua, the high priest, lends further credence to the hypothesis that they constitute the Order of which Melchizedek is a member and Yeshua is the high priest.

Taking this line of reasoning literally to its logical conclusion, as we must do, we see that Romans 8:29 and 1 Corinthians 3:18 tell us that every believer will be completely transformed into the image of Messiah, the Son of God. 1 Peter 2:5, 9 and Revelation 1:6; 5:10 confirm the fact that Believers shall be part of a royal priesthood. As stated above, in Revelation 5:5-10, the elders and the four beasts sing a new song which praises our Lord and God for making all believers, chosen by God out of the world, to be priestly kings as are the twenty-four elders.

In other words, the entire Spiritual Body of Messiah, individually and collectively, becomes priestly kings through and in Messiah after the Order of Melchizedek with Messiah as the High Priest. It may be that, through Yeshua, every member of His Spiritual Body gets the privilege and honor to exercise their duties as priestly kings after this auspicious Order (1 Peter 2:9, Revelation 1:6, 5:10). Praise be to God for the completeness and perfection of His finished work.

The Holy Scriptures often refer to every member of the Spiritual Body of Messiah as a saint (Romans 1:7, 1 Corinthians 1-2, 6:1-2, 2 Corinthians 1:1, Ephesians 1:1, Philippians 1:1, Colossians 1:2, Philemon 1:5) who will reign with Yeshua, being the King of saints (Revelation 15:3). Becoming a king and priest is a high calling that no child of God can earn. It is freely and graciously given out of love. We should be continually thankful to Almighty God that He has predestined us for such a high calling. Nothing should be more important to us than to realize our creative purpose in Yeshua HaMashiach. The Apostle Paul writes in Philippians 3:14: "I press toward the mark for the prize of the high calling of God in Yeshua, the Messiah."

It is one thing to live in the faith that we have eternal life through the sacrifice of Yeshua. It is yet another thing to know that we have been predestined to be members of the Spiritual Body of Messiah and to live physically, spiritually and gloriously in His Holy name as children of Almighty God who are imbued with our triune Godhead's mannerisms, attributes and characteristics and, thereby, are elevated to the high office of priestly kings assigned to reign with Messiah powerfully, humbly, and lovingly forever more.

There could not be a more perfect story of Godly love than our triune Godhead's love story with Mankind, Their highest creation. It has been God's eternal desire to be one with Mankind. Mankind was created with every Godly characteristic necessary to ensure that God and Mankind could be one, including God's greatest characteristic, love. However, God gave us the free will to choose selfless love. Unfortunately, our first parents chose love of self over love of others. Therefore, we had to be taught God's perfect love through a demonstration of sacrificial love that required God to become one of us and show, by the example of Yeshua's life, death, burial and resurrection, how Mankind should live in God's love.

The length, breadth, and depth of God's creative purpose for Mankind are far greater than could ever be imagined. The oneness that Mankind is to have with his God is so perfect and all-inclusive that God will be in us and we will be in God. Can there be any created purpose in or under heaven greater than this? Is this not worth our most loving obedience? Are you willing to give up all selfish desires to be like God and to suffer, to any extent required, to become one with Him to this extent? Are you willing to die to self so that you can live as one with God? The Holy Word of God loves us so much that He became one of us to show us exactly what it will be like to be one with God through loving obedience, and He suffered death so that we could realize His level of oneness with God as we were originally created to experience.

EPILOGUE

All that God created was initially perfect and good and that includes Mankind, God's greatest creation. We are the culmination of God's creative process. By that I mean, before Mankind's fall, all of creation was interconnected under Mankind's dominion. This was done so that, upon God's oneness with His highest creation, God would truly be the All-in-All. Thus, the perfection of all creation is directly dependent upon Mankind's perfection which, in turn, is itself directly dependent upon the eternal perfection of God. Permanent perfection is the attendant result of Mankind's oneness with his Creator because God is eternally perfect in all His ways.

Our triune Godhead made us in Their image and after Their likeness. From the moment of our creation, we resembled God in appearance and personality and were, therefore, perfectly designed to become one with Him. There was nothing unique about man, in his initial creative state, that would have prevented him from being a perfect physical temple of God. The incorporation of the righteous and holy characteristics of God into every human being enabled us to be congruous physical temples of God. This compatibility with God makes it possible not only for God to inhabit us but also for us to inhabit God. For it is written in Ephesians 2:19-22:

> Now therefore ye are no more strangers and foreigners, but fellow citizens with the saints, and of the household

of God; And are built upon the foundation of the apostles and prophets, Yeshua HaMashiach himself being the chief corner stone; In whom all the building fitly framed together groweth unto an holy temple in the Lord: In whom ye also are builded together for an habitation of God through the Spirit.

Our lives are intended to be mirror images of God's life so much so that the life of God becomes our lives and our lives become God's life. Praise be to God! However, God wanted each of us to willingly choose to experience this oneness with Him, not because of the awesome privileges and benefits attendant thereto, but because of a desire to obey the Word of God out of love, honor and respectful reverence. Just as a man and woman voluntarily pledge to love, honor and respect each other in a marriage ceremony, God requires every one of His children, Jew and Gentile alike, to make that kind of commitment to Him.

So, God decided to test Adam and Eve to determine if they would choose God's way to eternal perfection through obedient love or if they would choose their own way unto death through disobedient hatred. This test was conducted in the Garden of Eden, and it was very simple: Obey Me and live or disobey Me and die. In other words, demonstrate your God-given ability to love your Creator more than you love yourself through obedience, even if you believe that it is not in your interests to do so, and you will live. Otherwise, you will suffer death through eternal separation from God and eternal damnation. God imbued both Adam and Eve with free will and did not tell them about the fullness of their reward, so that the extent of their love of God would be the determining factor in this test of obedience. God knew what their choice would be and had predetermined to demonstrate what true Godly love is through His Word, Yeshua Messiah.

Satan, one of the greatest angelic beings created by God, albeit now fallen and the architect of all evil, wanted to be more than he was created to be. He wanted to be like God, and his prideful plan to rebel against God resulted in his ignominious fall. Nonetheless, Satan understood the fullness of God's creative process. He, therefore, understood God's creative purpose for Mankind, i.e., to be the physical temples through which God will manifest Himself throughout all of creation. Satan knew that God intended to physically rule the heavens and the earth by becoming one with His greatest creation through love.

Satan also knew that Mankind's oneness with God had yet to be perfected because he was aware of the Edenic test established by God to determine the extent of Mankind's love of God. Satan saw an opportunity to physically rule the heavens and the earth by becoming one with Mankind through sin. From this foundation, Satan sought to attack the very throne of God. He had to accomplish his union with Mankind before Adam and Eve ate from the Tree of Life and thereby perfect their oneness with God through loving obedience. Satan correctly reasoned that it would be impossible for Adam and Eve to perfect their oneness with God should they sin. He knew that God could have no part with sin. So, Satan became an active participant in God's test of Mankind's love for his Creator.

Had God decided to become eternally one with Adam and Eve at the moment of their creation, then a test would have been unnecessary and Satan would never have had an opportunity to attempt the usurpation of God's authority through Mankind. However, God wanted us to freely choose to love and worship Him because, through obedience, we demonstrate our love for God (John 14:15, 21, 23). Selfless love is the greatest characteristic of God (1 Corinthians 13:13). God wanted Mankind to show that selfless love is their greatest characteristic as well.

By persuading Adam and Eve to obey him and to disobey God, Satan was successful in causing them to fail God's test resulting in Adam and Eve and their offspring becoming servants of Satan through sin unto death (Romans 6:16), which is the wages of sin. God was aware of Satan's deceptive intervention into His love test of Adam and Eve. God did not prevent Satan's intrusion because, in the end, the decision to disobey out of love of self ultimately was made by Mankind and not Satan. Satan could tempt through deception but the decision rested with Adam and Eve just as it did with Yeshua in the wilderness (Luke 4:1-13).

God knew that Mankind had to experience true Godly love in order for us to appreciate it for what is actually is. Therefore, God chose to redeem us by lovingly allowing His Word to become man and to pay our death penalties. God's choice of selfless love unto death through Yeshua HaMashiach was the perfect example of Godly love because Yeshua said *"Greater love hath no man than this, that a man lay down his life for his friends"* (John 15:13). Yeshua is the living Word of God Who became flesh so that He could lovingly pay the ultimate price for the redemption of Mankind, whom He calls His friends (John 15:14-15). During His earthly life, Yeshua was perfected through loving obedience to God until He took His last breath. He thereby became the author of eternal salvation unto all who lovingly obey Him (Hebrews 5:9). In the end, loving obedience to God through Yeshua Messiah is still the only means to the salvation of Mankind. As it is written in Acts 4:12, "Neither is there salvation in any other: for there is none other name under heaven given among men, whereby we must be saved."

In John 17:21, 23-24, Yeshua prayed that the children of God, Jew and Gentile, be one with each other and with their triune God, that, just as He and God are in each other, the children of God be in both Yeshua and God. This prayer makes sense because our Father in heaven is God of both Jew and Gentile (Romans 3:29). Messianic Jewish and Gentile believers are, indeed, spiritually one as members of the Spiritual Body of Messiah but they have yet to be one in worship and praise in this world. However, we are rapidly approaching the day when Jewish and Gentile believers in Yeshua will be one in every respect. Today, Messianic Jews and Gentile believers are worldwide in number and efforts are underway to merge the two into one corporate body of born-again believers in answer to Yeshua's prayer in John 17:21.

Yeshua, through His life and death, made it possible for the world to have a better appreciation of what Godly love truly is. Yeshua, being God incarnate, wanted nothing more than the realization of God's creative purpose for man. In John 17, Yeshua prayed that we become one with God to the same extent that He is one with God, the Father. Yeshua's death, burial and resurrection provided the means through which His prayer would be answered. All who believe on His ultimate sacrifice for the forgiveness of their sins, in faith, become children of God.

Yeshua tells us that we must be humble like little children to enter the Kingdom of God (Matthew 18:1-5). As such, there is no ego to prevent our triune God living in us and we in Them. This oneness is initiated at the very moment of our spiritual rebirths, is lovingly perfected by God over time and is consummated at the marriage feast of the Lamb.

In the world that is to come, we will neither marry nor be given in marriage to each other (Luke 20:34-38). In fact, Yeshua tells us that whoever does the will of His heavenly Father is His brother, sister and mother (Matthew 12:49-50, Mark 3:31-35). Galatians 3:26-28 informs us that, as the children of God, we are one in Messiah and, therefore, are neither male nor female. This makes perfect sense because, if we are truly one in each other and in God, how can we marry ourselves?

Of interest is the passage contained in Luke 24:13-35 wherein Yeshua takes a form that was unrecognized by two of His disciples on the road to Emmaus. Of similar note is John 21:1-14 in which Yeshua was also unrecognized by Peter, James, John, Thomas, Nathanael, and two other disciples, men who certainly would know Yeshua when they saw Him. As mirror images of Yeshua, we, in our glorified states, will be able to take any form we want, whenever we want. This may include being male or female. Clearly, the interrelationships between the children of God, once perfected in and through Yeshua, will be nothing like we have ever seen or can imagine.

Even though the glorified children of God will not marry each other, we shall all be one through marriage with Yeshua HaMashiach, the second personage of our triune God. In Revelation 19:7-9, it is written:

> Let us be glad and rejoice, and give honour to him: for the marriage of the Lamb is come, and his wife hath made herself ready. And to her was granted that she should be arrayed in fine linen, clean and white: for the fine linen is the righteousness of saints. And he saith unto me, Write, Blessed are they which are called unto the marriage supper of the Lamb. And he saith unto me, These are the true sayings of God.

We, who are the children of God, are the bride of Messiah (2 Corinthians 11:2; Ephesians 5:25), and this marriage is an eternal, loving union between God's children and Yeshua HaMashiach (Matthew 25:1-13, 1 Thessalonians 4:16-17). Our collective and individual marriage to Yeshua makes us one with Him

(Galatians 3:28), just as a marriage between a man and a woman causes them to become one flesh (Genesis 2:24, 1 Corinthians 6:16, Ephesians 5:30-32). It officially completes God's answer to Yeshua's prayer that we become one with our triune Godhead (John 17:22). All Mankind, the Jew first and then the Gentile, is called to this marriage feast but few are chosen to be married to Yeshua Messiah (Matthew 22:2-14, Romans 1:16; 9:24).

In His high-priestly prayer, Yeshua prayed for the children of God (the Jew first and then the Gentile) who were given to Him out of the world by God. He did not pray for the world. In this prayer, Yeshua stated that those called by God received and believed the words that God gave Him to give to us. Because of this, we are no longer part of the world, just as Yeshua is not part of the world and the world hates us just as it hates Yeshua (John 17:5-8, 14, 16).

Indeed, all of God's children, who believe, in faith, the promises of God, confess that they are strangers and pilgrims on this earth (Psalm 39:12, Hebrews 11:13). We were separated from this world the moment we were spiritually reborn because the Spirit of Truth lives in us. John 14:17 tells us that the world cannot receive the Spirit of Truth because the world does not see Him nor does it know Him; but we know Him, for He dwells with us and in us. If we were of the world, the world would love us, but we were chosen out of the world, thus we are hated by the world (John 15:18-19). We are therefore instructed in 1 John 2:15-17:

> Love not the world, neither the things that are in the world. If any man love the world, the love of the Father is not in him. For all that is in the world, the lust of the flesh, and the lust of the eyes, and the pride of life, is not of the Father, but is of the world. And the world passeth away, and the lust thereof: but he that doeth the will of God abideth for ever.

Romans 8:1-4 tell us that we are not condemned because we are in Yeshua HaMashiach and walk after the Spirit, not after the flesh. The law of the Spirit of Life in Yeshua has freed us from the law of sin and death. We could never be righteous under the law of the flesh because our sin natures will cause us to inevitably sin. But we are made righteous because God sent His Son in the likeness of sinful flesh to condemn sin in the flesh for those of us who walk in the Spirit.

God will not impose redemption upon us. We must willingly accept Yeshua's sacrifice on our behalf. Paul, therefore, encourages us not to be conformed to this world (Romans 12:2), nor should we worry about worldly things such as what we should eat and drink, as the world does (Luke 12:29-30).

Friendship with this world is enmity with God. Whoever loves the world is an enemy of God (James 4:4). That is why the prophet Isaiah tells us, in Isaiah 2:22, that we are to "cease ye from man, whose breath is in his nostrils: for wherein is he to be accounted of?"

The death, burial and resurrection of Yeshua Messiah resulted in the redemption of all Mankind. At that point, the world and Satan were judged, and Satan was doomed to be cast out of heaven unto the earth (John 12:31). Yeshua told us that He had to leave so that the Comforter would come and "reprove the world of sin, and of righteousness, and of judgment: of sin, because they believe not on Me; of righteousness, because I go to my Father, and ye see Me no more; of judgment, because the prince of this world is judged." (John 16:8-11).

We, who are not of this world, wept when Yeshua left, but the world rejoiced. Our sorrow shall be turned into joy (John 16:20). When Yeshua left this world, He went to prepare a place for us (John 14:1-4). It is written:

Eye hath not seen, nor ear heard, neither have entered into the heart of man, the things which God hath prepared for them that love Him.

(1 Corinthians 2:9)

We *do* know that, as saints (separated holy ones), we shall judge the world and angels, who are ministering spirits sent to minister to the heirs of salvation (Psalm 149:5-9, 1 Corinthians 6:2-3). Yeshua tells us that we are not to rejoice in the fact that the spirits are subjected unto us, but rather that our names are written in heaven (Luke 10:20). The fact that we shall rule over all creation sheds immeasurable light on the nature of our predestined oneness with God when we are glorified and raised to our incorruptible states in Messiah Yeshua.

Adam and Eve were given dominion and authority over the earth. Upon our glorification in Yeshua, this dominion and authority shall be extended to all physical and spiritual creation. In our current redeemed but corruptible states, we are admonished not to judge anyone lest we be judged by the same measure of judgment meted out by us (Matthew 7:1-11). To do so now would be to condemn ourselves because we all have sinned and come short of the glory of God (Romans 3:23).

We will have incorruptible and immortal bodies (1 Corinthians 15:49-54). As mirror images of Yeshua, we shall be physical manifestations of God capable of performing all of the earthly works of Yeshua, including knowing the hearts of Mankind (Luke 5:22), traveling through matter (John 20:26), appearing and disappearing at will in and out of time (Luke 24:36-37), being capable of transfiguration (Matthew 17:1-2), healing all manner of sickness (Matthew 10:1), walking on water (Matthew 14:25-27), having authority over devils (Luke 9:1), raising the dead (John 11:38-44), feeding thousands with little or nothing (John 6:5-12), and changing water into wine (John 2:1-11). Incredibly, Yeshua told us that not only will we be able to do all that He did, but we will be able to do greater works than these (John 14:12). If only we could fully appreciate the tremendous wonder, magnitude,c and significance of our intended roles in God's Kingdom, we would run from this world as fast as our feet would carry us straight into the ever-waiting arms of our Lord and Savior, Yeshua Messiah.

If we keep in mind who we are, Whose we are, and of what Kingdom we belong, this present world becomes of no significance to us. All our efforts would be dedicated to seeking God's Kingdom. It is only when we give up all earthly desires that we obtain the desires of our hearts. It is only when we give up our lives that we gain a more abundant life. It is only when we stop trying to be God that we become one with Him.

Before creation week, God knew that Satan would succeed in convincing Adam and Eve to sin against God through disobedient selfish love. Even though God foreknew that they would choose death instead of life, God also knew that Adam and Eve, and certain of their offspring, would embrace His demonstration of Godly love through the sacrificial death, burial, and resurrection of Yeshua HaMashiach. Once this costly lesson has been learned and acted upon by a repentant Mankind, they are immediately restored as heirs to God's Kingdom and become pure love, holy and conformed to the image of the incarnate Word of God according to their creative purpose. The names of all Mankind were known by God and written in the Book of Life before the foundation of the world (Ephesians 1:4; 2 Timothy 1:9; Revelation 17:8). Throughout the history of Mankind, God has used trials and tribulations to draw His predestined children to Himself. For we know that all things work together for good to them that love God and are called according to His purpose (Romans 8:28).

Despite knowing, before creation week, of the fall of man, God did not alter His plan to inhabit and become one with Mankind, His highest creation. Instead, God proceeded with creation week and saw that it was good (Genesis 1:30-31). Mankind was created to have complete and total authority over all of creation with Yeshua as our head and God, the Father, over Yeshua, being the All-in-All. It is all inter-connected and flows down from the top. Consequently, Mankind's fall caused everything below us to slowly die.

God knew that a personal demonstration of perfect unconditional love was the only way to generate a repentant heart in Mankind. God, in His infinite grace and mercy, secured the restoration of Mankind to our original perfection by lovingly offering the second personage in a High Priestly holy sacrifice through His incarnation and ultimate sinless death for the sins of every human being born of Adam. The result of this demonstration of God's unconditional and uncompromising love is the ultimate restoration of Adam, Eve, and the chosen among their descendants, to our original estate thereby restoring the universe to its original order and perfection. Just as all the saved will be new creatures through Yeshua HaMashiach, all of creation will be new. The old man and the old creation will pass away.

At the end of creation week, it was Adam and Eve who had dominion over the earth. They lost that dominion when they sinned against God. Satan, who became one with them through sin, was given authority over the Kingdoms of the world through man (Luke 4:6). Satan was temporarily given this authority despite his own sin against God (Luke 4:5-7, 2 Corinthians 4:4). When Yeshua died and was resurrected, Satan's authority was taken from him and given back to Mankind through the person of Yeshua Messiah in Whom Mankind lives.

Up to now, I have been focused mainly on the physical oneness Mankind will enjoy with his triune Godhead. However, man will also enjoy a spiritual oneness with God that is as wondrous as anything imagined.

Since God is Spirit, Yeshua HaMashiach is His Spoken Word and we are members of Yeshua's Spiritual Body. When God speaks, He speaks His Word Who is comprised of the members of His Spiritual Body. We are the collective Word of God in and through Yeshua HaMashiach. That is why Yeshua can refer to us as His brothers and sisters. We are who He is.

Conversely, when we speak, as members of Yeshua's Spiritual Body, our words become Yeshua's words which are the words of God. When we praise God, He inhabits those praises. In Deuteronomy 10:21, it is written: "[God] is thy praise." Psalm 22:3 states: "But thou art holy, O thou that inhabitest the praises of Israel." Should these passages be taken literally? How can God inhabit the praises of His people?

To answer these questions, we must begin with the premise, discussed in earlier chapters, that oneness with God literally means that He spiritually lives in His children and His children spiritually live in Him. This mutual spiritual inhabitation will be perfected when we are glorified and God permanently indwells our future incorruptible bodies. Yeshua is our example of this incorruptible eternal oneness with God. When we walk in the Spirit and live in the Spirit (Galatians 5:16, 25), we yield our own desires to those of the Holy Spirit, allowing Him to effectuate His will through us.

Paul tells us to pray "always with all prayer and supplication in the Spirit" (Ephesians 6:18). This means that we are to continuously make prayerful requests, intercessions and praises

(1 Timothy 2:1-3). We do not know what we should pray for, or how we should pray, but the Spirit makes intercession for us when we pray (Romans 8:26). In fact, some suggest we should pray in tongues because the devil cannot interpret these prayers, only God will know the substance of these prayers. Psalm 40:3 tells us that God puts our praise to Him in our mouths. For the Holy Spirit to inspire our praise and prayers, we must have a mindset of a child, a willingness to be led. Yeshua confirms this fact in Mark 10:14-15 and Matthew 21:16. How many times have we started a prayer not knowing what to say, only to have the words flow from our mouths as if we had recited a well-rehearsed script. Only the Holy Spirit can do that.

When we pray in the Spirit, the Holy Spirit groans to God in our stead or inspires our prayers. If God literally prays to Himself for and through us, so, likewise, He praises Himself for and through us. We cannot yet understand why God chooses to use us in this manner. We can only revel in the joy of being used by God in whatever way He sees fit. So, let us praise the Lord with all our hearts while His breath of life is still in us because, in doing so, we honor Him by doing what we were created to do. The dead cannot praise God (Psalm 115:17). Indeed, the dead know not anything (Ecclesiastes 9:5-6; Job 14). Upon death, the thoughts of the dead perish (Psalm 146:4). All memory by and of them vanish (Ecclesiastes 1:11, 2:16, 8:10, 9:5-6, Job 7:8-10, Isaiah 26:14).

So that there is no misunderstanding, the above references concerning the dead specifically relate to what the dead can no longer do in the land of the living. Because the breath of life is no longer in them, they cannot praise God. Nor do they know anything concerning the land of the living. Their thoughts and memories vanish at their death. How many times have we heard it said that our departed loved ones continue to bless and spiritually support us from above. However, the Word of God tells us that this is not true. Once we give up the ghost, we give up anything and everything related to the land of the living.

The question then becomes what happens to the ghost that we give up? All of Mankind, including Yeshua, gives up the ghost upon death (Genesis 15:15; 25:8, 17; 35:29; 49:29, 33; Mark 15:37; Acts 5:5; 12:23). Genesis 35:18 states that the soul of Rachel departed upon her death. Genesis 35:29 informs us that we are gathered unto our people or join our ancestors. Isaiah 38:18-19 establishes that those, who go down into Sheol upon death, cannot praise God. According to Luke 16:19-31, while souls no longer have anything to do with the land of the living, they clearly have memories, and thoughts and can experience pain and pleasure. In this parable, Sheol is depicted as having two components: one for the condemned and one for the righteous, and these two places are separated by an impassible chasm. Psalm 16:10, 49:15, and Acts 2:31 tell us that, before Yeshua, the souls of the righteous descend into Sheol upon death but, because of Yeshua, they are not left there.

Upon giving up His Ghost upon death, Yeshua descended into the lower parts of the earth and brought the righteous out of Sheol (Ephesians 4:8-10). Sheol is no longer the place for those who die but are saved in Messiah. The Apostle Paul tells us that to be absent from the body is to be present with Messiah (2 Corinthians 5:5-8; Philippians 1:23-24). Ecclesiastes 12:7 tells us that our spirits return to God who gave it to us.

Our spiritual oneness with Yeshua HaMashiach, the Word of God, is more than we could ever imagine. As mentioned, the collective praise and prayers of the children of God, who comprise the Spiritual Body of Messiah, manifests itself in the form of words spoken by Messiah, Who, in turn, is the literal voice and

Word of God. In Ezekiel 43:2, the prophet describes God's voice as "a sound of many waters." John, in Revelation 14:2, describes a spiritual voice he heard from heaven as the "voice of many waters" and as the "voice of a great thunder." Revelation 19:6 tells us that John heard the voice of a great multitude, as the voice of many waters, and as the voice of mighty thunderings, praising God. John also describes Yeshua Messiah as the Son of Man, whose spiritual voice was as the sound of many waters (Revelation 1:15). According to these passages, when God and Messiah speak, Their spiritual voices are like the sound of many waters. What are the waters that are described here? Revelation 17:1,15 tell us that "waters" refer to "peoples, and multitudes, and nations, and tongues."

The peoples, multitudes, nations and tongues who compose the voice of God and Yeshua, the Word of God, must be the children of God who compose the Spiritual Body of Messiah. Thus, when Yeshua speaks, His voice is "as the sound of many waters," which are the collective praises and prayers of the members of His Spiritual Body. As Yeshua and God are one, and Yeshua is the literal voice and Word of God, the same voices that collectively compose the spiritual voice of Yeshua also collectively compose the spiritual voice of God. Yeshua is in the bosom of the Father (John 1:18). The words Yeshua spoke came from His Father (John 14:24).

The Holy Scriptures constantly remind us that we are members of the Spiritual Body of Yeshua HaMashiach. God spiritually speaks His Word, Yeshua, Who, in turn, spiritually speaks the members of His Spiritual Body. Yeshua was speaking literally when He said, if we are lukewarm in our walk with Him, He will spew us out of His spiritual mouth (Revelation 3:16). Can there be any more spiritual oneness between God and Mankind, His highest creation, than this?

The magnificence of our spiritual oneness with God is equaled by the awesome splendor of our physical oneness with God. Galatians 2:20 informs us that we were crucified with Yeshua and, therefore, we no longer live, but Yeshua lives in us through faith. 1 Corinthians 6:19-20 and 2 Corinthians 6:16 state we are the physical temples of the Holy Spirit that we must glorify God in our bodies and spirits because these are God's and that God dwells and walks in us.

This is the fulfillment of Yeshua's prophetic statement in John 14:20: "At that day, ye shall know that I am in my Father, and ye in me, and I in you." It is also the answer to Yeshua's prayer in John 17:21: "That they may all be one; as thou, Father, art in me, and I in Thee, that they also may be one in us…" Finally, it is the realization of Ephesians 4:4-6:

> There is one body, and one Spirit, even as ye are called in one hope of your calling. One Lord, one faith, one baptism, One God and Father of all, who is above all, and through all, and in you all.

Yeshua told Philip, in response to Philip's request for Yeshua to show him the Father, "Have I been so long time with you, and yet hast thou not known me, Philip? He that hath seen me hath seen the Father; and how sayest thou *then,* show us the Father?" (John 14:8-9).

Since we live in Yeshua and the Father and Yeshua and the Father live in us, if anyone asks us to show them the Father, our response should be the same as Yeshua's response to Philip. "Have we been with you so long and yet you do not know us? Anyone, who has seen us, has seen the Father!" To state it simply, we were created to be God in the flesh just as Yeshua is God in the flesh! This is so only because we are in Yeshua and we shall be mirror images of Him. This is the endgame of why

God created man in His image and likeness. This is the degree of oneness God has always intended for Mankind, His highest creation. Satan understood this and chose open rebellion to keep another created being from being exalted to an existence he so enviously desired.

Incredibly, the truth of this reality has never been properly preached. The absolute magnitude of our physical and spiritual oneness with God, in this world and the next, transcends reason and exceeds our wildest expectations. Please understand this: since there is no limit to our Triune Godhead, there is no limit to our oneness with Them.

In our yet to be perfected state of oneness with God, it may be impossible to wrap our heads around this actuality. The indescribably divine purpose God intends for Mankind cannot be rationalized given the wretched state of sinful man. It can only be explained by the boundless, perfect love that is God. Can the reconciled of Mankind do anything but prostrate ourselves before God in awe and wonder unwilling to do anything but His most perfect will?

It is impossible to contemplate and fully appreciate the complexity of this degree of spiritual and physical oneness until or unless it is experienced and we shall experience it because it is our predestination (Romans 8:29; Ephesians 1:5,11)!

Hallelujah and Amen!!!

Since the Holy Spirit inspires all praise (Ephesians 5:18-20) and, indeed, intercedes and makes prayerful praise for and through us (Romans 8:26-27), our praise and worship of God is initiated by God, our Father, inspired by the Holy Spirit, and spoken collectively by us through the personage of Yeshua HaMashiach, who is the spoken Word of God.

The words we speak while in this complete state of mutual, spiritual inhabitation and oneness with God have the living, faithful power of God in them. In fact, 1 Peter 4:11 tells us "If anyone speaks, they should do so as one who speaks the very words of God." All that we speak in faith, individually and collectively, will be realized because God lives in these words and, consequently, inhabits our God-inspired praises and prayers. God's words do not return to Him void. They accomplish His will (Isaiah 55:11).

If we take this line of thought to its literal conclusion, an amazing reality becomes clear. We have cited to Scriptural references that support the truth that our triune Godhead is the Alpha and Omega. Because the verb is in the present tense, they are the beginning, the end and everything in between at the same time. Every child of God, being members of the eternal, Spiritual Body of Messiah, is an integral component of our triune Godhead's eternal everything-in-the-present spiritual existence. It necessarily follows, then, from an eternal, spiritual perspective, every spiritually born-again member of Yeshua's Spiritual Body will, upon our perfection, experience the past, present and future at the same time. Perhaps, this may explain why the Prophet Ezekiel, some six hundred years before the birth of Yeshua, described the voice of God as the sound of many waters (Ezekiel 43:2) which we know represents peoples, multitudes, nations, and tongues. Our spiritual oneness with Almighty God is such that we, in and through our Savior, Yeshua, are one with the eternal I AM.

Adam and Eve were created so that the spiritual members of Yeshua could take on flesh and physically house the God Whose voice they are. Since every human being is an independent living soul, God gave each of us the free will to choose to remain a part of Him without knowing that we were a part of Him before the foundation of the world. Perhaps, this may also explain how we could be called by God and given God's purpose and grace in

Yeshua HaMashiach before the world began (Romans 8:28-29; 2 Timothy 1:9). Yeshua breathed the members of His Spiritual Body into Adam and Eve ensuring that every member, through procreation, would have the opportunity to choose God over self in the land of the living. Yeshua is the only human begotten of God. He is fully God and fully man. Mankind, as living souls, will never be fully God and fully human until our perfection (Ephesians 3:19).

Our oneness with God required us to demonstrate loving obedience while incognizant of our eternal, spiritual existence in God through Yeshua HaMashiach. God wanted us to freely choose to physically obey Him out of love. We chose otherwise and our selfish decision required the Word of God to take on flesh to demonstrate to us how to obey God out of selfless love, thereby redeeming us so that we could return to our pre-creation estate.

Once we embrace our redemption at Yeshua's physical and spiritual expense and are saved, we have been promised to sit with Him in heavenly places (Ephesians 1:20-22; 2:6). Indeed, we shall sit with Him in His throne as He now sits with His Father in His Father's throne (Luke 22:69; Revelation 3:21). This makes sense if we are, in fact, His Spiritual Body.

Envision, if you will, being able to look out upon the universe in our glorified states of oneness with God, from the perspective of the Throne of God, through the spiritual eyes of Yeshua as members of His Spiritual Body. Isn't this what Satan sought to do, independent of God, through selfish means? Yet, we get to do it through our Lord and Savior, Yeshua Messiah, not by our own actions but through the grace and mercy of God. How many of us truly understand the fullness of our oneness with God that was planned before the foundation of the world.

This is possible because, from a spiritual, everything-in-the-present perspective, the souls of the children of God have always been in God, through the Word of God. We became living souls upon our physical creation. Since our triune Godhead is the Alpha and the Omega at the same time, the members of the Spiritual Body of Yeshua are the present physical manifestation of the Alpha and the Omega through Yeshua HaMashiach. We were spiritually present with and in Him before we were breathed into the nostrils of Adam and became living souls through his blood line. Yeshua was able to bear our sins and die in our stead because we are eternal members of His Spiritual Body. We are redeemed because He sacrificed His physical Body and Blood unto physical death. As members of His Spiritual Body, we went through the sacrifice with Him spiritually, being redeemed thereby (Romans 6:3-11; Galatians 2:20; 5:24). Who better to redeem Mankind than the Personage of our triune Godhead Who housed the souls of Mankind?

Before his fall, Adam had the living power of God in his voice. When he named every living creature on the earth, that was the name thereof (Genesis 2:19-20). After Adam's fall, God no longer inhabited his words. Before the death and resurrection of Yeshua Messiah through the power of God, only men of God, who were anointed with the Holy Spirit, had the power of God in the words they spoke. For instance, because he spoke in faith through the Spirit that was upon him, Elijah was able to speak fire from heaven to kill the king's men pursuing him (2 Kings 1:9-15). Isaac could not take back his blessings upon his sons Jacob and Esau because, being anointed with the Spirit, his spoken words were true, faithful and sure (Genesis 27:30-39).

However, Footnote 2:1 of the Book of Acts in the *Thomas Nelson Study Bible* informs us that the power exhibited by these anointed Old Testament men of God was from without, temporary and exceptional. They could be led by the Spirit (Luke 2:27), but they could not be filled with the Holy Spirit because they were not spiritually born again with the Holy Spirit. Therefore, the Holy Spirit did not indwell them. In Old Testament times, the Holy Spirit could only come upon them and anoint them with His power.

It wasn't until the Pentecost, after the ascension of Yeshua, that the Holy Spirit indwelt Mankind, and the power of God began to live in and through us. In fact, true spiritual rebirth does not occur unless and until a spiritually baptized believer receives the Holy Ghost (Acts 8:12-17).

There are two forms of baptism discussed in the Holy Scriptures, one physical and one spiritual. John, the Baptist, told the people of his day, "I indeed have baptized you with water; but He shall baptize you with the Holy Ghost. (Mark 1:8). Physical baptism, for the believer in Yeshua, is a public affirmation of what took place spiritually upon their acceptance of Yeshua as their Lord and Savior. Our immersion into water symbolizes our death to self and our burial. Our emersion from the water symbolizes our resurrection from the dead in and through Yeshua. We are dead to self and alive as members of the Spiritual Body of Messiah. (Galatians 2:20). Our physical baptisms are symbolic demonstrations of our spiritual rebirths into the family of God through Yeshua HaMashiach.

More important, however, is our spiritual baptism. At the moment of our acceptance, in faith, of the death, burial and resurrection of Yeshua HaMashiach as atonement for our sins, the Holy Ghost quickens our spirits thereby engrafting us into the family of God. Our spirits are instantaneously reborn as one with our triune Godhead. God is a Spirit. Since our reborn spirits are one with Him, we are now His children. Our spiritual baptisms are the work of the Holy Spirit upon our repentance and acceptance of Yeshua HaMashiach as our Savior. Spiritual baptism is far more than a ritual or sacrament. It is the means by which the saved are made one with their Creator and sealed until the day of our Lord. Without spiritual baptism, physical baptism becomes meaningless. Spiritual baptism is required for anyone to become a spiritually born child of God. However, physical baptism is not mandatory. The sinner on the cross next to Yeshua was saved even though he was never physically baptized.

Yeshua, as the only begotten Son of God and the head of His Spiritual Body, is permanently filled with the Holy Spirit (Luke 4:1). His state of perfect oneness with God necessitated that whatever He asked of God would be given unto Him. For instance, Yeshua asked God the Father to raise Lazarus from the dead. Because Yeshua is in the Father and the Father in Him, Yeshua's prayer was granted, and Lazarus rose from the dead (John 11:17-46).

Yeshua tells us, in Matthew 17:19-21, that faith, with prayer and fasting, can cast out demons. The spiritually reborn person has the power to do all things through Yeshua HaMashiach, if he abides in Yeshua and asks in faith, wavering not (James 1:5-6). Footnote 2:1 of the Book of Acts in the *Thomas Nelson Study Bible* further tells us that this is so because the power demonstrated by the Spirit-filled children of God is from within, permanent and normal.

After God's ultimate love sacrifice for the forgiveness of sins, anyone, who, in faith, believes on the name of Yeshua Messiah, abides in God and God in him, therefore that person can ask anything of God, according to His Holy will and it will be granted unto him (Matthew 8:2-3; John 14:12-14; 15:16; 16:23-24). We are limited only by the extent of our faith. Love hopes for all things and never fails. Faith is the realization of all things hoped for. Our triune Godhead is love. Therefore, there is no limit to the faith of God. Our oneness with God has been perfected in and through Yeshua Messiah. Therefore, there is no limit to our faith as long as Yeshua abides in us and we in Him.

Footnote 14:13-14 of the *Thomas Nelson Study Bible*, referring to the references in these passages from the 14th chapter of the Gospel of John concerning the phrase "in my name", tells us that it literally means "as My agent." This type of agency is unique because the agent and the One the agent represents indwell each other so much so that they are one. The agent is asking his Greater Self to grant a request that the Greater Self has inspired him to make. Under these circumstances, the agent can never ask for anything that is not consistent with the will of his Greater Self. This is because they are the same entity.

Indeed, there is nothing that the agent does that is not also what his Greater Self does. Yeshua tells us as much when He says that He does nothing of Himself, only what He sees the Father do (John 5:19-20; 8:28). There is no distinction between the agent and his Greater Self. They are one to the extent that only one name is necessary to identify both agent and his Greater Self, and that is God. The agent, therefore, speaks with the authority and power of God. When we ask of God "in His name," as we have just defined that phrase, God cannot do anything but grant our prayer requests because He is granting prayers He has inspired us to pray.

We must conclude, therefore, that Yeshua's High Priestly prayer: That the chosen among Mankind, the Jew first and then the Gentile, become one with each other and with their Creator God, as set forth in John 17, was inspired by God with every intention of bringing it to pass. Yeshua, in loving, faithful obedience to a prayer request answered before the foundation of the world, gave His disciples power and authority over all devils and to cure diseases (Luke 9:1-2). Yeshua, being the Alpha and the Omega, knows the wonderful, perfect ending to this love story between God and Mankind, His highest creation. Now that we also know it, we must embrace it with every fiber of our being.

Bishop Clifford M. Johnson, Jr., who graciously serves as Bishop at Mount Pleasant Church and Ministries in Baltimore, Maryland, teaches us about a concept he calls "the principle of equivalent effect." It relates to the immutability of God; in other words, the unchanging nature of God (James 1:17). Therefore, if, upon a fervent request, God, the Father, responded a certain way in the past, He must do so again for us. The Holy Scriptures are replete with instances where God answered the prayers of His people, many times miraculously. Because God does not favor any one person over another and cannot change, what He does for one He has to do for all.

To the extent we beseech Him to do anything He has already done in the past in response to similar prayerful requests, we can rest assured that He will respond to our requests in a like manner. Because of His immutability, it is impossible for God to do anything other than generate a result that is equivalent to His past conduct. Since He has delivered, fed, saved, healed, empowered, inspired, blessed, and talked to His own in the past, the principle of equivalent effect tells us that we can live in the confidence that He will do the same for us.

The fulfillment of God's master plan for the restoration of all who will choose His free gift of eternal life instead of eternal death and damnation will be a testament to the consistency of His purpose and the reliability of His promises. We will be returned to our originally created estate in the image of Yeshua because God cannot do anything but be truthful to His Word. If we ask to be saved, we will be saved.

In response to Yeshua's prayerful request, we will be given incorruptible bodies that will house our triune Godhead, in and through which, we, along with our God, shall exercise dominion over all creation. In this glorified state, as members of the Spiritual Body of Messiah, we shall be exactly what Yeshua is, God in the flesh. Because we shall dwell in Yeshua and He in us, we will possess the attributes, characteristics and mannerisms of our great God and, therefore, will be uniquely capable of being one with Him. God's unchanging nature ensures that our elevation to His level will also be permanent and eternal.

Having these Godly qualities is not something that we should take lightly or acknowledge with half-hearted indifference. Satan and the rest of the fallen angels chose to rebel against God and suffer eternal damnation because they lacked such qualities. All that Yeshua is we shall become. The significance of that statement cannot be overstated. We shall possess the treasures of the Kingdom of God.

The honor and privilege of being the physical manifestation of God is only possible because we will humbly possess the attributes, characteristics and mannerisms of God, the most important of which is love. We are and will be holy because God is Holy.

We do not have to wait until our earthly lives end for us to experience great measures of this miraculous oneness with the Almighty. Indeed, Yeshua allowed some of His disciples to witness Mankind's glorification through Yeshua at the transfiguration while yet alive (Matthew 16:28-17:8; Acts 7:55-56). There are other instances in the Holy Scriptures in which men and women of God enjoyed deep personal relationships with God.

On two such occasions, the relationship between Mankind and God was so intimate that God took them up to heaven without them ever tasting physical death. One such relationship was that of Enoch, who was translated into heaven (Genesis 5:21-24). Footnote 5:21-24 of the *Thomas Nelson Study Bible* informs us that the Hebrew verb and preposition used to denote Enoch's "walk with God" signifies "to live in intimacy with God." According to this same footnote, the Hebrew word used for "translated" is the same word used in 2 Kings 2:3-5 that describes Elijah's translation into heaven without tasting death.

Even though the Comforter had yet to come into the world, these men experienced an anointed intimacy with God that most of us will only enjoy upon our perfection in and through Yeshua HaMashiach. Their oneness with God must have been such that, every morning when they arose and opened their eyes, Almighty God peered through their eyes. He spoke through their mouths. Our everlasting God touched with their fingers, smelled through their nostrils and heard through their ears. They were perfect physical temples for our Holy God in fulfillment of their creative purpose. Their anointing was so heavy that whatever they asked for was done because it was always according to God's will. We can also attain this degree of intimacy with God during our lifetimes if we give up all personal interests and let God be our everything in and through Yeshua Messiah.

Our spiritual rebirths begin our individual and collective intimate walks with God. The Holy Spirit searches all things, including the deep things of God and, as our spiritual walks with God progress, the Holy Spirit reveals these things to us (1 Corinthians 2:10). Our knowledge and understanding of God will grow to levels heretofore incomprehensible. There is no limit to God, and, therefore, there is no limit to our knowledge and understanding of God. Our growth in Him will be eternal in nature and substance.

Praise be to God for His perfect will and our role in it. We thank God not for what we will obtain through our union with Him, but because He loves us so much that He allows us to serve

Him in this most prestigious way despite our sin of disobedience. Mankind's sins demands physical and spiritual death. God became human and lovingly paid our death penalties. Now that Mankind has learned the what it means to be perfect love, through the most painful sacrifice of our Savior, we can embrace God's merciful offer of redemption through Yeshua Messiah whereby we and God become one.

God said: "Let us make man in our image, after our likeness." Despite the best efforts of Satan and fallen Mankind, nothing could be done to cause these words to return to God void. It is written in Isaiah:

Yea, I have spoken it, I will also bring it to pass; I have purposed it, I will also do it. (Isaiah 46:11) So shall my word be that goeth forth out of my mouth: it shall not return unto me void, but it shall accomplish that which I please, and it shall prosper in the thing whereto I sent it. (Isaiah 55:11)

The Holy Scriptures are replete with prophecies of Messiah being fulfilled in Yeshua (Genesis 3:15; 49:10; Exodus 12:1-51; Numbers 21:6-9; Psalm 22:1-31; 110:1-4; 118:22-24; Isaiah 7:14; 9:6-7; 11:1; 35:5-6; 40:3-5; 42:1-7; 52:13-53:12; 61:1-2; Daniel 7:13-14; Jonah 1:19-3:10; Micah 5:2; Zechariah 9:9; 12:10; Malachi 3:1; Matthew 12:39-40; Luke 11:30).

Since these inspired words of God shall not return to Him void, nothing could have stopped Yeshua, Who is the living Word of God, from completing His mission for the salvation of souls. We can take comfort in the knowledge that Yeshua's faithful prayer that Jew and Gentile be one with our triune Godhead will likewise not return to Him void. Jew and Gentile shall, indeed, be one in each other and be completely conformed to the image and likeness of God, through Yeshua Messiah, and enjoy the experience of being God and human as brothers and sisters of Yeshua, as was originally intended.

Grace and peace be multiplied unto you through the knowledge of God, and of Yeshua our Lord, According as his divine power hath given unto us all things that pertain unto life and godliness, through the knowledge of him that hath called us to glory and virtue:

Whereby are given unto us exceeding great and precious promises: that by these ye might be partakers of the divine nature, having escaped the corruption that is in the world through lust (2 Peter 1:2-4).

ABOUT THE AUTHOR

Born in Baltimore, Maryland, Ronald E. Richardson is a senior attorney with Murphy Falcon Murphy. He has practiced law for thirty-five years. He has been involved in various forms of products liability and personal injury litigation resulting in well over a billion dollars in settlements and verdicts. He has been named one of America's Top 100 Personal Injury Attorneys for the State of Maryland and one of the Top 100 Lawyers for the State of Maryland by the National Black Lawyers.

Mr. Richardson obtained B.S. and M.S. degrees in Criminal Justice from Northeastern University in Boston, a J.D. degree from Loyola Law School in Los Angeles and a Certificate in Biblical Studies from Capital Bible Seminary in Lanham, Maryland.

He is spiritually and professionally active in his community, serving in prayer ministries, mentorship programs and on various boards and committees. He is a former chair of the Deacon Board of Bel Forest Baptist Church.

He was inspired to publish his first book, *Oneness With God: A Christian Attorney's Analysis of What It Means to be Created in the Image and After the Likeness of God* in 2006 with Beckham Publications Group, Inc. This effort resulted in him becoming the first recipient of the Agape Gospel Academy Literary Award presented at the Apollo Theater in February 2007. Further inspiration has caused Mr. Richardson to publish this *Second Edition.*

Mr. Richardson has also assisted in the production of two documentary films: *Color at the Bar* and *Maryland State Bar Association: An Oral History.*

He is married to Ella and they have two children: Brea and Delsin.